SEXUAL OFFENCES ACT 2003

SEXUAL OFFENCES ACT 2003

A Guide to the New Law

Paul Lewis

The Law Society

The views expressed in this publication should be taken as those of the author only unless it is specifically indicated that the Law Society has given its endorsement.

The author has asserted the right, under the Copyright, Designs and Patents Act 1988, to be identified as author of this work.

© Paul Lewis 2004

ISBN 1–85328–965–5

Published in 2004 by the Law Society
113 Chancery Lane, London WC2A 1PL

Typeset by J&L Composition, Filey, North Yorkshire
Printed by Antony Rowe, Chippenham, Wiltshire

CONTENTS

8   Other offences   69

PART II   NOTIFICATIONS AND ORDERS   79

9   Notification requirements   81

PREFACE

A review of sexual offences legislation was long overdue, much of it being over 50 years old. In the intervening period the ambit of what is acceptable behaviour between individuals has changed markedly and what is now known about abuse and abusers was almost unthinkable in the 1950s.

The Sexual Offences Act aims to clarify and modernise the law in respect of sexual offences. What was surprising about the passage of the Bill through Parliament is that opinion and debate was not motivated by party political allegiances. Perhaps one opportunity that was missed was to consolidate all existing sexual offences in one piece of legislation in a manner similar to the Powers of Criminal Courts (Sentencing) Act 2000.

This book is intended to be a practical guide to the new legislation, guiding the reader through and highlighting the key points necessary to get to grips with the new offences. I hope that it achieves that aim.

Commencement orders for the various parts of the statute, and up to date information on the act can be obtained from the following websites www.crimeline.info and www.sexualoffencesact.com. Any news relating to the act will also be posted on those websites.

Crown copyright is acknowledged in this work. My gratitude also extends to those who have permitted their words to be used in this text and the editors and other staff at the Law Society whose assistance has also been invaluable.

My last and most important word of thanks is for my wife, Stephanie. Without her unending patience and understanding I would never have been able to indulge myself in the writing of this book. I dedicate this book to her.

Paul Lewis
December 2003

TABLE OF CASES

TABLE OF STATUTES

Page numbers in bold refer to text of the Act.

TABLE OF SECONDARY
LEGISLATION

PART I **OFFENCES**

1 INTRODUCTION

1.1 BACKGROUND TO THE SEXUAL OFFENCES ACT 2003

Reform of the legislation on sexual offences began with the recommendations made by the review teams published in two documents: *Review of Part 1 of the Sex Offenders Act 1997* (2001) and *Setting the Boundaries* (2000).

The Government then published the White Paper *Protecting the Public: strengthening protection against sex offenders and reforming the law on sexual offences* (Cm 5668) in November 2002 in response.

The White Paper set out the Government's intentions for reforming the law on sexual offences and for strengthening measures to protect the public from sexual offending.

Highlighting the need for reform the summary contained in *Setting the Boundaries* stated: 'it is a patchwork quilt of provisions ancient and modern, that works because people make it do, not because there is a coherence and structure' (paragraph 0.2).

The White Paper *Protecting the Public* sets the tone for the Sexual Offences Act 2003 (the Act).

> Public protection, particularly of children and the most vulnerable, is this Government's priority. Crime and the fear of crime have a damaging and dehabilitating effect on all who experience it. But sexual crime, particularly against children, can tear apart the very fabric of our society. It destroys lives and communities and challenges our most basic values.

The Act is in two parts. Part 1 is a clarification, revision and amendment of sexual offences. The current law 'is widely considered to be inadequate and out of date' as well as 'archaic, incoherent and discriminatory'[1], the revisions are designed to further strengthen the law on sex offenders and to modernise penalties and the law on sex offences in order to give the public greater confidence and better protection.

Much of the Government's concern has been a response to the loss of public confidence with frequent reference made to the low incidence of conviction on rape cases. Although the number of reported cases of rape has risen significantly, the number of successful prosecutions has risen only slightly.

It also seems to have been prompted by some high profile cases which have caused widespread public concern about the dangers that some sex offenders pose to the community in general, and to children in particular.

Introducing the second reading of the Bill, the then Home Office minister, Lord Falconer boasted:

> The bill provides for new offences that set out clearly what is acceptable sexual behaviour, together with appropriate penalties...our proposals will provide a clearer legal framework for juries as they decide the facts in each case.

The Home Secretary acknowledged that the Bill touched upon 'highly complicated and sensitive issues which test the balance between the role of government and the individual'.[2] He further stated, 'the sexual offences bill is the culmination of nearly four years' work and consultation. It is a difficult and sensitive task and the first time for 50 years that a government has had the courage to take it on'.[3]

Part 2 of the Act creates a new system of notification for sex offenders, replacing the provisions of the Sex Offenders Act 1997. Introduced is a system of annual reporting designed to strengthen existing provisions.

This part of the Act also introduces a series of preventative civil orders to restrict the movements and actions of relevant offenders where appropriate. The civil orders are draconian in parts, and the use of them will need to be closely monitored by the courts to prevent abuse.

The extensive use of civil orders reflects a government keen on preventative measures as part of its criminal justice strategy. The manner in which the Government has enacted legislation relating to Anti-social Behaviour Orders is an example of this.

The challenge of this part of the Act will be to balance the role of the individual and government. Sexual behaviour is a difficult and sensitive issue. Liberty, the human rights organisation, was particularly concerned that the Bill failed to 'strike an adequate balance between the individual's right to freedom of expression through sexual behaviour and the victim's right to be protected from unwelcome sexual contact'.

---

1 'Protecting the Public' Cm 5668 p.9.
2 Foreword to 'Protecting the Public' Cm5668.
3 Home Office Press Release, reference 204/2003; 14 July 2003.

1.2 IMPLEMENTATION

The Bill received Royal Assent on 20 November 2003 and is expected to be implemented in May 2004. In July 2003 the Home Secretary announced his intention to set up a ministerial committee including representatives from departments with responsibility for education, health, the law, employment and industry to ensure the effective and timely implementation of the Act and to monitor the impact of the Act's provisions following implementation.

1.3   MATTERS THAT FAILED TO MAKE IT TO THE STATUTE BOOK

1.3.1   Date rape

Drug-assisted rape has received considerable press coverage in recent years and is a real cause for concern. Creating a separate offence was mooted, but rejected as it might be thought of as a less serious form of rape both by jurors in terms of conviction rates and by judges in passing sentence. Indeed the evidence given to the review body responsible for publishing the document *Setting the Boundaries* concluded that rape by an acquaintance could not only be as traumatic as stranger rape, but that the betrayal of trust involved could cause further long term psychological damage to the victim or survivor.[1]

The Sentencing Advisory Panel also adopted this approach in its recent *Guidelines on Sentencing* in cases of rape.

Existing law includes an offence of administering drugs in order for a man to have unlawful sexual intercourse with a woman and carries a maximum penalty of two years.

The existing offence is retained and amended so that it covers the administering of drugs or other substances with intent to stupefy a victim in order that they can be subjected to an indecent act without their consent, and to increase the maximum penalty to 10 years' imprisonment.

---

1   At paragraph 0.10.

1.3.2   Consent

The Government originally intended to introduce a rebuttable presumption that consent was absent in cases of rape and sexual assault. It would have been incumbent upon the defendant to have shown that he acted reasonably and that the reasonable conduct relied upon would have been objectively judged as such by any objective third party in the circumstances.

This was a brave and bold move, which unsurprisingly attracted a great deal of criticism, not least of which because it was seen to move away from the so-called 'Golden thread of English Justice', that the prosecution must prove their case. It was also seen as insufficiently flexible as it did not take account of the particular characteristics of individual defendants, for example those with learning difficulties whose actions, whilst reasonable to them, would not be considered to be so by the objective standards of third parties. The compromise reached was an effort to be fair to victims and defendants alike.

The report, *Setting the Boundaries* recommended that an offence of sexual activity between minors be created. This would have applied to children under the age of 18 with those under the age of consent. It was intended to strike a balance between protecting children and also recognising that mutually agreed sex between contemporaries does, and will continue to, take place.

1.3.3   Anonymity in rape cases

The reason for anonymity for complainants in sexual cases was set out by the Heilbron Committee in 1975 (Cmnd 6352). Whilst it identified a number of factors, amongst the most important appears to have been the trauma associated with giving evidence in such trials.

Anonymity for the accused is not a novel concept, having been introduced by the Sexual Offences (Amendment) Act 1976 before its repeal by s.153(3) of the Criminal Justice Act 1988. A further attempt was made to reintroduce it in the Bill, citing the fact that sex crimes fall into an entirely separate category of their own and the stigma attached to such crimes, particularly when involving children, is enormous.[1]

The Government was pressed strongly on the subject, both by amendments made to the Bill in the House of Lords and by the Home Affairs Committee report. The Government's initial response was to reject it for precisely this reason, stating that there should be no distinction drawn between those accused of sex offences and other, very serious crimes, such as murder[2], preferring instead to amend the Guidance and Codes of Practice issued to the police and media representatives relating to such revelations.

A late amendment to the Bill, made against Government wishes, inserted a provision allowing for anonymity but the Government position finally prevailed and the clause was omitted. There is the possibility, however, that the issue will find its way back to the forefront of the political agenda in planned legislation to deal with witnesses in criminal cases.

---

1   Fifth Report of the Home Affairs Committee Report at para.76.
2   The Government Reply to the Fifth Report from the Home Affairs Select Committee Session 2002–2003 HC639 at p.8.

2 NEW SEXUAL OFFENCES

2.1 RAPE

2.1.1 Background to reform

Much debate took place in both Houses of Parliament regarding the issue of consent. The law previously provided that a man was guilty of rape if he knew that the other party was not consenting or was reckless as to the same. This subjective test, established in *DPP v. Morgan* [1976] AC 182, HL, did not require the defendant's mistaken belief in consent to be objectively judged. Provided that he honestly believed that the complainant was consenting, even if he had no reasonable grounds for that belief, then he was not guilty of rape.

As a result of the judgment in *Morgan*, the Heilbron Committee (Cmnd 6352, December 1975) was established to report on rape, in particular it concluded that the mental element in rape should be clarified. The Sexual Offences (Amendment) Act 1976 incorporated the findings of the committee in s.2:

> It is hereby declared that if at a trial for rape the jury has to consider whether a man believed a woman was consenting to sexual intercourse, the presence or absence of reasonable grounds for belief was a matter to which the jury is to have regard, in conjunction with any other relevant matters, in considering whether he so believed.

It is the Government's view that the subjective test created by s.2 is now outdated. The reason for the change was stated in the White Paper *Protecting the Public*:

> We believe the difficulty in proving that some defendants did not truly have an 'honest' belief in consent contributes in some part to the low rate of convictions for rape.

The Government's review also concluded that it was not unreasonable to require a person to take care that the other party to sexual activity is consenting, 'the cost to him is very slight and the cost to the victim of forced sexual activity is very high indeed' (Lord Falconer QC, then Home Office minister, now Lord Chancellor).

2.1.2 The new definition

The Sexual Offences Act 2003 (the Act) redefines the definition of rape to include oral and anal penetration. It becomes an offence for a person to intentionally penetrate (s.79(2)) with his penis the vagina (includes vulva as per s.79(9), see also *R. v. F* [2002] EWCA Crim 2936), anus or mouth of another person without that person's consent.

Penetration is a continuing act from entry to withdrawal, so that consensual intercourse will become rape if a woman or man ceases to consent during intercourse, and the other party continues with the necessary intent to complete the act. As under the Sexual Offences Act 1956 even the slightest penetration will be sufficient.

To maximise the protection offered by the criminal law, the definition of rape is widened to include surgically reconstructed male and female genitalia when a person has undergone an operation to change sex.

Oral peneration has been included within the definition of rape to indicate its seriousness. Existing legislation only permitted this to be charged as an indecent assault, carrying a maximum penalty of 10 years. The inclusion of oral penetration within the definition of rape prompted extensive debate, particularly within the House of Lords, and although creating a separate offence of oral penetration was mooted, it was ultimately rejected as unnecessary by over-complicating the situation and failing to reflect the seriousness of the act.

The White Paper *Protecting the Public* confirmed one of the principles underlying the new range of sexual offences that they should not be gender specific. However, as rape can only be performed by intentional penile penetration the new definition of rape will therefore not apply to circumstances where a woman compels a man to penetrate her without his consent.

However, this form of sexual offending will be caught within the scope of a new offence of causing another person to perform an indecent act without consent which will, in relation to sexual penetration, carry a maximum penalty of life.

2.1.3 Penalty

The offence continues to be triable only on indictment and carries a maximum sentence of life imprisonment.

2.1.4 Consent

Where the complainant does not consent the offence of rape will clearly be committed. The question of whether that party consented will remain a matter for the jury. Save in the circumstances specified below, there must always be some evidence of the lack of consent which can be put before the jury. The nature of such evidence will vary on a case by case basis.

The Act also provides that the defendant must 'reasonably believe' that the complainant consented. Whether a belief is reasonable and was introduced on amendment in the House of Lords, is to be determined having regard to all the circumstances, including any steps the defendant has taken to ascertain whether the complainant consents. (HL Deb, 17 June 2003, col.669).

The Government's message in changing the law was clear.

> The point of the test is to send out a clear signal to the public at large that where there is room for doubt as to whether the person with whom you are about to engage in sexual activity consents to that activity, then you should act reasonably to remove that doubt before continuing.

> www.homeoffice.gov.uk/justice/sentencing/sexualoffencesbill/faq.html

The burden is now clearly upon any person to take care to ensure that his partner is consenting and for him to be at risk of prosecution if he does not. However, the test remains sufficiently flexible to take account of individual characteristics of a defendant, such as learning difficulties or extreme youth which might affect the defendant's ability to understand whether or not the complainant is consenting.

There is now a clear obligation on someone who is about to have sexual intercourse with another person not to act negligently in terms of whether consent is present or not.

In determining whether the defendant's belief in consent was reasonable, it will be vital to consider the steps that he has taken to ascertain whether the other party consents. The purpose of this inclusion is to focus the court's attention on what is happening at the time of the offence and push to the margins of relevance factors like the previous sexual history of the complainant. There may still be instances when the previous sexual history of the complainant is relevant, and accordingly it will be admitted by the judge when the interests of justice require it. In 'date rape', for example, there may not be any independent evidence apart from the complainant's and the defendant's regarding the reasonable steps that the defendant did, or did not, take.

Once the defendant raises the issue of consent, the ultimate burden will remain on the prosecution to disprove the belief in consent.

Rebuttable presumptions about the absence of consent

For offences of rape, assault by penetration, sexual assault and causing a person to engage in sexual activity without consent, there are, in specified circumstances presumptions about the absence of consent, which the defendant will have an evidential burden to rebut.

The background to the reform was highlighted by Lord Falconer:

> In its consultation paper *Setting the Boundaries*, the independent review body proposed that there should be a statutory list of circumstances in which it could be

conclusively presumed by the jury that the complainant did not consent to sexual activity. The aim was to clarify existing case law and to incorporate it into statute, thereby allowing Parliament to give a clear indication to the courts and society at large about the circumstances in which sexual activity will not be condoned and in which there can be no doubt that a jury will pass a guilty verdict in relation to any defendant who is proved to have committed the relevant act.

Section 75 provides that when a defendant does an act to which that section applies (rape, indecent assault, etc.) and that the defendant was aware of the circumstances in subsection 2, the complainant is taken not to have consented, *unless sufficient evidence is adduced to raise an issue as to whether he consented to it, and that the defendant reasonably believed that he consented.*

The circumstances referred to by s.75(2) are that:

(a) any person was, at the time of the relevant act, or immediately before it began, using violence against the complainant or causing the complainant to fear that immediate violence would be used against him;

(b) any person was, at the time of the relevant act, or immediately before it began, causing the complainant to fear that violence was being used or that immediate violence would be used, against another person;

(c) the complainant was, and the defendant was not, unlawfully detained at the time of the relevant act;

(d) the complainant was asleep, or otherwise unconscious at the time of the relevant act;

(e) because of the complainant's physical disability, the complainant would not have been able at the time of the relevant act to communicate to the defendant whether the complainant consented;

(f) any person had administered to or caused to be taken by the complainant, without the complainant's consent, a substance which, having regard to when it was administered or taken, was capable of causing or enabling the complainant to be stupefied or overpowered at the time of the relevant act.

In such scenarios evidence must be adduced to raise the issue of consent. Home Office Minister, Baroness Asthal, explained:

In order for these presumptions not to apply, the defendant will need to satisfy the jury that there is a real issue about consent [or belief in consent] that is worth putting before the jury. The evidence relied on may be, for example, evidence that the defendant himself gives in the witness box, or evidence given on his behalf by a defence witness, or evidence given by the complainant during cross-examination. If the judge is satisfied that there is sufficient evidence to justify putting the issue of consent to the jury, then the issues will have to be proved by the prosecution in the normal way.

If the judge does not think that the evidence relied on by the defendant meets this threshold, he will direct the jury to find the defendant guilty, assuming that the jury is sure that the defendant did the relevant act, that the circumstances in subsection 2 applied and the defendant knew that (HL Deb, 17 June 2003, cols 670–671).

This clearly shifts the balance in favour of the complainant, although only once the circumstances referred to in subsection 2 are established. These provisions are not entirely new and re-enact provision made in case law. There are, though, potential dangers with this subsection, an example of which is the treatment of sleep – a possible scenario was given in the House of Lords:

> I am a little anxious about the treatment of sleep. Again I accept the general thinking behind the Bill; that having intercourse with someone who is asleep should in normal circumstances be regarded as an offence because consent cannot be given. However, there is one particular circumstance which to my knowledge has arisen in court and has become an issue, where the couple had had consensual intercourse and fallen asleep in bed side by side.

> In the middle of the night the woman reached out and made a gesture of affection, which the man interpreted as a gesture of consent. But it was not. She woke in the night, too drunk to remember how she got there, and screamed rape; as one might if one woke in the middle of the night and found a strange man beside one. But, until the lady indicated that she did not consent, there was a rebuttable presumption that she did. If a man makes love to a woman and goes to bed with her and falls asleep with her, he is entitled to presume that she consents until she tells him otherwise, and no longer. So the treatment of sleep in cases where there has been consensual intercourse immediately beforehand cannot be the same as the treatment of sleep in other circumstances.

Conclusive presumptions about the absence of consent

Where it is proved that the defendant acted in the manner described in s.75(2) there are a further two circumstances in which it will be conclusively presumed that the complainant did not consent and that the defendant did not believe in consent.

These arise where the defendant has induced sexual activity and in so doing he:

- intentionally deceived the complainant as to the nature or purpose of the relevant act; or
- induced the complainant to consent to the act by impersonating a person known personally to the complainant (s.76(2)).

These presumptions will apply to the offences of rape and sexual assaults strengthening s.142(3) of the Criminal Justice and Public Order Act 1994 which provided that 'a man . . . commits rape if he induces a married woman to have intercourse with him by impersonating her husband'. The protection of the law was extended to impersonation of a partner by R. v. *Elbekkay* [1995] Crim LR 163.

Placing conclusive presumptions about the absence of consent in the Act did not meet universal approval and were described in some quarters as overkill. When the circumstances now provided for by s.76 apply, it would be very doubtful that a jury, applying the objective test of consent, would think that consent actually existed. Indeed there is even the risk that a jury directed to consider rebuttable presumptions may be confused by legal jargon whereas the intention in the law was to bring clarity.

2.2   RAPE OF A CHILD UNDER 13

The review document *Setting the Boundaries* gave serious consideration as to whether the age of consent needed to be retained, and if so at what age. Opinion, perhaps not surprisingly, was sharply divided. It concluded that whilst the law will never prevent children from experimenting in sexual matters, the overriding public interest lay in retaining the age of consent in terms of child protection both from predatory adults and other children.

Having concluded in favour of retaining the age of consent the document recognised that there would still be situations in which children, in spite of the law, would consent to sexual relationships, and that this consenting behaviour was bound to be addressed by the law. The age in which consent could not be recognised in law would have to be below one in which it could be said safely that there was neither mutual agreement (because one or both parties was too young to possess the necessary knowledge, understanding and maturity to know what they were agreeing to) nor legal consent, where children should be protected from all sexual activity.

The result of the review is a new offence of raping a child under 13 introduced by the Act. For such an offence of rape it is unnecessary for the prosecution to prove the absence of consent.

The offence of sexual intercourse with a girl under 13 contrary to s.5 of the Sexual Offences Act 1956 is abolished. The offence of unlawful sexual intercourse with a girl under 16, and the so called 'young man's defence' that applied to it are also abolished.

This new offence applies to any defendant regardless of their age and as such attracted some criticism for bringing the full weight of the criminal law in cases where young people who are close in age are experimenting. Under the 1956 Act the offence of rape could be charged when consent was, de facto, absent, and the offence of unlawful sexual intercourse when it was not. Critics of the new offence point to the European perspective. For example, in Austria the common age of consent for males and females is 14; in Denmark, Finland and France it is 15; in Italy, on occasions, it can be 14; in Spain it is as low as 12, and in Sweden as low as 15.

The Government response was in these terms:

> A fundamental justification for the under-13 offence is the age and vulnerability of the victim. We do not think it is right that where the victim is 12 or under the question of consent should arise. There will be many cases where it would be utterly invidious for a 12 year old or under to have to give evidence in relation to consent. We therefore think that there needs to be a cut-off period. We think we have got the cut-off period right.

To ensure that the Government's objectives are met, the Crown Prosecution Service is to publish guidelines for prosecution (see para. 2.2.2).

How the offence may continue to work in practice was also explained by *Setting the Boundaries* (para. 3.5.11):

> In making this proposal we are not proposing statutory rape. The presumption of no consent applies to the 'consensual' offences of adult sexual abuse of a child, persistant sexual abuse of a child and sexual activity between minors. Rape and sexual assault by penetration are in essence offences where lack of consent has to be proved. We hope however the courts will find our arguments useful in cases involving the rape of children.

2.2.1   Consent

The issue of consent is immaterial, both in fact and in law.

2.2.2   Charging standards

To appease the criticism the Home Office minister Lord Falconer indicated that where sexual relationships between minors are not abusive, prosecuting either or both children is highly unlikely to be in the public interest. Nor would it be in the best interests of the children involved:

> In such cases, protection will normally best be achieved by educating the children and providing them and their families with counselling services. Even where the sexual activity is abusive, the Crown Prosecution Service may consider that it is not in the public interest to prosecute someone under 16 if other courses of action are likely to be more effective. The CPS has a discretion about whether or not to prosecute in such cases. We would expect it to continue to use that discretion wisely.

2.2.3   Knowledge as to age

Knowledge as to the age of the victim is also irrelevant, even if it is based upon reasonable grounds.

2.2.4   Penalty

The offence is triable only on indictment. A person guilty of an offence under this section is liable, on conviction, to imprisonment for life.

2.3   SEXUAL ASSAULTS

The offence of indecent assault provided by s.14 of the Sexual Offences Act 1956 is abolished. Amongst the faults that were perceived with it was that it covered too wide a range of sexual offending, from relatively minor assaults through to very serious violent attacks. In particular the Government wished to recognise that assaults by penetration can be just as damaging to victims as penile penetration. Under the 1956 legislation assaults involving some form of penetration could only be charged as an offence of indecent assault carrying a maximum penalty of 10 years' imprisonment.

All the behaviour that would previously have been charged as an indecent assault under the 1956 Act will remain criminal; however, it will be covered by two new sets of offences rather than one. These offences, in line with much in the 2003 Act, are not gender specific and can be committed by a male or female, against a male or female. They are assault by penetration (s.2) and sexual assault (s.3).

2.4   ASSAULT BY PENETRATION

Section 2 of the Act creates a distinct offence of assault by penetration. This offence is committed by the intentional, non-consensual penetration of vagina or anus with a body part or anything else. It does not, as is the case with rape, extend to oral penetration.

There is a clear overlap between rape and assault by penetration as any penetration with the penis would also amount to an assault by penetration. Where it is clear that the penis is the object with which somebody has been penetrated, a person will always be charged with rape. The two clauses were drafted as they were because there may be circumstances where it is not clear with what the victim was penetrated. If somebody is blindfolded, for example, there may be a reasonable assumption or a view about what happened, but it will not be clear (example given by Beverley Hughes at House of Commons committee stage). The distinction is deliberate and important and allows for that eventuality.

2.4.1   Sexual penetration

The penetration complained of must be sexual. Section 78 of the Act describes penetration as sexual if a reasonable person would consider that:

    (a) whatever its circumstances or any person's purpose in relation to it, it is because of its nature sexual, or
    (b) because of its nature it may be sexual and because of its circumstances or the purpose of any person in relation to it (or both) it is sexual.

An act will be sexual if it is objectively thought of as such, however the second limb of the test will cover behaviour that a particular individual may derive sexual pleasure from, even if it would appear strange or bizarre by objective standards.

2.4.2   Consent

The position is as that for rape described at para. 2.1. Both the rebuttable and conclusive presumptions about the absence of consent also apply to an offence committed under this section.

Whereas s.14(2) of the Sexual Offences Act 1956 prevented a girl under the age of 16 from giving consent, the new section makes no provision regarding the age of consent. Instead, non-consensual offences are likely to be charged under this section, whereas de facto consensual offences involving persons under 16 will now be charged as child sex offences. See Chapter 3 for further details of such scenarios.

2.4.3   Penalty

The matter is triable only on indictment. The maximum sentence upon conviction is life imprisonment.

2.5   ASSAULT ON A CHILD UNDER 13 BY PENETRATION

When a person intentionally penetrates the vagina or anus of a person under 13, with a part of his body or anything else and the penetration is sexual, a separate offence is committed contrary to s.6 of the Act.

2.5.1   Consent

Due to the age of the victim the issue of consent is removed from the jury, and an offence of strict liability is created.

2.5.2   Penalty

The matter is triable only on indictment. The maximum sentence upon conviction is life imprisonment.

2.6   INTENTIONAL SEXUAL ASSAULT

Section 3 of the Act introduces an offence of intentional sexual assault. This may take place by touching or penetration, provided that it is sexual in nature. Touching is considered sexual if a reasonable person would consider that (s.78):

(a) whatever its circumstances or any person's purpose in relation to it, it is because of its nature, sexual,or
(b) because of its nature it may be sexual and because of its circumstances or the purpose of any person in relation to it (or both) it is sexual.

An act will be sexual if it is objectively thought of as such. The second limb of the test will cover behaviour that an individual may derive sexual pleasure from even if it would appear strange or bizarre by objective standards.

It is submitted that there is a distinction between the definition of 'sexual' in this Act and that of indecent assault provided by the Sexual Offences Act 1956 and subsequent case law. In *R. v. Court* [1989] AC 28, HL, the test of what amounted to 'indecent' was explained as whether 'right-minded persons would consider the conduct indecent or not'. The test was to be applied with reference to modern standards of modesty and privacy.

Kissing in a public place may be considered sexual but not indecent by a reasonable bystander. This distinction might seem like a nicety in terms of the offences which involve an actual assault but the definition becomes more acutely relevant when dealing with the other offences created by the Act which can take place consensually.

Whether intentional or not, it is submitted that the definition of sexual is wider than that of indecent.

Touching is defined by s.79(8) in these terms:

> Touching includes touching
>
> (a) with any part of the body,
> (b) with anything else,
> (c) through anything,
>
> and in particular includes touching amounting to penetration.

2.6.1   Consent

The assault must take place without consent. The test of consent and the presumptions about the absence of consent are the same as for rape (see para. 2.1.4).

2.6.2   Penalty

The offence is triable either way. The maximum sentence on summary conviction is six months' imprisonment or a fine and upon conviction on indictment the maximum penalty is 10 years' imprisonment.

2.7   SEXUAL ASSAULT ON A CHILD UNDER 13

When the sexual assault is committed upon on a child under 13 years old, a distinct offence with separate sentencing powers is provided by s.7 of the Act.

2.7.1   Consent

Due to the age of the victim the issue of consent is removed from the jury, and an offence of strict liability is created.

2.7.2   Penalty

The offence is triable either way. On summary conviction the maximum sentence is six months' imprisonment, a fine or both. On conviction on indictment the maximum sentence is 14 years' imprisonment.

The maximum penalty available for this offence is sterner than that available when adults are assaulted in similar circumstances to reflect the comparative gravity of the offence.

2.8   CAUSING A PERSON TO ENGAGE IN SEXUAL ACTIVITY WITHOUT CONSENT

Existing legislation does not expressly provide for the prosecution of someone who forces another person to perform sexual or indecent acts. To remedy this loophole the Sexual Offences Act 2003 introduces a number of offences of causing a person to engage in sexual activity. Two new offences are created by the Act, applying to adults and children respectively.

Section 4 of the Act creates a specific offence of intentionally causing a person to engage in sexual activity without their consent. This offence will provide an equivalent to the charge of rape where, for example, a woman compels a man to have sexual intercourse with her, although the potential scope of the section is much wider than that.

2.8.1   Consent

The test for consent is the same as for rape, namely that there was no consent and the defendant did not believe that there was consent. Such belief is to be objectively judged (see para. 2.1.4).

2.8.2   Presumptions about the absence of consent

To prevent an abusive position this offence is covered by the provisions of ss.75 and 76 of the Act, (see para. 2.1.4) the circumstances in which there is a presumption against consent.

2.8.3   Penalty

The venue for trial and the court's sentencing powers will depend upon the activity alleged. When the activity concerned was, as described by s.4(4):

(a) penetration of B's anus or vagina,
(b) penetration of B's mouth with a person's penis,
(c) penetration of a person's anus or vagina with a part of B's body or by B with anything else, or
(d) penetration of a person's mouth with B's penis,

the matter must be tried on indictment. The maximum sentence in such a case is imprisonment for life.

When the conduct alleged is not encompassed by s.4(4) the offence is triable either way. In such circumstances the penalty on summary conviction is a fine, imprisonment for up to six months or both, and on conviction on indictment the maximum penalty is 10 years' imprisonment.

2.9   CAUSING A CHILD UNDER 13 TO ENGAGE IN SEXUAL ACTIVITY

A distinct offence against victims under 13 is created by s.8 of the Act. As in the corresponding provision for adults it is an offence to intentionally cause another person to engage in sexual activity when that person is under 13. To reflect the gravity of the offence, sentencing powers are increased and the matter is triable only on indictment.

2.9.1   Consent

Due to the age of the victim the issue of consent is removed from the jury, and an offence of strict liability is created.

2.9.2   Penalty

This offence must always be tried on indictment. The penalty available to the court will vary according to the conduct alleged. When, as defined at s.8(3), the activity involved:

(a) penetration of B's anus or vagina,
(b) penetration of B's mouth with a person's penis,
(c) penetration of a person's anus or vagina with a part of B's body or by B with anything else, or
(d) penetration of a person's mouth with B's penis,

the maximum penalty is life imprisonment.

In all other cases the maximum penalty is 14 years' imprisonment. Table 2.1 illustrates the position.

Table 2.1 Affect of age and conduct on mode of trial and penalty when offence is causing a person to engage in sexual activity

Age of complainant	Conduct alleged	Mode of trial	Penalty
Under 13 years	Penetration of B's anus or vagina; penetration of B's mouth with a person's penis, penetration of a person's anus or vagina with a part of B's body or by B with anything else, or penetration of a person's mouth with B's penis	Indictable only	Life imprisonment
Under 13 years	Any other conduct	Indictable only	14 years' imprisonment
Over 13	Penetration of B's anus or vagina, penetration of B's mouth with a person's penis, penetration of a person's anus or vagina with a part of B's body or by B with anything else, or penetration of a person's mouth with B's penis	Indictable only	10 years' imprisonment
Over 13	Any other conduct	Either way	6 months summarily and 10 years on

3 CHILD SEX OFFENCES

3.1 BACKGROUND

Whilst the pre-existing law offered a high level of protection to children it was open to criticism as being piecemeal and inconsistent. It did not cover consensual sexual activity between family members of the same sex falling short of incest nor did it offer children appropriate protection against step-parents, step-siblings, uncles and aunts.

Those anomalies were not the only inconsistency. The review document *Setting the Boundaries* (para 3.2.2) gave a number of examples:

- The level of penalties are out of kilter (e.g. unlawful sexual intercourse with a girl under the age of 16 carries a maximum penalty of two years yet an indecent assault on a girl of the same age carries a maximum penalty of 10 years).
- There are defences available to some but not all. The 'young man's defence' available to men charged with unlawful sexual intercourse on women as there is no equivalent offence against boys.
- There are also time limits attached to prosecutions for certain offences, such as unlawful sexual intercourse and gross indecency which required a prosecution to be brought within 12 months of the allegation. Time limits were criticised as arbitrary and did not assist in bringing cases as many children delayed in bringing cases until they felt in a safe environment to do so.

The Government response to that review is found in ss.9 to 15 of the Sexual Offences Act 2003 (the Act) which create a separate series of 'child sex offences' to cover activity between defendants and children younger than 16.

The offences in this section are distinguished from the offences of sexual assault, as consent is not in issue. Whilst it has been recognised that children younger than 16 are capable of reaching decisions about whether or not to engage in sexual behaviour, these provisions allow no flexibility.

Many potential problems may arise in circumstances in which two children are experimenting sexually but one or both is under 16 years of age. Clear charging standards will need to be issued by the Crown Prosecution Service to ensure that prosecutions are only brought in appropriate cases.

These sections also amend the law with respect to the defence of mistaken belief in the age of the child. A recent case before the House of Lords (*R. v. K.* [2002] 1 AC 462, HL) has altered the law by reading into statutory provisions a requirement for the prosecution to prove the absence of an honest although not necessarily reasonable belief that the child was 16 or over.

The Act introduces a test of reasonableness. When the child is aged between 13 and 16 it will now be for the prosecution to prove that the defendant did not have a mistaken belief in the child's age, or if he did, that it was not a reasonable belief.

Where the victim is under 13 the offence is one of strict liability as in these cases the defendant's belief in the age of the complainant will not be relevant.

3.2   SEXUAL ACTIVITY WITH A CHILD

The offence of sexual activity with a child under 16 years old is a separate offence from that of sexual assault created by s.3 of the Act, although the definition of 'sexual' and 'touching' remain the same.

Whilst there is an clear overlap between this offence and that of sexual assault created by s.3, the distinction is that consent is not an issue when the activity involves a child.

The offence is designed to operate in positions where there is a significant age difference between the parties to the sexual activity and thereby protect children from abuse.

3.2.1   Consent

The distinguishing feature between this offence and that of sexual assualt is that consent is not an issue. Accordingly, where a 15-year-old girl and her 18-year-old boyfriend engage in heavy petting to which they both consent, assuming that as her boyfriend he is aware of his girlfriend's age, he will be committing an offence punishable with up to 14 years' imprisonment.

Not suprisingly the offence has been criticised as criminalising perfectly normal adolescent behaviour, the knock-on effect of which will be to risk bringing into total disrepute the age of consent at 16. It may also have an effect by preventing young people in consensual relationships from seeking advice on contraception or lead to the more vulnerable being subject to abuse by a domineering partner of a similar age because of the secrecy involved.

The level of conduct that will be tolerated by society can be obtained from the present CPS charging standards. Those guidelines state that, if the victim consented, that would be relevant when considering the public interest in whether to prosecute. Other factors such as the age of the defendant in relation to the victim, emotional maturity, any element of seduction, the relationship between the parties, a duty of care and breach of trust are, rightly, taken into consideration now. The charging standards could not, because of obvious drafting considerations, be incorporated into the Act.

The Government's position was stated by Paul Goggins, Home Office minister at committee stage in the Commons.

> We are trying in these clauses to add more protection where consent is less clear than it is when one of the non-consensual offences applies. The balance is clearly a difficult one, but the objective in this part of the Bill is to add protection for children even when the activity engaged in is with other children.

3.2.2   Relevance of the complainant's age

In any case in which the complainant is between 13 and 15 years old, it will be for the prosecution to prove that the defendant did not believe that the complainant was over 16. The defendant's belief must be reasonable.

The defendant will have an evidential burden to establish that he reasonably believed that the complainant was over 16 years old. If he discharges that burden the prosecution will ultimately have to prove that he did not have such a belief. When the child is under 13 no issue arises as to the defendant's belief in the child's age.

3.2.3   Penalty – the importance of the age of the defendant (A) and the victim (B)

The penalty available and the mode of trial will depend upon the conduct alleged, and the age of the defendant.

When the activity involved (s.9(2)):

(a)   penetration of B's anus or vagina with a part of A's body or anything else,
(b)   penetration of B's mouth with a person's penis,
(c)   penetration of A's anus or vagina with a part of B's body, or
(d)   penetration of A's mouth with B's penis;

the matter is triable only on indictment and the maximum penalty is one of 14 years' imprisonment. In any other case involving an adult defendant the matter is triable either way, with a maximum sentence of six months on summary conviction and 14 years on indictment.

The Act draws a distinction between adults and youths in terms of sentence. When the offence is commited by children under 18, s.13 of the Act provides the offence is triable either way. On summary conviction it is punishable with a sentence of up to six months' imprisonment. The maximum sentence upon conviction on indictment is one of five years. Table 3.1 illustrates the position.

Table 3.1 Factors affecting mode of trial and penalty in relation to sexual activity with a child

Defendant's age	Complainant's age	Relevance of age/defences	Mode of trial and penalties
10–17 years per section 13	Under 13	None	Either way offence 6 months maximum if tried summarily, 5 years maximum on indictment
10–17 years per section 13	Over 13 but under 16	When complainant over 13. Reasonable belief that the complainant was over 16	Either way offence 6 months on summary conviction or 5 years on indictment
18 or over	Under 13	None	Where conduct involved: penetration of B's anus or vagina; penetration of B's mouth with a person's penis; penetration of a person's anus or vagina with a part of B's body or by B with anything else; or penetration of a person's mouth with B's penis; indictable only, maximum sentence 14 years. In any other case, either way offence, 6 months on summary conviction and 14 years on indictment.
18 or over	Over 13 but under 16 years old.	When complainant over 13. Reasonable belief that the complainant was over 16	Where conduct involved: penetration of B's anus or vagina; penetration of B's mouth with a person's penis; penetration of a person's anus or vagina with a part of B's body or by B with anything else; or penetration of a person's mouth with B's penis indictable only, maximum sentence 14 years. In any other case, either way offence, 6 months on summary conviction and 14 years on indictment.

3.3   CAUSING OR INCITING A CHILD TO ENGAGE IN SEXUAL ACTIVITY

The offence created by s.10 of the Act is causing a child to engage in sexual activity. It may be carried out:

- on the defendant, for example, where he causes the child to have sexual intercourse with him;
- on the child himself, for example, where the defendant causes the child to strip for his sexual gratification; or
- on a third person, for example, where the defendant causes the child to have sexual intercourse with his friend.

The offence may even be committed where the incitement takes place even if the sexual activity itself does not.

In *Fairclough* v. *Whipp* (1951) 35 Cr App R 138, DC, the defendant exposed his penis in the presence of a young girl and invited her to touch it, which she did. As she had done so on the invitation of the defendant, the matter could not be prosecuted as an indecent assault. This is precisely the sort of behaviour that the new offence is designed to protect against.

As is the case with the offence of sexual activity with a child created by section 9 of the Act, where the complainant is aged between 13 and 15, the prosecution must prove that the defendant did not reasonably believe that the complainant was over 16. The marriage exception will also apply.

3.3.1   Consent

Due to the age of the complainant it is not necessary for the prosecution to prove the absence of consent.

3.3.2   Relevance of the complainant's age

In any case in which the complainant is between 13 and 15 years old, it will be for the prosecution to prove that the defendant did not believe that the complainant was over 16. The defendant's belief must be reasonable.

The defendant will have an evidential burden to establish that he reasonably believed that the complainant was over 16 years old. When he does so the prosecution will ultimately have to prove that he did not have such a belief.

When the child is under 13 no issue arises as to the defendant's belief in the child's age.

3.3.3   Penalty – the importance of the age of the defendant (A) and the victim (B)

The penalty available and the mode of trial will depend upon the conduct alleged, and the age of the defendant.

When the defendant is an adult the activity involved (s.10(2)):

(a) penetration of B's anus or vagina;
(b) penetration of B's mouth with a person's penis;
(c) penetration of a person's anus or vagina with a part of B's body or by B with anything else; or
(d) penetration of a person's mouth with B's penis;

the matter is triable only on indictment and the maximum penalty is one of 14 years' imprisonment. In any other case involving an adult defendant the matter is triable either way, with a maximum sentence of six months on summary conviction and 14 years on indictment.

The Act draws a distinction between adults and youths in terms of sentence. When the offence is commited by children under 18, s.13 of the Act provides the offence is triable either way. On summary covnviction it is punishable with a sentence of up to six months' imprisonment. The maximum sentence upon conviction upon indictment is one of five years. Table 3.2 illustrates the position.

3.4   ENGAGING IN SEXUAL ACTIVITY IN THE PRESENCE OF A CHILD

Adults who intentionally engage in sexual activity in the presence of a child may also be committing an offence if the purpose of the activity was to obtain sexual gratification.

The offence will apply when the act is engaged in (s.11(1)(c)):

■   when another person (the child) is present or is in a place from which they can be observed; and
■   they knew, believed or intended that the child would be aware of it.

3.4.1   Relevance of age

As in the offence of causing or inciting a child to engage in sexual activity, where the child concerned is aged between 13 and 15, it is for the prosecution to show that the defendant did not reasonably believe that the child concerned was older than 16. The offence is one of strict liability when the child is under 13 years.

Table 3.2 Factors affecting mode of trial and penalty when causing or inciting a child to engage in sexual activity

Defendant's age	Complainant's age	Relevance of age/defences	Mode of trial and penalties
10–17 years per section 13	Under 13	None	Either way offence 6 months maximum if tried summarily, 5 years maximum on indictment
10–17 years per section 13	Over 13 but under 16	When complainant over 13. Reasonable belief that the complainant was over 16	Either way offence 6 months on summary conviction or 5 years on indictment
18 or over	Under 13	None	Where conduct involved: penetration of B's anus or vagina, penetration of B's mouth with a person's penis, penetration of a person's anus or vagina with a part of B's body or by B with anything else, or penetration of a person's mouth with B's penis; indictable only, maximum sentence 14 years. In any other case, either way offence, 6 months on summary conviction and 14 years on indictment
18 or over	Over 13 but under 16 years old.	When complainant over 13. Reasonable belief that the complainant was over 16	Where conduct involved: penetration of B's anus or vagina, penetration of B's mouth with a person's penis, penetration of a person's anus or vagina with a part of B's body or by B with anything else, or penetration of a person's mouth with B's penis; indictable only, maximum sentence 14 years. In any other case, either way offence, 6 months on summary conviction and 14 years on indictment

3.4.2 Penalty

In every case this offence is triable either way. The maximum sentence for an adult is six months' imprisonment upon summary conviction and 10 years' imprisonment upon conviction on indictment.

When the defendant is between 10–17 years old the maximum sentence is five years when tried on indictment and six months' imprisonment upon summary conviction.

3.5   CAUSING A CHILD TO WATCH A SEXUAL ACT

Section 12 makes it an offence for a person to intentionally cause a child to watch a third person, or to look at a photograph or pseudo-photograph (as defined in the Protection of Children Act 1978, clause 81(5)) of a person engaging in sexual activity.

The defendant must obtain sexual gratification from causing the child to watch the act.

3.5.1   Relevance of age

Where the child concerned is aged between 13 and 15, it is for the prosecution to show that the defendant did not reasonably believe that the child concerned was older than 16. The offence is one of strict liability when the child is under 13 years.

3.5.2   Penalty

In every case this offence is triable either way. The maximum sentence for an adult is six months' imprisonment on summary conviction and 10 years' imprisonment on conviction on indictment.

When the defendant is between 10–17 years old the maximum sentence is five years when tried on indictment and six months' imprisonment upon summary conviction.

3.6   ARRANGING OR FACILITATING A CHILD SEX OFFENCE

It will also be an offence for a person to intentionally arrange or facilitate something which, if done, will involve the commission of any of the child sex offences created by ss.9 to 13 of the Act.

The defendant may make the arrangements on behalf of himself, or on behalf of a third party. The child sex offence can be intended to take place in any part of the world. In all cases, what is important is the defendant's intent in making those arrangements.

By creating an offence of 'facilitating', Parliament meant this section to be very widely interpreted to include preparatory acts which would fall short of a criminal attempt. Examples envisaged here include:

1.   When a person approaches an agency requesting the agency to procure a child for sex. The offence is committed whether the child is procured for the person who approaches the agency or for anyone else and whether or not the activity takes place.

2. Where a person intentionally drives another person (X) to meet a child with whom he knows X is going to have sex. He may not intend X to have child sex, but he believes that X will do so if he meets that child.
3. Where, unbeknown to the participants, a policeman assumes the role of the child, thus making the commission of the offence impossible.

It follows, therefore, that the offence will be complete by the defendant's actions even if completion of it was ultimately impossible.

3.6.1 Defence

As stated above, the offence will include any act which 'facilitates' a child sex offence. On the face of these sections a person who provides a child with contraception as part of family planning advice, or a teacher who shows an educational film providing sex education will be committing an offence.

Subsection 2 of s.14 provides an exception for a person who acts to protect the child.

Subsection 3 defines the concept of 'acting for the protection of the child' as acting to protect a child from pregnancy or sexually transmitted infections, to protect the physical safety of a child or to promote the emotional well-being of a child by the giving of advice. It ensures that adults acting in a professional capacity have the confidence to know in advance that this exception exists when they provide the advice and support that is necessary to children.

An example of how this clause will operate was given, at the standing committee in the Commons, by Paul Goggins, the Home Office minister:

> Someone who is involved in providing sexual advice to teenagers might be aware that a 14-year-old girl is engaging in sexual activity. He or she might counsel her as necessary, but still know that the activity is taking place, and perhaps, from the child's reports, that serious physical harm or pain is occurring. We would not want that person, who is providing much-needed advice in desperate circumstances, to be caught by the provisions of the clause; that is why the exceptions are included.

It will be for the prosecution to show, once the defence was raised, that it could not possibly be said that the person's actions were for the sake of protecting the physical safety of the child.

A very fine line is drawn in the sand by subsection 3. Where a person is acting to cause or encourage the sexual activity there will be no defence.

3.6.2 Penalty

An either way offence is created, punishable on summary conviction by a term of imprisonment not exceeding six months or on indictment by a term of imprisonment not exceeding 14 years. This penalty will apply regardless of the age of the defendant.

3.7   MEETING A CHILD FOLLOWING SEXUAL GROOMING

3.7.1   Background

Pre-existing legislation meant that a person luring a child to meet them for a sexual purpose could rarely be charged, as no offence had actually occurred. The briefing paper prepared by Childnet International (see **www.childnet-int.org/ publications**) for the benefit of the Home Office provided a number of startling real life examples of this.

A further example of the failings of existing legislation can be demonstrated by s.1 of the Indecency with Children Act 1960, which created a specific provision of inciting a child to commit an act of gross indecency – the act of gross indecency was often difficult for the prosecution to prove. Charging a person with an attempt to commit an offence was likewise troublesome as evidence of an attempt to do such an act will always be difficult to obtain. The Act now provides for the making of Risk of Sexual Harm Orders when risk is anticipated, but the defendant has not progressed sufficiently to be charged with an attempt.

In an effort to make convictions easier to secure against defendants who behaved nefariously, but fell outside the arm of the law, section 16 of the Act, creates a new offence of meeting a child following sexual grooming.

3.7.2   Scope

An adult (defined as over 18 at s.16(1)) will commit an offence by meeting, or travelling with the intention of meeting, another person. He must have met or communicated with that person on *at least* two earlier occasions.

The person concerned must be under 16 (under s.17(3) the age is 17 in Northern Ireland) and the defendant must not reasonably believe them to be over that age.

The section is intended to cover situations[1] where an adult establishes contact with a child, for example, through meetings, telephone conversations or communications on the Internet with the intention of gaining the child's trust and confidence so that he can arrange to meet the child with the intention of committing a 'relevant offence'[2] against the child.

The course of conduct prior to the meeting may have an explicitly sexual content, such as the defendant entering into conversations with the child about the sexual acts he wants to engage them in when they meet or sending images of adult pornography. However, the meetings or communication need not have an explicitly sexual content and could, for example, simply be giving the child swimming lessons or meeting them incidentally through a friend.

The defendant may intend to do the act at any time during or after the meeting and in any part of the world, but the meeting itself must take place (or be arranged to take place in relation to the 'travelling to' limb of the offence) in England or Wales or Northern Ireland.

The offence will be complete either when the defendant meets the child or when he travels to the pre-arranged meeting with the intent to commit a relevant offence against the child. The evidence of the intent may be drawn from the communications between the defendant and the child before the meeting or may be drawn from other circumstances, for example, when the defendant travels to the meeting with ropes, condoms and lubricants.

Subsection 2(a) provides that the defendant's previous meetings or communications with the child can have taken place in or across any part of the world. This would cover, for example, the defendant e-mailing the child from abroad, or the defendant and the child speaking on the telephone in one country and then meeting in another.

The planned offence does not actually have to take place. It is so drafted to enable action to be taken prior to the child coming to any harm. This has been criticised as going too far by convicted people for what they might do rather than what they have done (see **www.trevor-mendham.com/civil-liberties/new-labour/sexual-offences.html**).

---

1 Example given at HL Deb, 1 April 2003, col 1256, by Lord Falconer of Thornton QC.
2 Defined by section 16(2)(b) as an offence under this part, an offence under paragraphs 61 to 92 of Schedule 3, or action done outside England, Wales and Northern Ireland that would be an offence if done in England and Wales.

3.7.3   Penalty

An either way offence is created, punishable on summary conviction to a term of imprisonment not exceeding six months, or upon conviction on indictment to a term of imprisonment not exceeding 14 years. The maximum penalty in Northern Ireland is 10 years, per s.15(4)(b).

4 ABUSE OF POSITION OF TRUST

4.1 BACKGROUND

The risks to children from sexual abuse are now better understood than ever before and in recent years a number of measures have been put in place to protect children from abuse.

By the provisions of the Sexual Offences Act 2003 (the Act) the Government is re-enacting the offence of 'abuse of a position of trust', provided by ss.3 and 4 of the Sexual Offences (Amendment) Act 2000 which prohibits sexual activity between those aged 18 or over and children under 18 who they are looking after in educational establishments and in various residential settings, such as prisons.

4.2 ABUSE OF A POSITION OF TRUST

4.2.1 Interpretation

The definition of position of trust is contained in ss.21 and 22 of the Act. They create a finite list of relationships in which a position of trust can exist. The list is open to amendment by the Secretary of State as he deems necessary from time to time.

There are two factors that will need to be proven for an offence to be committed under these provisions.

1. Did the defendant look after the child (under 18 years) in a place where a position of trust can arise? (Section 21(4) lists the places in which a position of trust existed. These include where an adult looks after a child at a school, a care home, prison, or hospital.)
2. Was the defendant responsible for caring for, training or supervising the child? A person will be involved in looking after another person on an individual basis if:
    –   he is regularly involved in caring for, training or supervising them; and
    –   during the course of his involvement regularly has unsupervised contact with the child alone (whether face to face or by any other means).

Examples

These new offences are designed to apply to personal advisers and those who care for, advise, supervise or train persons under 18 in the community on a one-to-one basis in pursuance of a court order made in the criminal justice system. This would include members of Youth Offending Teams provided they have sufficient contact and connection with the child, i.e. someone providing counselling or drug rehabilitation services to the child pursuant to the terms of a court order. It will also apply to a person at an educational establishment. This has been widely defined to include circumstances in which a member of the public is enrolled at one college and then sent to another college (with which the former has arrangements) for education.

It will not, on the face of it, cover caretakers. Although they may work in close proximity to children, they do not have a caring or training role in respect of them. This is a particularly significant omission with the Soham murder trial fresh in the memory.

The Act also fails to provide adequate protection for young people in groups such as Scouts and youth centres.

Any child under the age of 18 is protected by the abuse of a position of trust provision. The Act has been deliberately drafted in these terms to offer extended protection to children aged 16 and 17 in particular, as younger children will already be protected by the corresponding offences relating to child sex offences.

4.2.2   Scope of the offences

The prohibited behaviour in each of the clauses is identical to that prohibited by the child sex offences in ss.9, 10, 11 and 12 respectively, except that for these offences a 'position of trust' must also be established.

The specific offences are:

Section 16:   Abuse of a position of trust: sexual activity with a child.
Section 17:   Abuse of a position of trust: causing or inciting a child to engage in sexual activity.
Section 18:   Abuse of a position of trust: sexual activity in the presence of a child.
Section 19:   Abuse of a position of trust: causing a child to watch a sexual act.

4.2.3   Consent

Sections 16 to 19 will apply regardless of whether the parties acted consensually. Although the law presently provides that the age of consent is 16, for the purpose of these sections consent becomes irrelevant. Consequently a teacher engaging in a relationship with a 17½-year-old A level student will be guilty of an offence if that relationship involves sexual intercourse, sexual touching or even heavy petting even if that student clearly consents to the activity.

4.2.4   Defences

The age of the complainant

When the child is aged between 13 and 18 years old, the prosecution must prove that the defendant does not reasonably believe that the child was over 18.

When, however, the defendant looks after a child who is:

- detained by virtue of a court order (e.g. prison);
- in a care home, clinic, hospital, residential family centre;
- at an educational institution;

then, under subsection 3 of each offence, there will be a presumption that the defendant knew that the child was under 18 unless sufficient evidence is adduced by the defendant to raise an issue as to whether or not he reasonably believed it.

This provides the defendant with an evidential rather than legal burden which is then rebuttable by the prosecution. Where the child concerned is under 13 years old, the offence is committed regardless of any belief the defendant might have in relation to the child's age.

Knowledge of position of trust

Relationships in which the carer cannot be reasonably expected to know about the position of trust are also excluded. This is designed to cover cases where, for example, the institution at which the defendant works is very large or has a number of different sites and as such the defendant may not know that the child is at the institution, and technically within scope of the Act.

When, however, the defendant looks after a child who is:

- detained by virtue of a court order (prison);
- in a care home, clinic, hospital, residential family centre;
- in an educational institution;

there will be a presumption that the carer knew a position of trust existed, unless sufficient evidence is raised by him as to whether he did not know, or could not reasonably have been expected to know, of the position of trust.

Pre-existing relationships

Lawful pre-existing sexual relationships are excluded from criminal conduct. This applies when the sexual relationship immediately pre-dated the position of trust arising, and was otherwise lawful. In such circumstances it will be for the defendant to show, on the balance of probabilities, that such a relationship existed.

The marriage exception

When the defendant proves that he was lawfully married to the complainant he will be exempt from these sections by the defence provided at s.23. For the exception to apply the parties must be lawfully married at the time the conduct occurs and the person in 'care' must be over 16.

Whilst the age at which parties can lawfully marry in this country is 16 years old, the purpose of specifying the age of the party is to exclude foreign marriages from the section.

4.2.5   Penalties

All the offences created by this part of the Act are triable either way. Punishment on summary conviction is limited to a term of imprisonment not exceeding six months, a fine or both, and upon conviction on indictment to a term of imprisonment not exceeding five years.

5 FAMILIAL SEXUAL OFFENCES

5.1 BACKGROUND

It is recognised that the balance of power within the family and the close and trusting relationships that exist can make children particularly vulnerable to abuse within its environment. Much more is now known about the extent of abuse that can take place within families and institutions than was ever considered possible at the time of drafting earlier legislation.

A key theme of the Government's review was to provide clear sex offences that would protect individuals, but especially children and the more vulnerable, from abuse and exploitation (see para. 1.1.8 of *Setting the Boundaries*). As a result the Act creates two new offences relating to familial sexual activity to replace the existing gender-specific offences of incest by a man and incest by a woman.

5.2 SEXUAL ACTIVITY WITH A CHILD FAMILY MEMBER

The first of these new offences is created by s.25 of the Sexual Offences Act 2003 (the Act). Familial sexual abuse of a child will capture the sexual abuse and exploitation of children within the family unit. The offence protects children in a family relationship up to the age of 18 from any form of intentional touching that would be considered sexual (s.78) or indecent. It will cover sexual activity between family members of the same sex; oral sex or sexual acts falling short of penetration, thereby remedying a loophole in the former law of incest.

5.3 INCITING A FAMILY MEMBER TO ENGAGE IN SEXUAL ACTIVITY

The second new offence created by this part of the Act largely mirrors that of s.10: causing or inciting a child to engage in sexual activity.

The key element of the offence will be the incitement. As such, the offence will be complete regardless of whether such act actually takes place. It covers the scenario, for example, where the defendant induces a child to masturbate in front of him but is interrupted.

5.3.1   A family relationship – definition

The definition of family, as provided by s.27, has been drafted very widely to include blood relations and children who are adopted. There are three categories of person who may be considered to be in a family relationship.

1. When the defendant is the parent, grandparent, brother, sister, half-brother, half-sister, uncle, aunt or foster parent they will *always* be in a family relationship for the purposes of the Act.
2. Step-parents and foster parents, cousins and former step-brothers and step-sisters will also be included within the definition of a family relationship *if* they lived in the same household as the child *or* have been regularly involved in caring for, or being in sole charge of, the child.
3. Other care workers such as au pairs and nannies are brought within the definition of family relationship if they live in the same household *and* are regularly responsible for caring for, or being in sole charge of, the child.

In all cases the offender may be either an adult or another child as there is evidence to suggest that some adult familial relationships are the result of long-term grooming by an older family member.

5.3.2   Relevance of age

Sexual activity (as defined by s.78 of the Act) with a family member will be unlawful when the complainant is between 13 and 18, and the defendant does not reasonably believe that he is over 18. When the complainant is under 13 a strict liability offence will be created as knowledge of the child's age or belief in it will be irrelevant.

Where the prosecution show that the child was under 18, the defendant will have an evidential burden to adduce sufficient evidence to raise an issue as to whether he reasonable believed the child was over 18.

5.3.3   Defences

Pre-existing relationships

Lawful pre-existing relationships and those in which the parties are married are exempt upon the defendant proving the existence of the relationship or marriage.

Marriage exception

When the defendant proves that he was lawfully married to the complainant he will be exempt from these sections by the defence provided at s.28. For the exception to apply, at the time the conduct occurs, the parties must be lawfully married and the complainant aged over 16.

Knowledge of the family relationship

The conduct prevented by these sections will be unlawful when the defendant knows or could reasonably be expected to know that he has a 'family relationship'. Where the prosecution prove that the familial relationship exists the defendant will be taken to have known of the relationship unless he adduces sufficient evidence to raise an issue to the contrary. This might apply, for example where the defendant has not met the child before and therefore does not realise that she is his half-sister.

5.3.4   Penalty

As with other offences the penalty available and the mode of trial will depend upon the age of the defendant and the conduct alleged. When an adult is charged the offence will carry a maximum sentence of 14 years' imprisonment, but defendants under 18 face a maximum sentence of five years.

The position is demonstrated in Table 5.1.

Table 5.1 Factors affecting mode of trial and penalty concerning familial sexual offences

Offence	Defendant's age	Mode of trial	Penalty
Sexual activity with a child family member	Over 18	The offence is indictable only where the conduct involved: penetration of B's anus or vagina with a part of B's body or anything else; penetration of B's mouth with A's penis; penetration of A's anus or vagina with a part of B's body; penetration of A's mouth with B's penis. In any other case the offence is triable either way.	6 months on summary conviction. 14 years on conviction on indictment.
Sexual activity with a child family member	Under 18	Either way in all cases. 5 years on conviction on indictment.	6 months on summary conviction.
Inciting a child family member to engage in sexual activity	Over 18	The offence is indictable only where the conduct involved: penetration of B's anus or vagina with a part of B's body or anything else; penetration of B's mouth with A's penis; penetration of A's anus or vagina with a part of B's body; penetration of A's mouth with B's penis. In any other case the offence is triable either way.	6 months on summary conviction. 14 years on conviction on indictment.
Inciting a child family member to engage in sexual activity	Under 18	Either way in all cases. 5 years on conviction on indictment.	6 months on summary conviction.

6 OFFENCES AGAINST PERSONS WITH A MENTAL DISORDER

6.1 BACKGROUND

The Government's position in relation to persons with a mental disorder is clearly stated:

> Everyone has the right to a private life (and hence a sex life) and we have no wish to interfere with that right. However, society has a duty to protect those who do not have the capacity to consent to sexual activity and those who are, by reason of mental impairment, vulnerable to sexual abuse and exploitation. We intend to introduce measures that are proportionate and fair, that will provide protection whilst avoiding unnecessary interference in the private lives of vulnerable adults

www.homeoffice.gov.uk/justice/sentencing/sexualoffencesbill/faq.html

Previous legislation in the form of the Sexual Offences Acts of 1956 and 1967 and the Mental Health Act 1959 prohibited intercourse with a 'defective' and also prevent male staff employed in mental hospitals or homes from having intercourse with patients of either sex.

The legislation was seen as out of date and inadequate, providing in most cases for low penalties upon conviction and an insufficient umbrella of protection. Part of the difficulty was the need to prove that a person was 'defective'. As the law was confined to protecting persons with a severe mental impairment it failed to protect other vulnerable people who have some degree of ability or capacity to consent to sexual relationships but could be cajoled or targeted by others. The new legislation is designed to remove barriers to prosecution, for example, the need to obtain the consent of the Director of Public Prosecutions before a prosecution could be brought contrary to s.128 of the Mental Health Act 1983 has not been reflected in the new Sexual Offences Act (the Act).

The Act creates a series of offences designed to protect mentally vulnerable people. All the offences in these sections are concerned with the situation where a person (A) involves another person (B) in sexual activity where B has a mental disorder and because of that does not have the capacity to consent to the sexual activity. In all cases the sexual activity concerned must be intentional.

The definition of sexual activity is at s.78, which describes an act as sexual if a reasonable person would consider that:

(a) whatever its circumstances or any person's purpose in relation to it, it is because of its nature, sexual; or
(b) because of its nature it may be sexual and because of its circumstances or the purpose of any person in relation to it (or both) it is sexual.

An act will be sexual if it is objectively thought of as such. However, the second limb of the test will cover behaviour that an individual may derive sexual pleasure from even if it would appear strange or bizarre by objective standards.

6.1.1   The 'mental disorder'

The definition of mental disorder is at s.79(6) of the Act and has the same meaning given by s.1 of the Mental Health Act 1983. In each case the defendant must know, or could reasonably be expected to know, that the other party had a mental disorder and because of that condition or a reason related to it, it is likely that they would be unable to consent.

The Act refers to the person with the mental disorder being 'unable to refuse', the definition of what is meant by this is contained in subsection 2 of each offence (ss.30–33) as follows:

(2) B is unable to refuse if –
(a) he lacks the capacity to choose whether to agree to the touching (whether because he lacks sufficient understanding of the nature or reasonably foreseeable consequences of what is being done, or for any other reason), or
(b) he is unable to communicate such choice to A.

Consent will be a relevant issue in prosecutions under this part. Where there is clearly a lack of consent either an offence under this section of the Act could be charged or an alternative non-consensual sexual offence. Where the mental condition precludes the complainant from providing effective consent or communicating that choice they will be deemed not to have consented.

6.1.2   The offences created

The offences are divided according to the different types of sexual activity. The types of activity covered are the same as for the child sex offences together with an additional category involving inducements, threats or deceptions to the person with the mental disorder. These offences are further explained at paras. 6.2.–6.13.

6.2   SEXUAL ACTIVITY WITH A PERSON WITH A MENTAL DISORDER IMPEDING CHOICE AND CAUSING OR INCITING A PERSON WITH A MENTAL DISORDER IMPEDING CHOICE TO ENGAGE IN SEXUAL ACTIVITY

An offence will be committed under s.30 with an intentional sexual touching (s.79(8)) of a person with a mental disorder, whilst an offence under s.31 is complete by causing or inciting them to engage in sexual activity. Examples of an offence under s.31 include the situation where the defendant causes X (being a person with a mental disorder) to have sexual intercourse with him, where the defendant causes X to undress for the defendant's sexual gratification, or where the defendant causes X to have sexual intercourse with the defendant's friend.

By including 'inciting' within the definition of s.31 an offence will be committed even when the proposed sexual activity does not take place, for whatever reason.

6.2.1   Penalties

The penalties available for the offences created by ss.30 and 31 and the venue at which they can be tried depend upon the conduct alleged. When the touching involves:

(a) penetration of B's anus or vagina with a part of A's body or anything else;
(b) penetration of B's mouth with A's penis;
(c) penetration of A's anus or vagina with a part of B's body; or
(d) penetration of A's mouth with B's penis;

the maximum sentence is life imprisonment and the offence is triable only on indictment. When any other conduct is involved, the offence is triable either way and the maximum penalty is limited to six months' imprisonment on summary conviction and upon conviction on indictment to 14 years' imprisonment.

6.3   ENGAGING IN SEXUAL ACTIVITY IN THE PRESENCE OF A PERSON WITH A MENTAL DISORDER IMPEDING CHOICE

Such an offence occurs when a person intentionally engages in sexual (s.78) activity in the presence of a person with a mental disorder. The activity must take place when the person with the mental disorder is present or can observe the defendant. Mental disorder is defined at para. 6.1.1.

The Explanatory Notes to the Bill described s.32 as dealing with the situation where the defendant (A) has sexual intercourse in the presence of the complainant with a mental disorder (B), for the purpose of obtaining sexual gratification.

The offence is only committed, however, where A *knows* or *believes* that B is aware of the sexual activity or *intends* him to be aware of it. B might be aware of the sexual activity because he is watching it at A's behest or even because A is describing what he is doing to B. In all cases B must be unable to consent due to his condition.

6.3.1   Penalty

The offence is triable either way and carries a maximum penalty on summary conviction of six months' imprisonment and on conviction on indictment to a term of imprisonment not exceeding 10 years.

6.4   CAUSING A PERSON WITH A MENTAL DISORDER TO WATCH A SEXUAL ACT

Section 33 covers the situation where A causes B to watch a third person engaging in sexual activity or to look at an image of any person engaging in sexual activity for A's sexual gratification.

Image is defined by reference to s.79(5) as a moving or still image and includes an image produced by any means, and where the context permits, a three dimensional image.

Again, the offence is only complete if the victim has a mental disorder which the defendant does, or could be reasonably be expected to, know about. As a result of that disorder the victim must be unable to consent. Consent is defined at para. 6.1.1 above.

6.4.1   Penalty

The offence is triable either way and carries a maximum penalty on summary conviction of six months' imprisonment and upon conviction on indictment to a term of imprisonment not exceeding 10 years.

6.5   INDUCEMENTS TO A PERSON WITH A MENTAL DISORDER

The Act creates a series of offences (ss.34–37) which apply to a defendant who engages in, or is responsible for, sexual activity with a person with a mental disorder. In each case the activity must take place as a result of an inducement offered or given, or as a result of a threat or deception by the defendant.

In each case the defendant must know, or reasonably be expected to know, of the complainant's mental disorder. For these offences however, there is no need to prove that the complainant did not consent to the act.

6.6   INDUCEMENT, THREAT OR DECEPTION TO PROCURE SEXUAL ACTIVITY WITH A PERSON WITH A MENTAL DISORDER

Section 34 is concerned with the situation where a person (A) involves another person (B) in sexual activity where person B has a mental disorder (see para. 6.1.1).

The offence addresses the situation where A uses inducements, threats or deceptions to obtain B's agreement to the sexual activity. The Explanatory Notes that accompany the Act give examples of behaviour to be covered by this section that include A promising B presents of anything from sweets to a holiday; a threat might be A stating that he will hurt a member of B's family; and a deception might be A stating that B will get into trouble if he does not engage in sexual activity or persuading him that it is expected that friends should engage in sexual activity.

6.6.1   Penalty

The venue of trial and the penalty available to the courts will depend upon the conduct alleged. Life imprisonment is the maximum penalty when the conduct involves any of the following acts referred to in s.34(3) as follows:

(a) penetration of B's anus or vagina with a part of A's body or anything else,
(b) penetration of B's mouth with A's penis,
(c) penetration of A's anus or vagina with a part of B's body, or
(d) penetration of A's mouth with B's penis.

When any other conduct is involved the offence is triable either way and the maximum penalty is limited to six months' imprisonment on summary conviction and on conviction on indictment to 14 years' imprisonment.

6.7   CAUSING A PERSON WITH A MENTAL DISORDER TO ENGAGE IN OR AGREE TO ENGAGE IN SEXUAL ACTIVITY BY INDUCEMENT, THREAT OR DECEPTION

Section 35 deals with the situation where A causes B to agree to engage in sexual activity by means of an inducement, threat or deception, even if the offence is not carried out. Again B must have the mental disorder of which A knows or should reasonably know about.

6.7.1   Penalty

The venue of trial and the penalty available to the courts will depend upon the conduct alleged. When the conduct involves any of the following acts referred to in s.35(3) as follows:

(a) penetration of B's anus or vagina with a part of A's body or anything else;
(b) penetration of B's mouth with A's penis;
(c) penetration of A's anus or vagina with a part of B's body; or
(d) penetration of A's mouth with B's penis;

the offence is triable only on indictment and the maximum penalty is life imprisonment.

When any other conduct is involved the offence is triable either way and the maximum penalty is limited to six months' imprisonment on summary conviction and on conviction on indictment to 14 years' imprisonment.

6.8 ENGAGING IN SEXUAL ACTIVITY IN THE PRESENCE, PROCURED BY INDUCEMENT, THREAT OR DECEPTION, OF A PERSON WITH A MENTAL DISORDER

This offence, created by s.36(1) of the Act, is committed when the defendant (A) intentionally engages in sexual activity in a position from which he can be observed by the person with a mental disorder (B) who must be present because of an inducement offered or given, or a threat or deception used for the purpose of obtaining that agreement.

The defendant's conduct must be done in B's presence for the purpose of obtaining sexual gratification so behaviour by the defendant that is accidentally observed by B will not be covered by the section. The section is widely drafted to cover activity undertaken by the defendant over the Internet which B then views.

The offence is only committed where A *knows* or *believes* that B is aware of the sexual activity or *intends* him to be aware of it. Examples of this might be when B is aware of the sexual activity because he is watching it at A's behest or even because A is describing what he is doing to B.

In all cases B must have a mental disorder that is either known, or ought reasonably to have been known, to the defendant.

6.8.1 Penalty

The offence is triable either way and is punishable on summary conviction to a term not exceeding six months, or upon conviction on indictment to a term not exceeding 10 years.

6.9   CAUSING A PERSON WITH A MENTAL DISORDER TO WATCH A SEXUAL ACT BY INDUCEMENT, THREAT OR DECEPTION

Section 37 covers conduct when A (the defendant), for the purpose of sexual gratification, intentionally causes B (the person with a mental disorder) to watch another person engaging in sexual activity or to look at an image of a person engaging in sexual activity. The sexual activity (s.78) can involve the defendant or any other third party.

The offence is only complete when B agrees to watch because of an inducement, threat or deception, and when B has a mental disorder that is either known, or ought reasonably to have been known, to the defendant.

6.9.1   Penalty

The offence is triable either way and is punishable on summary conviction to a term of imprisonment not exceeding six months, and upon conviction on indictment to a term not exceeding 10 years' imprisonment.

6.10   CARE WORKERS

Sections 38 to 41 create separate offences that only apply to care workers. These offences will apply to defendants who have a relationship of care with the mentally-disordered persons. To reflect the position of trust that exists in cases of this nature consent can never be an issue. In such cases the existence of a mental disorder by itself will be sufficient and it will be no defence to say that the mentally-disordered person did or could provide consent to the act with the defendant.

6.10.1   Relationship of care – 'Interpretation'

The relationships of care that are covered by these offences are explicitly set out at s.42. The section will operate to extend protection from those looking after the complainant personally as in all cases the defendant must have functions to perform that are likely to bring him into regular 'face to face' contact with the person with the mental disorder.

Examples include where A is a member of staff in a care home and B is a resident there (s.42(2)); where A is a receptionist at the clinic that B attends every week (s.42(3)(b)); or where A takes B on outings every week (s.42(4)). It will not apply when the defendant is employed at an institution which provides services to the mentally-disordered person when their paths are unlikely to cross in the course of that employment.

6.11   CARE WORKERS – SEXUAL ACTIVITY WITH A PERSON WITH A MENTAL DISORDER

Section 38 of the Act protects persons with a mental disorder from sexual activity with a care worker. It will apply when the defendant intentionally touches the person with the mental disorder and the touching is sexual (as defined in s.78).

The definition of mental disorder is provided by s.79(6) of the Act.

In all cases the defendant must know, or could reasonably be expected to know, about the complainant's mental disorder (see para. 6.11.3).

6.11.1   Consent

The presence or absence of consent is irrelevant to a conviction under this section. Once it is established that the victim has a mental disorder it is assumed that he does not have the capacity to consent.

6.11.2   Defences

Awareness of condition

The provisions about the defendant's awareness of the complainant's mental disorder are contained in s.38(2) in these terms:

> (2) Where in proceedings for an offence under this section it is proved that the other person had a mental disorder, it is to be taken that the defendant knew or could reasonably have been expected to know that the person had a mental disorder unless sufficient evidence is adduced to raise an issue as to whether he knew or could reasonably have been expected to know it.

Subsection 2 of all the sections within this part of the Act create a rebuttable presumption of fact by the defendant that he did not know of the mental disorder. If he discharges this evidential burden it is then for the prosecution to prove that he could reasonably have been expected to know about the complainant's mental disorder.

The creation of a rebuttable presumption reflects the position of trust that the defendant is in as a care worker for the complainant. The test of knowledge of the mental disorder is clearly more stringent than that to be applied generally to persons who commit offences against persons with a mental disorder but who are not in a position of care (those offences covered by ss.30–37 of the Act). In those circumstances it is for the prosecution to prove that the defendant knew, or could reasonably be expected to have known, of the mental disorder.

The marriage exception

It is a defence, provided by s.43 of the Act, for the defendant to prove he was lawfully married at the time of the sexual activity to the person with a mental disorder.

This defence will only operate when the person with the mental disorder was over 16 years old, taking foreign marriages outside the scope of protection offered by this defence.

Existing sexual relationships

Under s.44 where the defendant can prove on the balance of probabilities that a lawful relationship existed between the parties which immediately pre-dated the position of care he will not be guilty of an offence created by these sections.

The defence is drafted in a particular way, the consequence of which is to make sexual relationships between carer and dependant that pre-existed the commencement of the Act criminal conduct.

6.11.3   Penalty

A person guilty of this offence is liable to a term of imprisonment, the precise term of which will depend upon the activity alleged. When the conduct involves any of the following acts referred to in s.39(3):

(a) penetration of B's anus or vagina with a part of A's body or anything else;
(b) penetration of B's mouth with A's penis;
(c) penetration of A's anus or vagina with a part of B's body; or
(d) penetration of A's mouth with B's penis;

the offence is indictable only and the maximum penalty is 14 years' imprisonment.

In any other case the offence is triable either way with a maximum sentence of six months if tried summarily and 10 years on indictment.

6.12   CARE WORKERS – CAUSING OR INCITING SEXUAL ACTIVITY

Under s.39(1), care workers intentionally causing or inciting a person in their care with a mental disorder to engage in sexual activity will be guilty of an offence provided by the Act. The act will not have needed to take place if a person is charged under the incitement part of this section.

The definition of sexual activity is provided for by s.78 of the Act and is drafted very widely to provide the maximum protection to mentally vulnerable victims.

6.12.1   Defences

Awareness of condition

The provisions about the defendant's awareness of the complainant's mental disorder are contained in s.39(2) in these terms:

> (2) Where in proceedings for an offence under this section it is proved that the other person had a mental disorder, it is to be taken that the defendant knew or could reasonably have been expected to know that the person had a mental disorder unless sufficient evidence is adduced to raise an issue as to whether he knew or could reasonably have been expected to know it.

Subsection 2 of all the sections within this part of the Act create a rebuttable presumption of fact by the defendant that he did not know of the mental disorder. If he discharges this evidential burden then it is for the prosecution to prove that he could reasonably have been expected to know about B's mental disorder or learning disability.

The creation of a rebuttable presumption reflects the position of trust that the defendant is in as a care worker for the complainant. The test of knowledge of the mental disorder is clearly more stringent than that to be applied generally to persons who commit offences against persons with a mental disorder but who are not in a position of care (those offences covered by ss.30–37 of the Act). In those circumstances it is for the prosecution to prove that the defendant knew or could reasonably be expected to have known, of the mental disorder.

The marriage exception

It is a defence, provided by s.43 of the Act, for the defendant to prove he was lawfully married at the time of the sexual activity to the person with a mental disorder.

This defence will only operate when the person with the mental disorder was over 16 years old, taking foreign marriages outside the scope of protection offered by this defence.

Existing sexual relationships

Where the defendant can prove on the balance of probabilities that there existed a lawful relationship between the parties which immediately pre-dated the position of care he will not be guilty of an offence created by this section.

The defence is drafted in a particular way, the consequence of which is to make sexual relationships between carer and dependant that pre-existed the commencement of the Act criminal conduct.

6.12.2 Penalty

A person guilty of this offence is liable to a term of imprisonment, the precise term of which will depend upon the activity alleged. When the conduct involves any of the following acts referred to in s.39(3) as follows:

(a) penetration of B's anus or vagina with a part of A's body or anything else;
(b) penetration of B's mouth with A's penis;
(c) penetration of A's anus or vagina with a part of B's body; or
(d) penetration of A's mouth with B's penis;

the offence is indictable only and the maximum penalty is 14 years' imprisonment.

In any other case the offence is triable either way with a maximum sentence of six months if tried summarily and 10 years on indictment.

6.13 CARE WORKERS – SEXUAL ACTIVITY IN THE PRESENCE OF A PERSON WITH A MENTAL DISORDER AND CAUSING SUCH A PERSON TO WATCH A SEXUAL ACT

When a care worker intentionally engages in sexual activity in the presence of a mentally-disordered person in his care he commits an offence created by s.40 *provided that he engages in it for the purpose of sexual gratification (s.40(1)(c) and* it is done.

(i) when another person (B) is present or is in a place from which A can be observed, and
(ii) knowing or believing that B [the person with the mental disorder] is aware, or intending that B should be aware, that he is engaging in it.

6.13.1 Defences

Awareness of condition

The provisions about the defendant's awareness of the complainant's mental disorder are contained in s.40(2) in these terms:

(2) Where in proceedings for an offence under this section it is proved that the other person had a mental disorder, it is to be taken that the defendant knew or could reasonably have been expected to know that the person had a mental disorder unless sufficient evidence is adduced to raise an issue as to whether he knew or could reasonably have been expected to know it.

Subsection 2 of all the sections within this part of the Act create a rebuttable presumption of fact by the defendant that he did not know of the mental disorder. If he discharges this evidential burden then it is for the prosecution to prove that he could reasonably have been expected to know about B's mental disorder.

The creation of a rebuttable presumption reflects the position of trust that the defendant is in as a care worker for the complainant. The test of knowledge of the mental disorder is clearly more stringent than that to be applied generally to persons who commit offences against persons with a mental disorder but who are not in a position of care (those offences covered by ss.30–37 of the Act). In those circumstances it is for the prosecution to prove that the defendant knew or could reasonably be expected to have known of the mental disorder.

The marriage exception

It is a defence, provided by s.43 of the Act, for the defendant to prove he was lawfully married at the time of the sexual activity to the person with a mental disorder.

This defence will only operate when the person with the mental disorder was over 16 years old, taking foreign marriages outside the scope of protection offered by this defence.

Existing sexual relationships

Where the defendant can prove on the balance of probabilities that there existed a lawful relationship between the parties which immediately pre-dated the position of care he will not be guilty of an offence created by this section.

The defence is drafted in a particular way, the consequence of which is to make sexual relationships between carer and dependant that pre-existed the commencement of the Act criminal conduct.

6.13.2   Penalty

The offence under s.40 is always an either way offence. No distinction is made between the activity that takes place as is the case with the other sections within this part of the Act.

A person guilty of this offence is liable to a term of imprisonment not exceeding 6 months on summary conviction, or on conviction on indictment to a term of imprisonment not exceeding seven years.

6.14   CARE WORKER CAUSING A PERSON WITH A MENTAL DISORDER TO WATCH A SEXUAL ACT

The offence provided for under s.41 of the Act is committed by a person when the defendant:

> For the purpose of obtaining sexual gratification, intentionally causes another person to watch a third person engaging in an activity or to look at an image of any person engaging in an activity.

The other person must have a recognised mental disability and be in the care of the defendant.

6.14.1   Defences

Awareness of condition

The provisions about the defendant's awareness of the complainant's mental disorder or learning disability are contained in s.41(2) in these terms:

> (2) Where in proceedings for an offence under this section it is proved that the other person had a mental disorder, it is to be taken that the defendant knew or could reasonably have been expected to know that the person had a mental disorder unless sufficient evidence is adduced to raise an issue as to whether he knew or could reasonably have been expected to know it.

Subsection 2 of all the sections within this part of the Act create a rebuttable presumption of fact by the defendant that he did not know of the mental disorder. If he discharges this evidential burden then it is for the prosecution to prove that he could reasonably have been expected to know about B's mental disorder.

The creation of a rebuttable presumption reflects the position of trust that the defendant is in as a care worker for the complainant. The test of knowledge of the mental disorder is clearly more stringent than that to be applied generally to persons who commit offences against persons with a mental disorder but who are not in a position of care (those offences covered by ss.30–37 of the act). In those circumstances it is for the prosecution to prove that the defendant knew or could reasonably be expected to have known of the mental disorder.

The marriage exception

It is a defence, provided by s.43 of the Act, for the defendant to prove he was lawfully married at the time of the sexual activity to the person with a mental disorder.

This defence will only operate when the person with the mental disorder was over 16 years old, taking foreign marriages outside the scope of protection offered by this defence.

Existing sexual relationships

Where the defendant can prove on the balance of probabilities that there existed a lawful relationship between the parties which immediately pre-dated the position of care he will not be guilty of an offence created by this section.

6.14.2   Penalty

The offence under s.41 is always an either way offence. No distinction is made between the activity that takes place as is the case with the other sections within this part of the Act.

A person guilty of this offence is liable to a term of imprisonment not exceeding six months on summary conviction, or on conviction on indictment to a term of imprisonment not exceeding seven years.

7 OFFENCES RELATING TO PROSTITUTION, PORNOGRAPHY AND TRAFFICKING

7.1 BACKGROUND

Many of the laws detailing sexual conduct are outdated and discriminatory. Some failed because they were gender discriminatory, but mostly they failed to reflect a changing society in which the exploitation of people in the sex industry has become far more common and the methods employed by those who do it far more sophisticated that was ever imagined in 1956.

The review document, *Setting the Boundaries*, identified a number of loopholes in existing legislation which did not allow for adequate protection of children and adults in the 21st Century.

Section 28 of the Sexual Offences Act 1956, the offence of causing the prostitution of a girl under 16, was limited in scope as it could only apply to the person in charge of the child and carried a very low penalty.

The offences of living off the earnings of a prostitute were used with mixed success by police forces, with some finding the offences too difficult to comprehend and readily use.

The Sexual Offences Act 2003 creates a new regime of offences relating to prostitution which are simple to use and have effective punishments. Many of the old offences were outdated in that they could only be committed by one sex. Offences including keeping a brothel (Sexual Offences Act 1956, s.5), kerb crawling (Sexual Offences Act 1985, s.1) and soliciting (Street Offences Act 1959, s.1) remain contrary to law but have been amended to include both men and women who commit such acts, so that they can be dealt with in an 'equitable fashion' (as defined in the Police Research Series Paper 134 (Home Office, 2000)).

7.2   TAKING OR DISTRIBUTING INDECENT PHOTOGRAPHS OF CHILDREN – PROTECTION OF CHILDREN ACT 1978

The Protection of Children Act 1978 (POCA) created a series of offences relating to the possession of indecent photographs of children under 16 years old (POCA, s.1(1)(a)–(c)).

Section 45 of the Sexual Offences Act 2003 amends the definition of 'child' for the purposes of the Protection of Children Act 1978, to include a child under 18 years old. Under the revised section it will now also be an offence to take, permit to take, show, distribute or possess with intent to distribute an indecent photograph (including a pseudo-photograph) of a child aged 16 or 17. These amendments will not apply to photographs taken or made before commencement of this section of the Act.

7.2.1   Defences

Marriage

It will be open for the defendant to prove on the balance of probabilities that at the time of charge, he was married to the person within the photograph. The 'marriage exception' also applies to couples who live together as partners in an 'enduring family relationship'. In all cases it will be for the defendant to prove, again on the balance of probabilities, that the 'child' concerned was aged 16 or over.

The defence will only be available when the parties were married at the time of charge. The wording of the section is a little ambiguous referring to the past tense of 'were married'. Although on one interpretation it could refer to the parties having been married at any time in the past, it is submitted that this cannot be correct. This is largely because of the distinction drawn between the defence available under the Sexual Offences Act 2003, s.45 and that available under s.160 of the Criminal Justice Act 1988 (CJA 1988) also amended by this act. Under CJA 1988, s.160, the defence will arise when the defendant can prove he was married to the complainant at the time of charge (inserted by s.45(3) of this Act) and also at the time the photograph was taken (s.45(1)). This distinction is purposeful and must clearly limit the defence to a charge under the Protection of Children Act 1978, s.1 to the time of charge.

The reason for the distinction is that the scope of the Protection of Children Act is wider than the CJA 1988, s.160, as it covers distribution of such photographs. It will therefore protect children under 18 from having their photographs displayed once they leave a relationship.

In any case the marriage defence will only apply when the photograph shows either the child alone or with the defendant, but not if it showed any other person.

Distribution

Where the offence charged is contrary to s.1(1)(b) – distribution – of POCA the defendant will not be guilty unless it can be shown that the distribution was to a person other than the child concerned.

Exception for criminal proceedings and investigations

In order to effectively investigate and prosecute those who use and trade in indecent images of children it is occasionally necessary for the police and others, such as the Internet Watch Foundation, to look at and make copies of such images from the Internet. This can constitute an offence of 'making child pornography', to which there is currently no defence in law. Although the exercise of discretion by the Crown Prosecution Service in authorising such prosecutions means that the risk of prosecution in such circumstances is very small, the Government believe that children will be better protected if action is taken to remove this obstacle. There is, therefore, a limited defence to the charge of making child pornography to cover these circumstances, while ensuring that it will not protect users of child pornography themselves.

Section 46 of the Act inserts a new s.1B in the Protection of Children Act 1978 in order to permit such photographs to be held by authorised bodies such as the police for the purposes of prevention, detection or investigation of any crime. Any authorisation may be subject to conditions to keep or destroy the material in a particular way. It is likely to be relevant to undertakings given by solicitors who are served the documents in criminal proceedings, not to distribute them.

Section 46(1) of the Act provides details of the individuals and organisations who will be exempt under this provision.

7.2.2   Consent

When a person is charged with an offence of taking a photograph of a child under s1(1)(a) of the Protection of Children Act 1978 an evidential burden will rest upon the defendant to introduce evidence as to whether the child consented or whether he reasonably believed the child consented to the taking of that photograph. When he does so it will be for the prosecution to rebut that assertion.

However, where the offence alleged is contrary to the Protection of Children Act 1978, s.1(1)(c) – the possession of such photographs with a view to them being distributed or shown – the prosecution must simply prove the absence of consent and no legal or evidential burden is placed upon the defendant.

7.3   POSSESSION OF INDECENT PHOTOGRAPH OF A CHILD – CRIMINAL JUSTICE ACT 1988

The offence of possession of indecent photographs of a child contrary to the Criminal Justice Act 1988, s.160, will also be amended to include photographs of 16 and 17 year olds.

7.3.1   Defence

The existing defences in relation to knowledge of possession of the photograph and legitimate excuse for such possession provided by CJA 1988, s.160(2) are retained.

Marriage

The Sexual Offences Act 2003 adds to the defences available to a person charged under CJA 1988, s.160, as a marriage exception will now apply.

The marriage defence will apply in a similar way to the offences contrary to the Protection of Children Act 1978 (see para. 7.2.1), however, in this case the defence will only arise if the parties were married or in an enduring family relationship at the time the photograph was obtained, and when the defendant is charged.

7.3.2   Consent

When a person is charged with an offence contrary to s.160 of the Criminal Justice Act 1988, an evidential burden will rest upon the defendant to introduce evidence as to whether the child consented or whether he reasonably believed the child consented to the photograph being in the defendant's possession. If he does so then he will not be guilty of an offence under this section unless the prosecution are able to rebut that assertion.

7.4   ABUSE OF CHILDREN THROUGH PROSTITUTION AND PORNOGRAPHY

7.4.1   Background

Adults and children can be sexually exploited for the gain (financial or otherwise) of others. Indeed, there is increasing concern about the role of transnational and organised crime in trafficking people for sexual exploitation. The Government's clear aim was that:

> . . . both children and adults should be protected not only from those who seek to abuse them directly but also from those whose intention is to exploit them. Many adults are exploited in prostitution. Some may have been trafficked to this country explicitly for the purposes of exploitation while others may have become subject to

exploitation within this country, through being enticed by a pimp or for whatever other reason. People who sexually exploit children for their own gain – irrespective of whether they participate in any sexual activity with the child – are responsible for that abuse and should be treated accordingly.

(Protecting the Public, 2002)

The Act creates new offences with severe penalties signalling the Government's intentions to take action against the perpetrators of such crimes.

7.5   PAYING FOR SEXUAL SERVICES OF A CHILD

Section 47 creates a separate and distinct offence from prostitution due to the age of the victim. It becomes an offence for any person intentionally to obtain the sexual (as defined at s.78) services of a child (under 18 years) for himself or another person. It is an offence where those services have been paid for or where payment has been promised even of the act does then not take place.

Payment is widely defined by s.47(2) to include:

> . . . any financial advantage, including the discharge of an obligation to pay or the provision of goods and services gratuitously or at a discount.

The offence is intended to apply where payment for the services is made or promised and payment is made either directly to the child concerned or to a third party, for example a pimp, or where he knows that another person has paid for the services or promised such payment.

7.5.1   The relevance of age

Where the child is aged between 13 and 17, the offence will not be committed by a person who reasonably believes that the child is 18 or over. No evidential burden will be placed upon the defendant as it will be for the prosecution to prove that he does not reasonably believe that the child is 18 or over.

However, where the child is under 13, a person will commit the offence regardless of any reasonable belief he may have about the child's age.

7.5.2   Penalty

The level of penalty, and venue for trial will depend on the age of the parties and the act alleged.

Where the offence is committed against a person under 13 (B), and the offence involved:

(a)   penetration of B's anus or vagina with a part of A's [the defendant's] body or anything else;

(b) penetration of B's mouth with A's penis;

(c) penetration of A's anus or vagina with a part of B's body; or

(d) penetration of A's mouth with B's penis;

the offender is liable upon conviction on indictment to life imprisonment. Where any of the acts listed above are committed against a person aged between 13 and 16 (save in Northern Ireland where the age is 17, Table 7.1 should be read accordingly), the offence is also triable only on indictment. The maximum sentence upon conviction is 14 years' imprisonment. When any other conduct is involved the offence becomes triable either way. On summary conviction the maximum penalty is six months' imprisonment. The maximum penalty on conviction on indictment is 14 years.

When the child involved is aged 16 or 17 years old an either way offence is created regardless of the conduct alleged. The maximum penalty is six months on summary conviction and seven years on indictment.

The position is illustrated in Table 7.1.

7.6   CAUSING OR INCITING CHILD PROSTITUTION OR PORNOGRAPHY

The offence is aimed at persons who recruit into prostitution or pornography (whether on a one-off basis or longer term) those who are not currently involved in it.

Section 48 makes it an offence for a person to intentionally cause or incite a child under 18 into prostitution or involvement in pornography anywhere in the world.

Pornography is defined by s.51(1) as an indecent moving or still image of that person. No definition of indecent is provided in the Act. It is suggested that the test remains the same as for indecent assault. It can be contrasted with the term sexual which appears in much of the Act and is defined at s.78.

Prostitute is defined by s.51(2) as

> . . . a person who, on at least one occasion and whether or not compelled to do so, offers or provides sexual services to another person in return for payment or a promise of payment to A or a third person . . .

There is no need for the defendant or another person to actually benefit from this financially or otherwise thereby making the offence easier to prove (earlier drafts of the Act had this provision).

Table 7.1 Factors affecting mode of trial and penalty for offence of paying for sexual services of a child

Age of child	Conduct	Venue of trial	Maximum sentence
Under 13	Penetration of B's anus or vagina with a part of A's body or anything else; penetration of B's mouth with A's penis; penetration of A's anus or vagina with a part of B's body; or penetration of A's mouth with B's penis.	Indictable only	Life imprisonment
Under 13	Any other sexual conduct not listed above	Either way	On summary conviction to a term not exceeding 6 months a fine or both. On conviction on indictment to a term not exceeding 14 years.
Aged 13 to 15	Penetration of B's anus or vagina with a part of A's body or anything else; penetration of B's mouth with A's penis; penetration of A's anus or vagina with a part of B's body; or penetration of A's mouth with B's penis.	Indictable only	14 years' imprisonment
Aged 13 to 15	Any other sexual conduct not listed above	Either way	On summary conviction to a term not exceeding 6 months a fine or both. On conviction on indictment to a term not exceeding 14 years.
Over 16 but under 18	Any sexual conduct	Either way	On summary conviction to a term not exceeding 6 months, a fine or both. On conviction on indictment to a term not exceeding 7 years.

7.6.1 Examples

The offence would therefore be committed by someone who makes a living from the prostitution of others and encourages new recruits to work for him or another (whether those recruits do actually then engage in prostitution or not). It could also cover where A and B live together and A compels B to become involved in pornography in order to pay their rent.

7.6.2   The relevance of age

Where the child is between 13 and 17, the offence will not be committed by a person who reasonably believes that the child is 18 or over. No evidential burden will be placed upon the defendant as it will be for the prosecution to prove that he does not reasonably believe that the child is 18 or over.

However, where the child is under 13, a person will commit the offence regardless of any reasonable belief he may have about the child's age.

7.6.3   Penalty

The offence is triable either way. A person guilty of this offence is liable by s.48(2):

    (a) on summary conviction, to a term of imprisonment not exceeding 6 months or a fine or both;

    (b) on conviction on indictment to a term of imprisonment not exceeding 14 years.

7.7   CAUSING OR INCITING PROSTITUTION FOR GAIN

Section 52 makes it an offence for a person (A) to intentionally cause or incite another person into prostitution (as defined at s.52(2)) anywhere in the world where A does so for, or in expectation of, gain for himself or for a third party. Gain is widely defined to include financial advantage, the discharge of an obligation to pay for goods or services or any goodwill which is likely in time to bring a financial advantage (s.54).

This offence is not specifically limited to where the person incited into prostitution is aged over 18, however, because of the corresponding offence of inciting child prostitution (s.48) it is clearly aimed at cases where the person is an adult.

Although prostitution by adults aged 18 or over is not an offence in itself, this offence is intended to capture those who, for gain, recruit others into prostitution, whether this be by the exercise of force or otherwise.

7.7.1   Penalty

This is an either way offence. A person guilty of an offence under this section is liable on summary conviction to a term not exceeding six months and on conviction on indictment to a term not exceeding seven years.

7.8   CONTROLLING A CHILD PROSTITUTE OR A CHILD INVOLVED IN PORNOGRAPHY

It an offence (s.49) for a person to intentionally control the activities of a child under 18 relating to prostitution or pornography. The offence applies regardless of whether there is any benefit or gain either directly for the defendant or for a third party.

The scope of the offence is potentially very wide indeed as an offence will be committed if the prostitution or pornography takes place in any part of the world.

The offence is committed even if the child's activities in relation to prostitution or pornography are controlled for part of the time by another person. An example of the behaviour that might be caught by this offence is where the defendant requires or directs the child to charge a certain price or to use a particular hotel for her sexual services or to pose for a certain photographer and the child subsequently complies with this request or direction.

7.8.1   The relevance of age

Where the child is between 13 and 17, the offence will not be committed by a person who reasonably believes that the child is 18 or over. No evidential burden will be placed upon the defendant as it will be for the prosecution to prove that he does not reasonably believe that the child is 18 or over. However, where the child is under 13, a person will commit the offence regardless of any reasonable belief he may have about the child's age.

7.8.2   Penalty

A person guilty of an offence under this section is liable on summary conviction to a term not exceeding six months and upon conviction on indictment to a term not exceeding 14 years.

7.9   ARRANGING OR FACILITATING CHILD PROSTITUTION OR PORNOGRAPHY

The Act creates an offence at s.50 for a person to intentionally arrange or facilitate the involvement of a child in prostitution or pornography. This offence would cover, for example, taking the child to a place where he will be used to make pornography or making arrangements for the child's prostitution to take place in a particular room. The act must be done intentionally and if so done does not require any payment or gain to have been received by the defendant.

7.9.1   The relevance of age

Where the child is between 13 and 17, the offence will not be committed by a person who reasonably believes that the child is 18 or over. No evidential burden will be placed upon the defendant as it will be for the prosecution to prove that he does not reasonably believe that the child is 18 or over. However, where the child is under 13, a person will commit the offence regardless of any reasonable belief he may have about the child's age.

7.9.2   Penalty

A person guilty of an offence under this section is liable on summary conviction to a term not exceeding six months and on conviction on indictment to a term not exceeding 14 years.

7.10   CONTROLLING PROSTITUTION FOR GAIN

Section 53 makes it an offence for a person to intentionally control another person's activities relating to prostitution where he does so in the expectation of gain for himself or a third party. This section will apply to protect adults in the prostitution industry and is not gender specific. It will not be an offence, unlike the corresponding provision for children, to arrange or control activities relating to pornography. In such cases there must be evidence of gain or an expected gain either for the defendant or another. As for other offences, gain is widely drafted to include financial advantage or the goodwill of any person which in the future is likely to bring such advantage (s.54).

7.10.1   Penalty

To reflect the fact that the offence is primarily directed at protecting adults the courts' sentencing powers are more limited than those created by section 49 protecting children. A person guilty of an offence under this section is liable on summary conviction to a term not exceeding six months and on conviction on indictment to a term not exceeding seven years.

7.11   KEEPING A BROTHEL USED FOR PROSTITUTION

The Sexual Offences Act 1956 is amended by the insertion of a new s.33A. It is an offence for a person to keep, manage or act or assist in the management of, a brothel to which people resort for practices involving prostitution. This will apply whether or not it is also used for other purposes. The meaning of prostitution is that given at s.51(2) of the Sexual Offences Act 2003.

The offence will be triable either way. The maximum penalty on summary conviction will be six months' imprisonment or a fine and on conviction on indictment the maximum penalty is seven years' imprisonment.

7.12   EXTENSION OF GENDER-SPECIFIC PROSTITUTION OFFENCES

Prostitution itself is not illegal in this country but existing offences cover some of the behaviour related to it, such as soliciting for the purposes of prostitution. These offences are reformed with the aim of making them gender neutral. Section 36 of the Sexual Offences Act 1956 (permitting premises to be used for the purposes of prostitution) is amended to take account of whether any prostitute concerned is male or female (Sexual Offences Act 2003, Sched.1, para.1).

The Street Offences Act 1959 and the Sexual Offences Act 1985, governing loitering and soliciting for the purpose of prostitution is now extended to both men and women (Sexual Offences Act 2003, Sched.1, paras 2 and 4).

A full list of amendments can be found in Schedule 1 to the Act (see Appendix).

7.13   TRAFFICKING

7.13.1   Background

The sex industry is growing rapidly all over the world. The International Labour Organisation has suggested that the sex sector is a significant component in many economies. The International Office of Migration estimated that in 1995 half a million women were trafficked into the EU and the use of children in prostitution has grown significantly in recent years (*Setting the Boundaries*, para. 7.1).

The growth of human trafficking linked to sexual exploitation has caused worldwide concern. The EU Joint Action on Trafficking in Human Beings and Sexual Exploitation of Children called on EU Member States to review their laws on the sexual exploitation of children and on trafficking.

In response the Government have already introduced a new offence of trafficking to control prostitution in the Nationality, Immigration and Asylum Act 2002. That legislation was somewhat of a stop-gap measure and needs to be updated to take account of the changes created by this Act.

In setting the background for further reform the Government reported:

> We will therefore also be introducing an offence of trafficking for commercial sexual exploitation, which will cover recruiting, harbouring, and facilitating the movement of another person for the purposes of commercial sexual exploitation. It will carry a maximum penalty of 14 years' imprisonment. This offence will implement the commitment made by the Government to introduce new offences of trafficking for sexual exploitation in line with the UN protocol and the EU framework decision

on trafficking. It will apply to persons trafficked from one place to another within the UK as well as across international borders.

The White Paper 'Secure Borders Safe Haven', published earlier this year, set out a comprehensive approach for victims of trafficking in order to help them give evidence against the traffickers who have brought them here to exploit them.

We will make arrangements for their protection and support by providing access to safe accommodation and services such as medical care, legal advice, and counselling. We recognise that in some cases it may be appropriate for them to remain here; however, in many cases it will be more appropriate for them to return home, and to help them do so we will provide additional support and ensure that they have suitable accommodation to return to. We are working with the voluntary sector to set up these arrangements and hope to set up a pilot scheme next year.

In addition we are currently developing advice for immigration officers, police and others potentially dealing with trafficking and its victims. This will raise awareness of the difference between people who are trafficked into this country and those who seek to enter the country illegally of their own will, and to help them to treat trafficking victims more fairly.

(Protecting the Public, 2002)

7.14   TRAFFICKING INTO, WITHIN AND OUT OF THE UK FOR SEXUAL EXPLOITATION

The Act creates three separate offences for a person to intentionally arrange or facilitate the arrival in the United Kingdom (s.57), traffic within the United Kingdom (s.58) and traffic out of the United Kingdom (s.59) with the purpose of committing a 'relevant offence' (see para. 7.14.1), either in the UK or elsewhere.

These provisos are intended to protect against the position where the defendant uses the UK as a mid-point in a journey elsewhere. Bringing a person to the UK with the intention that they then go on to Europe to be subject to a relevant sexual offence (such as being involved in child pornography as protected by s.49) will therefore be an offence.

Travel within the United Kingdom will also be a specific offence created by s.58. The offence of trafficking out of the United Kingdom is designed to cover the situation where the victim is in the UK, either because he is ordinarily resident here or because he has been trafficked here, but is then trafficked by the defendant to another part of the world to be sexually exploited.

Facilitating is to be widely interpreted so that any person intentionally providing assistance in the chain will be subject to the Act. This could be by providing finance or fake documentation, or even a cover story presented to the authorities to facilitate entry to the UK.

What is important is the intention of the defendant in bringing the person to the UK. An offence would still be committed even if the person does not go on to be made subject to a relevant offence provided that the defendant intends that he should be the victim of an offence.

The new offences requires *mens rea* on behalf of any defendant. The Explanatory Notes confirm that airline companies, road hauliers, etc. who are transporting someone without any criminal intent are not captured within the ambit of the section.

7.14.1   Relevant offence

The relevant offence is defined at s.60(1) as an offence relating to this part of the Act or the taking of photographs or images within this part together with an offence under s.1 of the Protection of Children Act 1978.

This offence re-enacts, with amendments, the offence in s.145 of the Nationality, Asylum and Immigration Act 2002. It includes acts done outside England, Wales and Northern Ireland which, if they had been done in those countries, would constitute an offence. This includes an act which does not necessarily constitute an offence in the country in which it is done.

7.14.2   Jurisdiction

The offences created in this part of the Act apply to anything done within the United Kingdom or by an individual or company incorporated within the UK. Accordingly, the offences will cover behaviour committed by any person in the UK and any such behaviour outside the UK by any body incorporated under UK law such as a UK company. The offences may also be committed by any British person or national when abroad, irrespective of whether or not the activity is a criminal offence under the law in the country in which it is committed (this list is not exhaustive, see s.60(3)). For example, travelling to Thailand to make arrangements to bring a person back to the UK for the purposes of prostitution will be an offence even though it is not committed on British soil.

7.14.3   Penalty

A person guilty of an offence under these sections is liable under subsection 2 of each section:

(a) on summary conviction to imprisonment for a term not exceeding 6 months or a fine not exceeding the statutory maximum or both;

(b) on conviction on indictment, to imprisonment for a term not exceeding 14 years.

8 OTHER OFFENCES

8.1 ADMINISTERING A SUBSTANCE WITH INTENT

When re-defining rape in section 1 of the Sexual Offences Act 2003 (the Act), consideration was given to creating a separate offence of date rape. The rise in 'date rape drugs' in recent years is of growing concern, and is tackled by s.61 of the Act which makes it an offence for a person to intentionally administer a substance, or cause a substance to be taken by another person. The defendant must know that the other person does not consent to taking that substance.

The intention of the person administering the substance must be to stupefy or overpower another, so as to enable any person to engage in sexual activity that involves the victim.

Sexual activity is defined in s.78, an example in a s.61 offence could involve the defendant having sexual intercourse with, or masturbating another; or causing another person to commit a sexual act upon himself. The intended sexual activity need not involve the defendant. Nor is it actually necessary for sexual activity to take place under s.61. The offence would be committed in any case where the substance is administered to another person with the relevant intent.

8.1.1 Application

Whilst the primary application of this section is to cover so-called date rape drugs, the offence has wider application to cover the use of any other substance administered with the relevant intention. It would cover 'spiking' drinks with alcohol, provided that the person whose drinks were spiked did not know he was consuming alcohol. It would not cover A encouraging B to get drunk so that A could have sex with B, where B knew that he was consuming alcohol, as B had consented to drinking alcohol.

There is no limit upon the method of administering the subject. Whilst spiked drinks are most commonly considered, injection or covering a person's face with a cloth impregnated with the substance would also be an offence.

The offence applies where the substance is administered personally or through a third party, for example, whereby a person persuades a friend to administer the substance to the victim because it is easier to do so.

8.1.2   Penalty

A person guilty of an offence under these sections is liable under s.61(2):

(a) on summary conviction, to imprisonment for a term not exceeding 6 months or a fine not exceeding the statutory maximum or both;
(b) on conviction on indictment, to imprisonment for a term not exceeding 10 years.

8.2   COMMITTING AN OFFENCE WITH INTENT TO COMMIT A SEXUAL OFFENCE

Section 62 makes it an offence for a person intentionally to commit any criminal offence with intent to commit any 'relevant sexual offence'. Relevant sexual offence includes any offence within this Act and relates to aiding, abetting, counselling or procuring the same.

This offence is intended to deal with circumstances in which the defendant commits a criminal offence but does so with the intention of committing a subsequent sexual offence, regardless of whether or not the substantive sexual offence is committed.

Notwithstanding the application of s.62, nothing within the Act would prevent a defendant being charged with the substantive sexual offence, if committed, in addition to this offence.

8.2.1   Penalty

The sentencing powers provided by this section vary according to the severity of preparatory conduct alleged. Where such conduct is false imprisonment or kidnap the offence is triable on indictment only, carrying a maximum sentence of life imprisonment.

In all other cases the offence is triable either way. A person guilty of such an offence is liable:

(a) on summary conviction, to imprisonment for a term not exceeding 6 months or a fine not exceeding the statutory maximum or both;
(b) on conviction on indictment, to imprisonment for a term not exceeding 10 years.

The effect of this section is to increase the courts' sentencing powers. A defendant who assaults a woman with the intention thereafter of raping her may, depending upon the level of the assault, be liable to a sentence of imprisonment as low as six months whereas if he were convicted under s.62 he would be liable to 10 years' imprisonment.

Some of the examples given by the Government as intended to be covered by this section, such as false imprisonment, already carry a maximum penalty of life imprisonment but it is intended to bring within the scope of law any other criminal offence which is preparatory to a sexual offence.

8.3   TRESPASS WITH INTENT TO COMMIT A SEXUAL OFFENCE

Aggravated burglary, with the intent to commit rape, was already an offence but it did not require a person convicted to register under the Sex Offenders Act 1997. That lacuna has been remedied by a new provision provided by s.63(1)(a). A person commits an offence if he trespasses with the intent to commit a relevant sexual offence on the premises and knows or is reckless as to whether he is a trespasser. This gives effectively the same definition of trespasser as s.9(1)(b) Theft Act 1968. This offence is effectively the replacement of the offence of burglary when the intention was to commit rape. Schedule 7 repeals the words 'or raping any person' from s.9(2) Theft Act 1968. It is, however, wider in scope as it will apply to any sexual offence, whereas the offence of burglary required an intent to commit rape.

No definition of trespasser is provided within the Act. Earlier drafts suggested a person 'enters as a trespasser' if he enters without the owner's or occupier's consent. Premises are defined by s.63(2) to include a structure or part of a structure. This will apply to a tent, vehicle or vessel or other temporary or movable structure and is likely to be interpreted in the same wide manner as 'building' has been in reference to allegations of burglary.

This offence is intended to capture, for example, the situation where a person enters a building owned by another, or goes into a garden or garage without consent, intending to commit a sexual offence against the occupier, and applies regardless of whether or not the substantive sexual offence is committed.

8.3.1   Intent

The defendant must have the intent to commit a relevant sexual offence at the time he enters the structure, part of a structure or land that he enters as a trespasser. The Explanatory Notes that accompanied the Act give the following example – A may enter B's property on B's invitation, but B may make it clear that A is not to go into a particular part of that property. A will commit the offence if he has the intent to commit a relevant sexual offence when he enters the prohibited part of the property – he need not have had that intent when he first entered the property on B's invitation.

The intent is likely to be inferred from what the defendant says or does to the victim or intended victim (if there is one) or from items in possession of the defendant at the time he commits the trespass (for example, condoms, pornographic images, rope, etc.).

8.3.2   Penalty

A person guilty of such an offence is liable on summary conviction to imprisonment for a term not exceeding six months or a fine not exceeding the statutory maximum or both or upon conviction on indictment, to imprisonment for a term not exceeding 10 years.

Whereas an offence of burglary carried a maximum penalty of 14 years' imprisonment in the case of a dwelling house burglary, no such corresponding provision is made in the amended legislation.

8.4   SEX WITH AN ADULT RELATIVE

The Act creates two new offences designed to replace the old offence of incest created by s.10 of the Sexual Offences Act 1956. The new offences are 'Penetration of an adult relative' (s.64) and 'Sex with an adult relative who is consenting to penetration' (s.65).

Part of the problem with the law of incest was that it applied to a limited number of family relationships – in the case of a man, with his grand-daughter, daughter, sister or mother – and failed to take account of sexual intercourse in a wider familial relationship such as between uncle and niece.

Sections 64 and 65 of the Act make it an offence for a person aged 16 or over to intentionally penetrate sexually, or to consent to being penetrated by a close relative who is aged 18 or over if he knows or could reasonably have been expected to know that they are close relatives.

The requirement that the other party is aged 18 is to distinguish this offence from the other familial sex offences created and explained in Chapter 5.

Penetration can be of the vagina, anus or other part of the body by the penis or by anything else. When the penetration is of the mouth it must be by the penis.

For the offence to be committed the penetration must be 'sexual' (s.78). This requirement ensures that penetration for some other purpose, for example, where one sibling helps another to insert a pessary for medical reasons, is not caught by this offence. There is no requirement that either party is aware of the other's age.

8.4.1   Consent

Section 64 applies in the absence of consent whereas s.65 applies where there is consent between the parties.

Unlike the offences of sexual assault and rape, a reasonably held belief in consent by the defendant will not provide a defence in law. Where there is any suggestion that one party was not consenting, then charges of rape and sexual assault will be a more appropriate starting point, although there is nothing to prohibit the two charges being put as alternatives.

8.4.2   Definition of 'relative'

Subsection 2 of both ss.63 and 64 defines 'relative' for the purposes of the offence as parent, grandparent, child, grandchild, brother, sister, half brother or half sister. Adoptive relatives are excluded from this offence. Schedule 4 makes a consequential amendment to the Adoption and Children Act 2002, to the effect that the provision in the 2002 Act that makes an adoptive child the child of the adoptive parents, does not apply in relation to these offences. Therefore, for example, it will not be an offence under these clauses for an adoptive brother and sister aged over 18 to have sexual intercourse.

8.4.3   Defence

Knowledge of the family relationship

Subsection 3 of each offence creates a rebuttable presumption of fact that the defendant will need to discharge. It will be taken that the defendant knew or could have reasonably been expected to know of the relationship between the parties unless sufficient evidence is raised to the contrary. The burden will then shift to the prosecution.

8.4.4   Penalty

A person guilty of offences contrary to ss.64 and 65 is liable on summary conviction to imprisonment for a term not exceeding six months or a fine not exceeding the statutory maximum or both and upon conviction on indictment, to imprisonment for a term not exceeding two years.

8.5   SEXUAL ACTIVITY IN A PUBLIC LAVATORY

An offence will be committed contrary to s.71 of the Act if a person intentionally engages in sexual activity in a lavatory to which the public have access, whether on payment or otherwise.

8.5.1   Sexual activity defined

An activity is considered sexual if a reasonable person would consider that it was sexual in all the circumstances but regardless of the purpose in it (s.71(2)). The definition of sexual within this section is clearly an objective test alone and differs from the definition of sexual activity within the rest of the Act which also encompassed a subjective alternative.

The offence is clearly designed to cover sexual liaisons and not changing nappies which would involve the touching of a child's genitalia or medical emergencies.

8.5.2 Penalty

Schedule 5 to the Act provides an amendment to the Police and Criminal Evidence Act 1984 (PACE) to provide a power of arrest for this offence. The offence is triable summarily only and carries a maximum penalty of a fine up to level five, six months' imprisonment or both.

8.6 EXPOSURE

At present, exposure or 'flashing' can be charged under the Vagrancy Act 1824, s.4 or the Town Police Clauses Act 1847, s.28. Charges can also be brought under the common law offence of outraging public decency.

The offence under s.66 of the Act introduces a new gender neutral offence of intentional exposure of genitals. It relates to the exposure of both male and female genitalia in circumstances where the accused knows or intends that someone will see them and be caused alarm or distress. This is designed to catch those whose behaviour is specifically intended to shock another person and would not be used to criminalise, for example, naturists in regulated environments, although it could apply to streakers at sporting events.

There is no need to prove that the defendant was acting with a sexual motive. All he need do is intentionally expose his genitals with the intention of causing alarm or distress.

The offence will be committed regardless of whether the exposure is seen by others. For example, if a person exposes his genitals to some passers-by, as long as he intends that someone will see them, he commits the offence regardless of whether they actually see his genitals or whether they have been alarmed or distressed by seeing them.

Schedule 5 to the Act provides an amendment to PACE to provide a power of arrest to this offence.

8.6.1 Penalty

A person guilty of such an offence is liable on summary conviction to imprisonment for a term not exceeding six months, or a fine not exceeding the statutory maximum or both and upon conviction on indictment, to imprisonment for a term not exceeding two years.

8.7   VOYEURISM

A new offence of voyeurism (s.67) is introduced to cover cases where a person, for the purpose of sexual gratification, observes another doing a private act and that person does not consent to being observed in those circumstances of privacy.

The rationale behind the Act is clear. The Government's paper *Protecting the Public* stated:

> We would want cases where a photographer takes indecent photographs of someone without their consent and, for example, posts them on the Internet or in a pornographic magazine to be treated particularly seriously by the courts.

This offence is not designed to apply to journalists where they are pursuing legitimate journalistic activity. In such circumstances the observing or taking of images will not be done for sexual gratification.

8.7.1   Definition of a private act

A person is doing a private act as provided for by s.68(1) when:

(a) the person's genitals, buttocks or breasts are exposed or covered only with underwear,
(b) the person is using a lavatory, or
(c) the person is doing a sexual act that is not of a kind ordinarily done in public.

The voyeurism must take place without the consent of the person being viewed. As such it will not be an offence to take pictures or video images with an adult who consents to them being taken, although child sex offences or offences relating to images of children as per the Protection of Children Act 1978 will apply if the person observed is under 18 years old.

Section 67(2) makes it an offence to operate equipment for the purposes of such an observation. It will cover cases where, for example, a camera or two-way mirror is secretly installed and will apply to audio and video equipment alike. As the act must be done for sexual gratification it will not apply to an observation made, for example, in the course of a police observation on premises.

Section 67(3) also provides that it will be an offence to record the private act without consent, when the purpose of the recording was for the sexual gratification of the defendant or a third party.

An offence may therefore be committed contrary to subsections 2 or 3 by viewing material recorded or shown via computer or webcam. In all cases the defendant must know that the person being observed does not consent to that observation. The effect of this is that where the image is a recorded one and the person observed did not consent to it being so recorded at the time but later does give his consent for the defendant to look at it for his sexual gratification, the defendant will be committing an offence, although it is difficult to imagine a scenario when a prosecution will arise in these circumstances.

Those who adapt a structure by installing such equipment will also be guilty of an offence under s.67(4). This will apply to peepholes.

The act must take place in a 'structure', a term further explained at s.68(2) as including a tent, vehicle or temporary or movable structure. There is no requirement that the structure provides a reasonable expectation of privacy.

Schedule 5 to the Act provides an amendment to PACE to provide a power of arrest for this offence.

Examples

The kind of acts the offence could cover include a landlord secretly observing his tenants bathing or using the toilet in their bathrooms or having sexual intercourse or masturbating in their bedrooms, or a person looking through a peephole at people dressed only in their underwear in the changing room of a clothes shop or a tented cubicle at a market stall.

It would also be an offence for A to film B undressing in a swimming pool changing room intending that someone else (C) should look at the film for their own sexual gratification, where C knows that B does not give the relevant consents.

8.7.2   Penalty

A person guilty of such an offence is liable on summary conviction to imprisonment for a term not exceeding six months, or a fine not exceeding the statutory maximum or both and on conviction on indictment, to imprisonment for a term not exceeding two years.

8.8   INTERCOURSE WITH AN ANIMAL

Sexual activity with animals is generally recognised to be profoundly disturbed behaviour. This offence is related solely to penile penetration in relation to animals and does not replace existing legislation covering cruelty to animals.

Section 69 makes it an offence for a man intentionally to penetrate the vagina or anus (explained further at s.79(10)) of a living animal with his penis where he knows or is reckless as to whether that is what he is penetrating.

Subsection 2 makes it an offence for a person to intentionally cause or allow her vagina or his or her anus to be penetrated by the penis of a living animal where he or she knows or is reckless as to what they are being penetrated by.

Schedule 5 to the Act provides an amendment to PACE to provide a power of arrest for this offence.

8.8.1   Penalty

The offence will be triable either way. A maximum penalty of six months' imprisonment will be available on summary conviction. On indictment the maximum penalty will be two years' imprisonment.

8.9   SEXUAL PENETRATION OF A CORPSE

Perhaps surprisingly, there was no law that covered sexual interference with human remains, although there is no indication that such activity is anything but extremely rare. The Government's position is that this behaviour is so deviant as to warrant the intervention of the criminal law. A new offence of sexual interference with human remains is created by s.70 of the Act.

It becomes an offence for a person to intentionally penetrate any part of the body of a dead person with any part of his body or any other object. The penetration must be sexual.

The offence is committed when a defendant knows or is reckless as to whether he is penetrating any part of a dead body. This is intended to cover when he knows he is penetrating a dead body, for example in a mortuary, or where he is reckless as to whether the other party is alive or dead.

It will not cover situations where A penetrates B fully believing B to be alive, but in fact B is dead, or where B unexpectedly dies during intercourse.

The definition of sexual is given in s.78. This is to exclude legitimate penetration of corpses, for example, that which occurs during an autopsy.

Schedule 5 to the Act provides an amendment to PACE to provide a power of arrest for this offence.

8.9.1   Charging standards

The *Protecting the Public* document helpfully states that:

> Where a defendant is suspected of killing their victim, the first priority will clearly be to charge murder or manslaughter. Where there is evidence of sexual penetration of the body after death, it is important that the sexual deviance of the offending behaviour is properly recognised by a separate indictment of sexual interference with human remains. This will ensure that a defendant who is found guilty on both charges is sentenced accordingly and is treated and monitored as a sex offender both in prison and after release. The offence could also apply to cases in which the offender had no contact with the victim prior to death but sexually abused their corpse.

8.9.2   Penalty

The offence will be triable either way. A maximum penalty of six months' imprisonment will be available on summary conviction. On indictment the maximum penalty will be two years' imprisonment.

8.10   OFFENCES OUTSIDE THE UNITED KINGDOM

As a response to the growing trend of sex tourism, the Government is keen to crack down on sexually deviant behaviour, wherever it takes place.

Any person who was a British citizen or resident after 1 September 1997 will commit an offence under s.72 by doing an act outside the UK which is both an offence in the country in which it is committed and would be a sexual offence in England and Wales if it were done in any part of the United Kingdom.

Schedule 2 to the Act lists the sexual offences to which this section applies. These offences only relate to offences against victims who were under 16 at the time of the offence. All the child sex offences, together with rape, and the taking of indecent photographs will fall within the ambit of this section.

The exact description of the offence does not need to be the same in both countries. For example, the provisions would apply to someone who raped a child in another country regardless of how that offence was described under the law in that country.

8.10.1   Procedure

It is to be assumed that the overseas offence is equivalent to one under Schedule 2 unless that is challenged by the defendant. The Act provides that the court will lay down rules governing the timetable of such notices, but they must state the grounds for objection and require the prosecution to prove the same. The court has a discretionary power to waive the service of the notice (s.72(5)).

Where the matter is heard in the Crown Court, the judge alone will decide whether the appropriate conditions are met.

PART II NOTIFICATIONS AND ORDERS

9 NOTIFICATION REQUIREMENTS

9.1 INTRODUCTION

The second part of the Sexual Offences Act 2003 (the Act) is the Government's response to public concern regarding the system of registration that existed after the Sex Offenders Act 1997 (the 1997 Act) creating the obligation upon sex offenders to register their details with the police and to renew them periodically.

According to the first multi-agency public protection arrangements (MAPPA) reports there were 18,500 registered sex offenders living in the community on 31 March 2002.

The Home Office consultation on the Sexual Offences Bill stated that:

> In June 2000, the Home Office announced a review of the Sex Offenders Act 1997 to identify any areas of weakness in the legislation and to maximise its effectiveness. A range of organisations, including government departments, relevant professional organisations and children's charities were actively involved in the review process.
>
> Just a few weeks later, following the tragic death of Sarah Payne, widespread public concern was expressed about the dangers posed by sex offenders. In response, the Government introduced, in autumn 2000, a number of amendments to the then Criminal Justice and Courts Services Bill to strengthen the Sex Offenders Act. These anticipated some of the work of the Review.
>
> The Review team completed its work and published its recommendations for public consultation in July 2001. Over 50 organisations responded and many of their responses simply supported the proposals in the Review
>
> www.homeoffice.gov.uk/justice/sentencing/sexualoffencesbill/consultation.html

Liberty's response to the Bill on 29 January 2003 was to suggest that registration should be by order of a judge at the time of sentencing: the judge should decide whether or not the offender is a risk and only if they are should they be put on the register.[1] The judge knows the details of the case, of any previous convictions, will have any psychiatric and other reports, etc. and so is the person best placed to make this vital assessment. The reason for this, they state, is that only a fraction of the 18,500 names currently on the Register pose a real threat to children or the wider public. The Register should be cleared of (for example) people involved in consensual gay sex, so that the Register is properly focused on people who pose a real danger, and so the authorities who use the Register and monitor those on it can concentrate on real dangers. Unfortunately, the register still contains the names, for example, or people involved in consensual gay sex when over 18 from before the law changed.

The Government resisted calls for public access to the names of people on the register, the so-called 'Sarah's Law' saying:

> We believe that public access to the register drives sex offenders underground. This is the very opposite of what we are trying to achieve, as it would make it more difficult to monitor sex offenders. However, members of the public will soon be recruited to contribute to the strategic management of the MAPPA.
>
> **www.homeoffice.gov.uk/justice/sentencing/sexualoffencesbill/faq.html**

It seems that such an approach is justified as the compliance rate (around 97 per cent) (*Protecting the Public*, 2002) is higher than that in the USA (50 per cent), where the public are allowed access to the register.

Part 2 of the Act also creates a series of civil orders that can be used against sex offenders, or potential sex offenders. This extends and reviews the powers to make sex offender orders available under s.1 of the Crime and Disorder Act 1998.

Between 1 December 1998 and 1 March 2001 a total of 92 Sex Offender Orders had been awarded. Thirty-eight out of 43 forces had applied for an order and the success rate of applications at court was high (94 per cent). Almost half (46 per cent) had been prosecuted for subsequent breach. Whilst the response to such orders has generally been positive the study identified a number of problems arising principally from geographical constraints over the legal powers and who legally can apply for an order.[2]

Part 2 of the Act is designed to address all of these issues and to carry effective and meaningful penalties in the event of a breach of an order.

1   www.liberty-human-rights.org.uk/press/press-releases-2003/sexual-offences-bill-liberty-response.shtml.
2   Source – The Police Perspective on Sex Offender Orders: A preliminary review of Policy and Practice. Police Series Research Paper 155, Katy Knock.

9.2   THE NOTIFICATION REQUIREMENTS

There remains a widespread misconception regarding the duty to register. Many people think of it in terms of the judge making an order, where in fact he has no power to do so, registration simply follows as a consequence of conviction (Att.-Gen.'s Reference (No. 50 of 1997) (*R. v. V.*) [1998] 2 Cr App R (S) 155).

9.3   THE RELEVANT OFFENDER

All those persons who were required to notify under the provisions of the 1997 Act will now be required to do so under this legislation together with any person convicted,[1] cautioned or found guilty by reason of insanity in respect of any of the trigger offences. It will not apply to those whose notification period ends before the commencement of this section.

The definition of conviction is widened to include sentences of conditional discharge,[2] and reference to caution is to include a reprimand or warning within the meaning of s.65 of the Crime and Disorder Act 1998.

---

1   Also to include persons under a disability as defined by s.135 of this Act and a finding of guilt under Court Martial.
2   s.14(1) of the Powers of Criminal Courts (Sentencing) Act 2000 (which deems a conviction with a conditional discharge not to be a conviction) does not apply by virtue of s.134(1) of this Act.

9.4   THE TRIGGER OFFENCES

The offences which create an obligation to notify are listed in Schedule 3 to the Act. These are exclusively sexual offences and list all those offences that were formally set out in Schedule 1 to the 1997 Act together with some of the additional offences created by this Act.

Schedule 3 creates a series of absolute and conditional offences. The absolute offences, such as rape and assault by penetration, will place an absolute obligation on any offender to notify regardless of the sentence received. There are, however, within Schedule 3 a list of conditional offences. These are offences that, following a conviction, may require an offender to register, but the obligation to notify will depend upon the penalty imposed upon the defendant.

One such example is the offence of sexual assault, created by s.3 of this Act. In such a case, Schedule 3, para.18 provides that an obligation to notify will arise:

(a) where the offender was under 18, he is or has been sentenced in respect of the offence, to imprisonment for a term of at least 12 months;

(b) in any other case–

(i)   the victim was under 18, or
(ii) the offender, in respect of the offence or finding, is or has been–

(a) sentenced to a term of imprisonment,
(b) detained in hospital, or
(c) made subject to a community sentence[1] of at least 12 months.

Not all conditional requirements are the same, for example, some of the familial sexual offences will trigger notification when the offender is aged over 18 and sentenced to a period of imprisonment for a period of at least 12 months.

A community penalty in such a circumstance will not trigger notification as it does in the case of sexual assault given above.

The choice of 12 months' imprisonment in the case of youths was not an accident. It was designed to reflect the mid-range of seriousness, falling as it does at the middle of the available detention period permitted by a detention and training order.

This will lead to a degree of flexibility and ensure that those offences that take place in unusual circumstances, such as experimentation between teenagers who are de facto consenting even though the law prevents consent being given, do not result in a registration requirement. It is submitted that the appropriate starting point for any court is to sentence upon the facts of the case and not to take into account that a reduced sentence will lead to a lesser registration period.

This does, however, create an anomalous position that a youth convicted of an offence and sentenced to a supervision order for a period of six months will not be obliged to register, whereas the same youth cautioned for the offence would be so obliged. This is a matter which will need to be at the forefront of the mind of those advising suspects at the police station.

The Secretary of State has a residual power to alter any of the offences listed within Schedule 3.

---

1   Defined by para.96 of Schedule 3, with reference to the Powers of Criminal Courts (Sentencing) Act 2000. The definition is provided at s.33(2) of that Act and will include, but is not limited to, curfew orders and drug treatment and testing orders.

9.5   OFFENCES CARRYING AN ABSOLUTE REQUIREMENT TO REGISTER

This is the list for England and Wales, separate offences apply to Scotland and Northern Ireland.

An offence under section 1 of the Sexual Offences Act 1956 (c. 69) (rape).

An offence under section 5 of that Act (intercourse with girl under 13).

An offence under section 1 of the Indecency with Children Act 1960 (c. 33) (indecent conduct towards young child).

An offence under section 54 of the Criminal Law Act 1977 (c. 45) (inciting girl under 16 to have incestuous sexual intercourse).

An offence under section 3 of the Sexual Offences (Amendment) Act 2000 (c. 44) (abuse of position of trust), if the offender was 20 or over.

An offence under section 1 or 2 of this Act (rape, assault by penetration).

An offence under any of sections 4 to 6 of this Act (causing sexual activity without consent, rape of a child under 13, assault of a child under 13 by penetration).

An offence under section 15 of this Act (meeting a child following sexual grooming, etc.).

An offence under any of sections 30 to 37 of this Act (offences against persons with a mental disorder impeding choice, inducements, etc. to persons with mental disorder).

An offence under section 61 of this Act (administering a substance with intent).

9.6   OFFENCES WITH A CONDITIONAL REQUIREMENT TO REGISTER

An offence under section 6 of the Sexual Offences Act 1956 (intercourse with girl under 16).

An offence under section 10 of that Act (incest by a man).

An offence under section 12 of that Act (buggery).

An offence under section 13 of that Act (indecency between men).

An offence under section 14 of that Act (indecent assault on a woman).

An offence under section 15 of that Act (indecent assault on a man).

An offence under section 16 of that Act (assault with intent to commit buggery).

An offence under section 1 of the Protection of Children Act 1978 (c. 37) (indecent photographs of children).

An offence under section 170 of the Customs and Excise Management Act 1979 (c. 2) (penalty for fraudulent evasion of duty, etc.) in relation to goods prohibited to be imported under section 42 of the Customs Consolidation Act 1876 (c. 36) (indecent or obscene articles).

An offence under section 160 of the Criminal Justice Act 1988 (c. 33) (possession of indecent photograph of a child).

An offence under section 3 of the Sexual Offences (Amendment) Act 2000 (c. 44) (abuse of position of trust).

An offence under section 3 of this Act (sexual assault).

An offence under section 7 of this Act (sexual assault of a child under 13).

An offence under section 13 of this Act (child sex offences committed by children or young persons).

An offence under section 14 of this Act (arranging or facilitating the commission of a child sex offence).

An offence under any of sections 16 to 19 of this Act (abuse of a position of trust).

An offence under section 25 or 26 of this Act (familial child sex offences).

An offence under any of sections 38 to 41 of this Act (care workers for persons with mental disorder).

An offence under section 47 of this Act (paying for sexual services of a child).

An offence under section 62 or 63 of this Act (committing an offence or trespassing, with intent to commit a sexual offence).

An offence under section 64 or 65 of this Act (sex with an adult relative).

An offence under section 66 of this Act (exposure).

An offence under section 67 of this Act (voyeurism).

An offence under section 69 or 70 of this Act (intercourse with an animal, sexual penetration of a corpse).

In each case the criteria are different and reference ought to be made to Schedule 3 for full details.

9.7   THE NOTIFICATION PERIOD

The table below describes the categories of relevant person and the period that applies to him. The 'relevant date' is the date of conviction, caution or finding of insanity.

Table 9.1 Section 82 notification periods

Description of relevant offender	Notification period
A person who, in respect of the offence, is or has been sentenced to imprisonment for life or for a term of 30 months or more	An indefinite period beginning with the relevant date
A person who, in respect of the offence, has been made the subject of an order under section 210F(1) of the Criminal Procedure (Scotland) Act 1995 (order for lifelong restriction)	An indefinite period beginning with that date
A person who, in respect of the offence or finding, is or has been admitted to a hospital subject to a restriction order	An indefinite period beginning with that date
A person who, in respect of the offence, is or has been sentenced to imprisonment for a term of more than 6 months but less than 30 months	10 years beginning with that date
A person who, in respect of the offence, is or has been sentenced to imprisonment for a term of 6 months or less	7 years beginning with that date
A person who, in respect of the offence or finding, is or has been admitted to a hospital without being subject to a restriction order	7 years beginning with that date
A person within section 80(1)(d)	2 years beginning with that date
A person in whose case an order for conditional discharge or, in Scotland, a probation order, is made in respect of the offence	The period of conditional discharge or, in Scotland, the probation period
A person of any other description	5 years beginning with the relevant date

The significant alteration to the table produced by the Sex Offenders Act 1997 is the requirement that those cautioned for such an offence will now be obliged to register for a period of two years.

The notification period for a person under 18 at the relevant date will be one half of that period listed above. A 17 year old convicted and sentenced to 18 months' detention and training will therefore be obliged to report for a period of five years.

In calculating the relevant period, consecutive terms of imprisonment are to be added together and calculated accordingly. Where terms are partly concurrent, for example, when an offender is sentenced to a period of imprisonment for a Schedule 3 offence and part way through that term is sentenced to a further period, the notification period is to be calculated by combining the total sentence minus any overlapping term.

9.8   THE INITIAL NOTIFICATION

Within a period of three days from the relevant date (in calculating any such period any time spent in custody does not count) the offender must notify the police of the information listed in s.83(5) of the Act. The information consists of the relevant offender's:

- date of birth;
- national insurance number;
- name on the relevant date, and where he used more than one name on that date, each of those names;
- home address on the relevant date;
- name on the date that notification is given and where he used more than one name, each of those names;
- home address on the notification date;
- address of any other premises in the United Kingdom at which at the time notification is given he regularly resides of stays.

Notification will take place at prescribed police stations within each offender's local police area. A person giving notification of a change of address may give that notice at a police station in the area of his new address.

The requirement to provide 'oral notification' (s.87(1)(b)) to an authorised police officer (such person will be authorised by the officer in charge at each station) will mean that the report must be in person. Each notification must be acknowledged in writing and will be in the prescribed form that the Secretary of State may direct.

The details which the defendant is now to provide are significantly greater than those required under the 1997 Act, which simply required a person's name and address to be provided to the police. The definition of 'home address' has been broadened to include itinerant and homeless offenders. The timescale for notification has also been reduced from 14 days (1997 Act, s.2(1)) to three days.

9.9   CHANGE OF DETAILS

The Act also requires that a relevant offender notify the police of his release from custody or any change of name or address within a period of three days of that change. Where an offender intends to change name or address in the future he may notify the police in advance providing also the date that the change of details will have effect from.

If, for whatever reason, the anticipated change does not take place then the police must be told within a period of six days from the date of proposed change that the change has not taken place.

Section 84 also requires the offender to notify the police of his having stayed at any address other than his home address in the United Kingdom for an aggregate period of seven or more days within any 12 month period.

9.10   PERIODIC NOTIFICATION

The Act provides for a system of periodic notification to ensure that the records kept by the authorities are as up to date as possible. This will apply to offenders who are still required to notify the police pursuant to the Sex Offenders Act 1997 at the time of the commencement of this section of the Act.

The offender must re-notify the police of the details set out above within one year of the last time he was required to notify or, (for the first year only) if later, commencement of this part of the Act and annually thereafter on a rolling basis.

The rolling system of notification set up by the Act means that each time an offender notifies the police of a change in his details, the requirement to report again annually runs from the date on which the change was notified.

When the offender is in custody or abroad they have three days from their release or return to the United Kingdom in which to report.

9.11   OFFENDERS OUTSIDE THE UNITED KINGDOM

The Act provides the Secretary of State with powers to make regulations to govern relevant offenders who leave the UK. The information to be provided is likely to be wide in scope, but at a very minimum offenders will be required to provide the details of when they leave the UK and the date on which they intend to arrive in the foreign country. This is designed to prevent sex tourism and enable the passing of information to foreign governments.

9.12   NOTIFICATION ORDERS

In addition to the requirement to provide information, s.97 provides a Chief Constable with the power to apply to the Magistrates' Court for a Notification Order or an Interim Notification Order. This will apply to offenders who were convicted abroad and who now live in that police area and also offenders who are 'intending' to travel to the area. Upon the court being satisfied that the relevant conditions set out in s.97(2)–(4) are met it must make the order.

Such orders will only apply to foreign convictions[1] and cautions after 1 September 1997, the commencement date for the 1997 Act, save where the offender is still to be dealt with from a conviction preceding that date.

The purpose and power arising from such an application will be to require the offender to register under the provisions of this Act. An order will therefore only be available against a person who would be subject to a notification requirement if convicted in this country.

When, therefore, a person is convicted and sentenced abroad to a period of imprisonment of four months on 1 January 2000, the notification requirement imposed by the Act is seven years (see table at s.82 of the Act and para 9.7 of this book). If he comes to the UK on 1 January 2004 an order can only be made for a maximum of three years. If he were to arrive in the UK on 2 January 2007, no order would be possible.

Any requirement to notify arising from such an order will take effect within three days of the service of the order.

Application can also be made for an interim order imposing the same obligations upon the offender. Whereas the making of a full order is mandatory when the requisite conditions are met, an interim order may be made when the court 'considers it just to do so' (s.100(3)). The interim order will last for the period specified in the order and expire upon hearing the main application.

Section 101 permits a defendant to appeal to the Crown Court against the making of a notification order or interim notification order.

It is not clear from the Act how representation for such applications is to be funded. As the provisions are similar to Anti-social Behaviour Orders and Football Banning Orders it is likely that funding may be made available under a Criminal Defence Service CDS3 form.

---

1   A finding equivalent to not guilty by reason of insanity is included within this definition.

9.13   POLICE POWERS ARISING FROM NOTIFICATION

Where any notification is given, the relevant offender must, if requested to do so, allow the police to photograph any part of him,[1] to take his fingerprints or to do both for the purpose of identifying him.

The Act does not create a reasonableness test on behalf of the police.

---

1   The Explanatory notes to the Act state that this will include an iris scan, but on the face of the legislation could be much wider.

9.14   YOUNG OFFENDERS – PARENTAL DIRECTIONS

Section 89 of the Act allows the court dealing with the offender to direct a person with parental responsibility for the offender to comply with the notification requirements that apply to the offender until either the offender attains the relevant age[1] or until a date before that specified by the court. The parent must ensure that the young offender attends the police station with him.

The Court with the power to make an order will vary according to the nature of the offence and offender. The position is illustrated in Table 9.2.

Table 9.2 Power of court according to offence and offender

Description of person	Court which may make the direction
An offender within s.80(1)(a)–(c) (those convicted, but not cautioned of a Schedule 3 offence) An offender within s.81(a)–(c) – (persons subject to the notification requirements of the 1997 Act)	The Court which deals with the offender in respect of the offence or finding
A relevant offender within s.129(1)(a)–(c) Breach of a risk of sexual harm order (RSHO) or interim RSHO (see Chapter 12)	The Court which deals with the offender in respect of the offence or finding
A person who is the subject of a notification order, interim notification order, sexual offences prevention order or interim sexual offences order	The Court which makes the order
A relevant offender who is the defendant to an application under s.89(4) (application for an order made on complaint)	The Court which hears the application

---

1   18 in England, Wales and Northern Ireland and service law; 16 in Scotland.

9.15   PARENTAL DIRECTION ORDERS ON COMPLAINT

Where a court, for whatever reason, decides not to make such an order at the time of dealing with the young offender, a magistrates' court for the area in which the relevant offender resides or intends to reside, may on complaint of a chief officer of police make a direction requiring the parent to notify (s.89(4)).

The Act does not make it clear precisely whom this order will be sought against and whether the parent, child or both will be subject to the summons. Section

89(1) makes it clear that the order shall apply in respect of 'an individual having parental responsibility' and in such circumstances. Presumably a local authority would not fall within this definition. There is no guidance within the Act as to the burden and standard of proof to be applied in dealing with such applications nor is there any indication as to how such responses are to be funded. This is a particularly relevant consideration as such applications may by their very nature involve a conflict of interest between parent and child, since it is likely to be the child's conduct that has caused the parent to be summonsed.

9.16   PARENTAL DIRECTIONS: VARIATIONS, RENEWALS AND DISCHARGES

A court may vary, renew or discharge a parental direction. This may be required where there is a change in residence as a result of a divorce or where the parent can no longer control the young offender and is unable to ensure that he attends with the parent to notify. In these circumstances the court may consider that the liability for his failure to attend should revert to the young offender himself.

Applications can be made by the parent, young offender, the police or, in any other case the prosecution. Applications are made to the magistrates' court, save where the Crown Court or Court of Appeal made the order. In such cases the appropriate court is the Crown Court.

9.17   NOTIFICATION OFFENCES

Any person commits an offence, if without reasonable excuse, he fails to comply with any of the notification requirements imposed upon him, or in complying with the notification requirements he provides false information (s.91).

'Reasonable excuse' is likely to be interpreted in the same manner as the Bail Act 1976 and would include illness or in the case of an adult with a responsibility to bring a young offender to the police station, having made all reasonable efforts to persuade the young person to attend the police station.

9.18   PROCEDURE

Proceedings can be commenced in any court where the person charged with the offence resides or is found. A certificate of conviction from the convicting court or certification of a caution by a constable shall in each case be evidence of the facts contained within the certificate. In the case of police the certificates will be in a form to be prescribed by the Secretary of State.

9.19   PENALTY

A person guilty of such an offence is liable on summary conviction to a term not exceeding six months, a fine or both. On conviction on indictment to a term of imprisonment not exceeding five years.

This marks a significant increase in the penalties available to the court, as the 1997 Act allowed a maximum sentence of six months on an offence triable only summarily.

9.20   INFORMATION ABOUT RELEASE OR TRANSFER

The Act provides that those involved in the prevention, detection, investigation or prosecution of such offences may pass on information to specified bodies such as the police and Director General of National Criminal Intelligence Service (NCIS) for the purpose of verifying such information.

The Act also permits the Secretary of State to make regulations to ensure those who are temporarily responsible for the offender to pass on information regarding the release of that person. This section re-enacts many of the provisions of the 1997 Act, subject to amendments necessary by the insertion of provisions into this Act. It will be used, for example, to require a prison governor or hospital director to pass on information to the police about the release or transfer of a prisoner or patient.

9.21   ENDING OF NOTIFICATION FOR REPEALED HOMOSEXUAL OFFENCES

The Act has repealed many of the homosexual offences, particularly gross indecency between men and buggery. Schedule 4 provides that persons with convictions for such offences will no longer be subject to the notification requirements imposed by the Sex Offenders Act 1997.

Certain categories of offender will be eligible to be removed from the notification requirements. The relevant offender may apply to the Secretary of State for a decision as to whether it appears that the person with whom the act of buggery or gross indecency was committed was aged over 16 at the time and consented.

Applications must be in writing and state:

(a) the name, address and date of birth of the offender;
(b) his name and address at the time of the conviction, finding or caution;
(c) so far as is known to him, the time when and the place where the conviction or finding was made or the caution given and, for a conviction or finding, the case number;
(d) such other information as the Secretary of State may require.

In making a decision the Secretary of State must take account of any representations and any available record of the investigation, but is 'not to seek evidence from any witness' (Schedule 4, para.3(1)). Any decision will be given in writing and takes effect from the date upon which it is given.

A right of appeal lies to the High Court on application, who are also prohibited from hearing evidence on the matter. There is no appeal from the decision of the High Court.

9.22   OTHER STATUTES

Notification requirements are designed to work in harmony with other legislation to control sex offenders. Extended post supervision licence remains a tool available to courts at the time of sentencing, to effectively monitor and track sex offenders between their annual periods of notification. These areas are designed to work in harmony with MAPPA to manage the risks posed by offenders in the community.

10 SEXUAL OFFENCES PREVENTION ORDERS

A Sexual Offences Prevention Order (SOPO) is a civil order replacing and amending those orders available under section 5 of the Sexual Offenders Act 1997.

10.1 THE TEST

Orders are available to the court at the time of conviction or, on application, post-conviction if it is necessary to protect the public or any particular members of the public from serious sexual harm from the defendant. Section 106(3) describes this as:

> . . . serious physical or psychological harm, caused by the defendant committing one or more of the offences listed in Schedule 3.

10.2 AGAINST WHOM MAY AN ORDER BE MADE

A SOPO can only be sought against a person convicted of an offence listed in Schedule 3 or 5 to this Act. Schedule 3 is a list of specified sexual offences whilst Schedule 5 contains a list, designed to coincide with the definition of dangerous offenders within the Criminal Justice Act 2003 as it went before Parliament. Schedule 5 includes, but is not limited to, murder, kidnap, and offences of assault occasioning actual bodily harm.

10.3 PROCEDURE

A SOPO can be made at the time of the defendant's conviction for an offence listed in Schedules 3 or 5 to this Act if it is necessary to make such an order for the purpose of protecting the public or any particular members of the public from serious sexual harm by the defendant.

Applications can also be made post-conviction by the chief police officer for the area in which the relevant offender resides or intends to come, provided that the person has 'acted in such a way as to give reasonable cause to believe that it is necessary for such an order to be made' (s.104(5)(b)). Such behaviour does not appear to be limited to criminal conduct.

Such application can be made to any magistrates' court whose commission area includes any part of the applicant's police area, or any place in which it is alleged that the person acted in the way referred to.

There is no doubt that the proceedings are civil in nature and are consequently governed by ss.51–57 of the Magistrates' Courts Act 1980.

10.4   INTERIM ORDERS

Section 109 of the Act allows for an interim order to be made on complaint, provided that the court 'considers it just to do so'. The interim order may be made when a full application has been made but not yet determined.

Interim orders must be for a fixed duration specified in the order which will cease on determination of the main application if it has not already expired.

10.5   SCOPE OF ORDER

The SOPO can prohibit the defendant from doing anything described in the order that is 'necessary to protect the public from serious sexual harm by the defendant'. It must be noted that there is no power to require the defendant to do acts, only not to do them. The SOPO must last for a fixed period not less than five years starting with the date of service of the order, or for an indefinite period. Only one order can be in place at any one time and where a further order is made the earlier order ceases to have effect.

Such an order might prevent the defendant from having contact with children under 16, from approaching any school premises, or from contacting his victims. A SOPO will work in tandem with the notification requirements of this Act.

Where the defendant was already subject to a notification order, that order will remain in place for the period of notification or the period of the SOPO, whichever is the greater.

Defendants who were not subject to a notification order will become subject to the notification requirements for the period of the order.

10.6   VARIATION, RENEWAL AND DISCHARGE

An application can be made by the defendant or chief constable to renew or vary an order or interim order by imposing only those conditions which are necessary to protect the public from serious sexual harm by the defendant. Section 108(2) defines chief constable as 'the chief officer of police for the area in which the defendant resides or is intending to come or where an order is made under s.104(5) (post conviction) the chief officer who made the application'.

The application should be made in most cases by complaint to the magistrates' court where the defendant resides or for the commission area of the applying chief constable. The exception to this will be when the Crown Court or Court of Appeal made the order, in which case the appropriate application is to the Crown Court.

Before making the order the court ought to hear from the party making the application and also the chief of police, also as defined by s.108(2) above.

Any orders presently in place under s.5A of the Sex Offenders Act 1997 (restraining orders) or those made under s.2 or s.20 of the Crime and Disorder Act 1998 (sex offender orders) will be varied and discharged using the procedures described above.

A court must not discharge an order before the end of five years from the date upon which the order was made without the consent of the defendant and the police.

10.7   APPEALS

A defendant may appeal to the Crown Court against the making of a SOPO or interim SOPO made in the magistrates' court. Orders imposed at the Crown Court ought to be appealed to the Court of Appeal.

A defendant can also appeal against the decision of the court on application to vary, renew or discharge the order. In such cases the appeal lies to the Crown Court, save where the application for such an order was made to the Crown Court in which case the appeal should be made to the Court of Appeal.

10.8   PENALTY FOR BREACH

A person commits an offence if, without reasonable excuse, he does anything that he is prevented from doing by a SOPO or interim SOPO or any restraining order or sex offender order currently in place under the Crime and Disorder Act 1998 or the Sex Offenders Act 1997.

The offence is punishable on summary conviction to a term of imprisonment not exceeding six months, a fine or both, and upon conviction on indictment to a term not exceeding five years.

It must be noted that by virtue of s.113(3) of the Act the court is expressly prevented from sentencing a person so convicted to a conditional discharge.

11 FOREIGN TRAVEL ORDERS

11.1 BACKGROUND

The foreign travel notification regulations were introduced in June 2001 under the Sex Offenders Act 1997 to enable the police to know when a sex offender is planning to travel abroad for eight days or more. The police can then notify other jurisdictions if they believe there is a risk posed by the defendant.

The review of sexual offences provided an ideal opportunity for reviewing the foreign travel requirements to improve their effectiveness. In a 2003 press release Home Office minister Hilary Benn said:

> ... under current legislation the courts do not have the power to stop an offender who has been convicted of sexual offences against children from travelling abroad to abuse children. We believe this is wrong and that it should be addressed.

The result of the review is a tightening of the notification requirements (see Chapter 9) and additionally giving the power conferred by s.114 of the Act, to allow for a civil order preventing a defendant from travelling abroad.

11.2 THE TEST

Orders can be made if it is necessary to protect children or any particular child under 16 from serious sexual harm from the defendant. Section 115(2) describes this as:

> ... serious physical or psychological harm, caused by the defendant doing, outside the United Kingdom, anything which would constitute an offence listed in Schedule 3 if done in any part of the United Kingdom.

11.3 AGAINST WHOM AN ORDER CAN BE MADE

An order can be made against any defendant who is has been convicted[1] or cautioned[2] in respect of a relevant offence,[3] *and* who behaves:

. . . in such a way as to give reasonable cause to believe that it is necessary for such an order to be made (s.114(1)(b)).

Orders can be also be made against a person who was dealt with (by way of conviction or caution, etc.) prior to the commencement of this Act and against persons convicted of a like offence whilst abroad which would constitute a relevant sexual offence were it committed in the United Kingdom.

---

1   Includes a finding of not guilty by reason of insanity, or having been found to be under a disability at the time of the act.
2   Includes reprimand and warning.
3   Defined by s.116(2) and includes some of the offences listed in Schedule 3.

11.4   PROCEDURE

An order may be made on complaint to the magistrates' court by the chief constable for the area in which the defendant resides or intends to come to.

There is no power of arrest conferred by the Act so that an offender who appears at an airport to board a plane abroad cannot on the face of it be stopped from going.

11.5   SCOPE

The order has effect for a fixed period of not more than six months (s.117(1)) specified in the order and under s.117(2) can prevent a defendant from either:

(a) travelling to any country outside the United Kingdom named or described in the order,
(b) travelling to any country outside the United Kingdom other than a country named or described in the order, or
(c) travelling to any country outside the United Kingdom.

The order can only contain such prohibitions as are necessary for protecting children from serious sexual harm from the defendant outside the UK. Only one order can be in place at any time and where a further order is made the earlier order ceases to have effect.

There is no power to make an interim foreign travel order.

Foreign Travel Orders can be made that run alongside Sexual Offences Prevention Orders (SOPOs).

11.6   VARIATION, RENEWAL AND DISCHARGE

The provisions in relation to foreign travel orders almost mirror those of the SOPOs and are contained in s.118 of the Act. An application can be made to the magistrates' court by the defendant or chief constable for the area in which the defendant resides, or intends to reside, or the force officer who made the original application.

The renewal or variation of an order may be made once any interested party has been given an opportunity to be heard. The court may then make any order that it considers appropriate. An order may be renewed or varied so as to impose additional conditions only if it is necessary to protect children from serious sexual harm by the defendant outside the United Kingdom.

11.7   APPEALS

The defendant may appeal to the Crown Court against the making of a Foreign Travel Order or the refusal to make a variation, renewal or discharge of the order by s.119 of the Act.

On appeal the court may make such order as it considers 'just'. No further guidance is given as to the procedure for making such applications or the burden and standard of proof in such applications.

11.8   PENALTIES FOR BREACH

It is an offence to do an act that breaches the order without reasonable excuse.

The offence is punishable on summary conviction to a term of imprisonment not exceeding six months, a fine or both, and upon conviction on indictment to a term of imprisonment not exceeding five years.

It must be noted that by virtue of s.122(3) the court is expressly prevented from sentencing a person so convicted to a conditional discharge.

12 RISK OF SEXUAL HARM ORDERS

12.1 BACKGROUND

The order is a preventative civil order with startling and draconian consequences. It is designed to apply to circumstances where the behaviour of an adult gives reason to believe that the child is at risk from the defendant and that intervention at an early stage is necessary to protect the child (Home Office, Provisional Draft Guidance on Risk Of Sexual Harm Orders, March 2003, para.12).

It is not surprising that they have attracted a great deal of criticism. Liberty has defined these orders as 'an affront to any notion of traditional British justice' in that 'they permit the badge of paedophilia and, accordingly, broad and ill-defined prohibitions . . . to be placed upon a person who has never been convicted of any criminal offence. No criminal offences need even to be anticipated' (EV 82).

When giving evidence to the House of Commons Home Affairs Select Committee, Ian Berry, Chairman of the Police Federation said, 'it may well be classed as overkill' (Q.91 to that committee and referred to within the fifth report).

12.2 THE TEST

Such orders will apply to persons aged 18 or over (the only civil order to have a minimum age requirement), who on at *least two* previous occasions have done an act within s.123(3) of the Sexual Offences Act 2003 and as a result of those acts there is 'reasonable cause to believe that it is necessary for such an order to be made'.

It is not necessary for the defendant to have convictions for sexual offences or any other offences. The acts referred to within s.123(3) are:

(a) engaging in sexual activity involving a child or in the presence of a child;
(b) causing or inciting a child to watch a person engage in sexual activity or to look at a moving or still image that is sexual;
(c) giving a child anything that relates to a sexual activity or contains reference to such activity;
(d) communicating with a child, where any part of the communication is sexual.

Sexual activity is as defined by s.124(5) as an activity that a reasonable person would, in all the circumstances, but regardless of any person's purpose, consider to be sexual. The test is therefore objective not subjective.

12.3   PROCEDURE

The application is made to the magistrates' court for the area where the defendant resides or acted in the way alleged above. The application is made by the chief constable for the area in which the person resides or intends to reside.

Draft guidance has been published by the Home Office (March 2003) on Risk of Sexual Harm Orders (RHSOs) that confirms that although the orders are civil in nature the burden of proof will be to the criminal standard of beyond reasonable doubt, reflecting a similar position to Anti-social Behaviour Orders (R. (McCann) v. Manchester Crown Court [2002] UKHL 39; [2002] 3 WLR 1313).

12.4   SCOPE

The order can either last for a fixed period of at least two years or be indefinite. The only conditions that can be imposed are those protecting children from serious physical or psychological harm from the defendant doing acts within s.123(3) (see para.12.2).

Only one order can be in place at any one time and where a further order is made the earlier order ceases to have effect.

12.5   INTERIM ORDERS

Section 126 provides for the making of interim RSHOs. Again these are made on complaint to the magistrates' court and will be made if the court 'considers it just to do so'. No further guidance is given as to the procedure for making such an application or the burden and standard of proof to be applied in such circumstances.

Interim orders will last for a fixed period and cease to have effect upon the hearing of the main application. Applications to vary or discharge interim orders can also be made in the same manner as applications relating to the substantive order.

12.6   VARIATION, RENEWAL AND DISCHARGE

Such applications follow the same procedure as for SOPOs and foreign travel orders. An application can be made to the magistrates' court by the defendant, or the chief constable for the area in which the defendant resides or intends to reside, or the force officer who made the original application.

The renewal or variation of an order may only impose those conditions which are necessary to protect children from serious sexual harm by the defendant outside the United Kingdom.

Any interested party ought to be given an opportunity to be heard before any order is made.

Section 125(5) provides that a court must not discharge an order within two years of the making of that order without the consent of the defendant or, when the application is made by the chief officer of police, that officer.

12.7   APPEALS

The defendant may appeal by virtue of s.127 of the Act to the Crown Court against the making of a RHSO or an interim RHSO or the refusal to make a variation, renewal or discharge of the order.

In hearing the application the court will make such order as is necessary and as appears to be just. Again no further guidance as to the procedure to be followed and the burden and standard of proof applicable for such an application is contained within the Act.

12.8   PENALTIES FOR BREACH

It is an offence to do an act that breaches the order or interim order without 'reasonable excuse' (s.128). It is suggested that the same test as applies to an offence of failing to surrender to bail, contrary to the Bail Act 1976, will apply to a breach alleged under this section.

The offence is punishable on summary conviction to a term of imprisonment not exceeding six months, a fine or both, and upon conviction on indictment to a term of imprisonment not exceeding five years.

It must be noted that, by virtue of s.128(3), the court is expressly prevented from sentencing a person so convicted to a conditional discharge.

In addition to those powers a person convicted or cautioned for an offence of breaching such an order will from the date of conviction be subject to the notification requirements of this Act (see Chapter 9).

A person who is already subject to the notification requirements will continue to be subject to those requirements for the period of notification or the period of the RHSO, whichever is the greater.

13 MISCELLANEOUS PROVISIONS CONTAINED WITHIN THE ACT

The Act makes a number of minor and consequential amendments, which are listed within Schedule 5.

13.1 EARLY RELEASE

These include amending the Criminal Justice Act 1982 to exclude from early release provisions some of the offences created by this Act. Included are rape, assault by penetration, rape or assault by penetration of a child under 13 and offences of sexual activity against a person with a mental disorder.

13.2 POWER OF ARREST

Schedule 5 to the Act also amends the Police and Criminal Evidence Act 1984 (PACE) to provide a power of arrest for offences of sexual activity in a public lavatory, exposure, voyeurism, intercourse with an animal and sexual penetration of a corpse. The powers of arrest arising from the Obscene Publications Act 1959 are extended to include many of the offences within this Act.

13.3 BAIL

The Criminal Justice and Public Order Act 1994 (CJPOA) created a list of offences when, on the face of it, bail was to be withheld (CJPOA, s.25). Added to the list to which that section applies are the offences of:

- assault by penetration;
- causing a person to engage in sexual activity without consent;
- rape of a child under 13;
- assault of a child under 13 by penetration;
- causing a child under 13 to engage in sexual activity involving an act of penetration;
- sexual activity of a person with a mental disorder;

- causing or inciting a person with a mental disorder to engage in a sexual activity involving penetration; or
- any attempt to commit the offences listed above.

13.4   CROSS EXAMINATION OF CHILD WITNESSES

Amendment is made to the Youth Justice and Criminal Evidence Act 1999 (YJCE). Section 35 of that Act outlines the offences where a defendant is prevented from cross-examining a witness in person. Any offence that falls within Part 1 of this Act will now be included within s.35.

13.5   DETENTION FOR AN EXTENDED PERIOD

Section 91 of the Powers of Criminal Courts (Sentencing) Act 2000 (PCC(S)A) lists those offences for which a person under 18 may be sentenced on indictment for a period in excess of two years, the current maximum permitted by the introduction of detention and training orders. Included in the new list are offences of sexual assault, sexual activity with a child family member, inciting a child to engage in sexual activity and child sex offences that are committed by young people.

The list of offences in PCC(S)A, s.109, in which a life sentence is given for a second similar offence are also taken to include many of the offences listed above.

13.6   REPEAL OF SEXUAL OFFENCES

A full list of all the repeals and revocations can be found at Schedule 7 to the Act. Those that are perhaps worthy of particular note are listed below.

The whole of the Sex Offenders Act 1997.

The Sexual Offences Act 1956 as follows:

- Sections 1–7 – Intercourse by force, intimidation, etc.;
- Sections 9–17 – Intercourse with defectives, Incest, Unnatural offences, Assaults, Abduction;
- Sections 19–32 – Abduction, Prostitution, Procuration etc., Solicitation;
- Sections 41–47 – Power of arrest and search, Interpretation;
- In Schedule 2, paragraphs 1–32 – Table of Offences with mode of prosecution and punishment, etc.

The Sexual Offences Act 1967 as follows:

- Section 1 – Amendment of law relating to homosexual acts in private;
- Section 4 – Procuring others to commit homosexual acts;
- Section 5 – Living on earnings of male prostitution;
- Sections 7 and 8 – Time limit and restriction on prosecutions;
- Section 10 – Past offences.

Sexual Offences Amendment Act 1976 as follows:

- Section 1(2) – Meaning of 'rape' etc.;
- Section 7(3) – Citation, interpretation, commencement and extent.

Sexual Offences (Amendment) Act 2000 as follows:

- Section 1(1), (2) and (4). – Reduction in age at which certain sexual acts are lawful;
- Section 2(1) to (3) and (5) – Defences available to persons who are under age;
- Sections 3 and 4 except so far as extending to Scotland. – Abuse of position of trust;
- Section 5 – Notification requirements for offenders under section 3.

PART III THE SEXUAL OFFENCES ACT 2003

Appendix
SEXUAL OFFENCES ACT 2003

2003 CHAPTER 42

CONTENTS

PART 1   SEXUAL OFFENCES

Rape

PART 2   NOTIFICATION AND ORDERS

An Act to make new provision about sexual offences, their prevention and the protection of children from harm from other sexual acts, and for connected purposes.

[20th November 2003]

BE IT ENACTED by the Queen's most Excellent Majesty, by and with the advice and consent of the Lords Spiritual and Temporal, and Commons, in this present Parliament assembled, and by the authority of the same, as follows:-

PART 1   SEXUAL OFFENCES

Rape

1 Rape

(1)   A person (A) commits an offence if –

    (a)   he intentionally penetrates the vagina, anus or mouth of another person (B) with his penis,

    (b)   B does not consent to the penetration, and

    (c)   A does not reasonably believe that B consents.

(2) Whether a belief is reasonable is to be determined having regard to all the circumstances, including any steps A has taken to ascertain whether B consents.

(3) Sections 75 and 76 apply to an offence under this section.

(4) A person guilty of an offence under this section is liable, on conviction on indictment, to imprisonment for life.

Assault

2 Assault by penetration

(1) A person (A) commits an offence if –

    (a) he intentionally penetrates the vagina or anus of another person (B) with a part of his body or anything else,

    (b) the penetration is sexual,

    (c) B does not consent to the penetration, and

    (d) A does not reasonably believe that B consents.

(2) Whether a belief is reasonable is to be determined having regard to all the circumstances, including any steps A has taken to ascertain whether B consents.

(3) Sections 75 and 76 apply to an offence under this section.

(4) A person guilty of an offence under this section is liable, on conviction on indictment, to imprisonment for life.

3 Sexual assault

(1) A person (A) commits an offence if –

    (a) he intentionally touches another person (B),

    (b) the touching is sexual,

    (c) B does not consent to the touching, and

    (d) A does not reasonably believe that B consents.

(2) Whether a belief is reasonable is to be determined having regard to all the circumstances, including any steps A has taken to ascertain whether B consents.

(3) Sections 75 and 76 apply to an offence under this section.

(4) A person guilty of an offence under this section is liable –

    (a) on summary conviction, to imprisonment for a term not exceeding 6 months or a fine not exceeding the statutory maximum or both;

    (b) on conviction on indictment, to imprisonment for a term not exceeding 10 years.

Causing sexual activity without consent

4 Causing a person to engage in sexual activity without consent

(1) A person (A) commits an offence if –

    (a) he intentionally causes another person (B) to engage in an activity,

    (b) the activity is sexual,

    (c) B does not consent to engaging in the activity, and

    (d) A does not reasonably believe that B consents.

(2) Whether a belief is reasonable is to be determined having regard to all the circumstances, including any steps A has taken to ascertain whether B consents.

(3) Sections 75 and 76 apply to an offence under this section.

(4) A person guilty of an offence under this section, if the activity caused involved –

    (a) penetration of B's anus or vagina,

    (b) penetration of B's mouth with a person's penis,

    (c) penetration of a person's anus or vagina with a part of B's body or by B with anything else, or

(d)   penetration of a person's mouth with B's penis,

is liable, on conviction on indictment, to imprisonment for life.

(5)   Unless subsection (4) applies, a person guilty of an offence under this section is liable –

(a)   on summary conviction, to imprisonment for a term not exceeding 6 months or to a fine not exceeding the statutory maximum or both;

(b)   on conviction on indictment, to imprisonment for a term not exceeding 10 years.

Rape and other offences against children under 13

5 Rape of a child under 13

(1)   A person commits an offence if –

(a)   he intentionally penetrates the vagina, anus or mouth of another person with his penis, and

(b)   the other person is under 13.

(2)   A person guilty of an offence under this section is liable, on conviction on indictment, to imprisonment for life.

6 Assault of a child under 13 by penetration

(1)   A person commits an offence if –

(a)   he intentionally penetrates the vagina or anus of another person with a part of his body or anything else,

(b)   the penetration is sexual, and

(c)   the other person is under 13.

(2)   A person guilty of an offence under this section is liable, on conviction on indictment, to imprisonment for life.

7 Sexual assault of a child under 13

(1)   A person commits an offence if –

(a)   he intentionally touches another person,

(b)   the touching is sexual, and

(c)   the other person is under 13.

(2)   A person guilty of an offence under this section is liable –

(a)   on summary conviction, to imprisonment for a term not exceeding 6 months or a fine not exceeding the statutory maximum or both;

(b)   on conviction on indictment, to imprisonment for a term not exceeding 14 years.

8 Causing or inciting a child under 13 to engage in sexual activity

(1)   A person commits an offence if –

(a)   he intentionally causes or incites another person (B) to engage in an activity,

(b)   the activity is sexual, and

(c)   B is under 13.

(2)   A person guilty of an offence under this section, if the activity caused or incited involved –

(a)   penetration of B's anus or vagina,

(b)   penetration of B's mouth with a person's penis,

(c)   penetration of a person's anus or vagina with a part of B's body or by B with anything else, or

(d)   penetration of a person's mouth with B's penis,

is liable, on conviction on indictment, to imprisonment for life.

(3) Unless subsection (2) applies, a person guilty of an offence under this section is liable –

    (a) on summary conviction, to imprisonment for a term not exceeding 6 months or to a fine not exceeding the statutory maximum or both;

    (b) on conviction on indictment, to imprisonment for a term not exceeding 14 years.

Child sex offences

9 Sexual activity with a child

(1) A person aged 18 or over (A) commits an offence if –

    (a) he intentionally touches another person (B),

    (b) the touching is sexual, and

    (c) either –

        (i)   B is under 16 and A does not reasonably believe that B is 16 or over, or

        (ii) B is under 13.

(2) A person guilty of an offence under this section, if the touching involved –

    (a) penetration of B's anus or vagina with a part of A's body or anything else,

    (b) penetration of B's mouth with A's penis,

    (c) penetration of A's anus or vagina with a part of B's body, or

    (d) penetration of A's mouth with B's penis,

is liable, on conviction on indictment, to imprisonment for a term not exceeding 14 years.

(3) Unless subsection (2) applies, a person guilty of an offence under this section is liable –

    (a) on summary conviction, to imprisonment for a term not exceeding 6 months or to a fine not exceeding the statutory maximum or both;

    (b) on conviction on indictment, to imprisonment for a term not exceeding 14 years.

10 Causing or inciting a child to engage in sexual activity

(1) A person aged 18 or over (A) commits an offence if –

    (a) he intentionally causes or incites another person (B) to engage in an activity,

    (b) the activity is sexual, and

    (c) either –

        (i)   B is under 16 and A does not reasonably believe that B is 16 or over, or

        (ii) B is under 13.

(2) A person guilty of an offence under this section, if the activity caused or incited involved –

    (a) penetration of B's anus or vagina,

    (b) penetration of B's mouth with a person's penis,

    (c) penetration of a person's anus or vagina with a part of B's body or by B with anything else, or

    (d) penetration of a person's mouth with B's penis,

is liable, on conviction on indictment, to imprisonment for a term not exceeding 14 years.

(3) Unless subsection (2) applies, a person guilty of an offence under this section is liable –

    (a) on summary conviction, to imprisonment for a term not exceeding 6 months or to a fine not exceeding the statutory maximum or both;

    (b) on conviction on indictment, to imprisonment for a term not exceeding 14 years.

11 Engaging in sexual activity in the presence of a child

(1) A person aged 18 or over (A) commits an offence if –

    (a) he intentionally engages in an activity,

    (b) the activity is sexual,

    (c) for the purpose of obtaining sexual gratification, he engages in it –

        (i)   when another person (B) is present or is in a place from which A can be observed, and

        (ii)   knowing or believing that B is aware, or intending that B should be aware, that he is engaging in it, and

    (d) either –

        (i)   B is under 16 and A does not reasonably believe that B is 16 or over, or

        (ii)   B is under 13.

(2) A person guilty of an offence under this section is liable –

    (a) on summary conviction, to imprisonment for a term not exceeding 6 months or a fine not exceeding the statutory maximum or both;

    (b) on conviction on indictment, to imprisonment for a term not exceeding 10 years.

12 Causing a child to watch a sexual act

(1) A person aged 18 or over (A) commits an offence if –

    (a) for the purpose of obtaining sexual gratification, he intentionally causes another person (B) to watch a third person engaging in an activity, or to look at an image of any person engaging in an activity,

    (b) the activity is sexual, and

    (c) either –

        (i)   B is under 16 and A does not reasonably believe that B is 16 or over, or

        (ii)   B is under 13.

(2) A person guilty of an offence under this section is liable –

    (a) on summary conviction, to imprisonment for a term not exceeding 6 months or a fine not exceeding the statutory maximum or both;

    (b) on conviction on indictment, to imprisonment for a term not exceeding 10 years.

13 Child sex offences committed by children or young persons

(1) A person under 18 commits an offence if he does anything which would be an offence under any of sections 9 to 12 if he were aged 18.

(2) A person guilty of an offence under this section is liable –

    (a) on summary conviction, to imprisonment for a term not exceeding 6 months or a fine not exceeding the statutory maximum or both;

    (b) on conviction on indictment, to imprisonment for a term not exceeding 5 years.

14 Arranging or facilitating commission of a child sex offence

(1) A person commits an offence if –

    (a) he intentionally arranges or facilitates something that he intends to do, intends another person to do, or believes that another person will do, in any part of the world, and

    (b) doing it will involve the commission of an offence under any of sections 9 to 13.

(2) A person does not commit an offence under this section if –

    (a) he arranges or facilitates something that he believes another person will do, but that he does not intend to do or intend another person to do, and

    (b) any offence within subsection (1)(b) would be an offence against a child for whose protection he acts.

(3) For the purposes of subsection (2), a person acts for the protection of a child if he acts for the purpose of –

    (a) protecting the child from sexually transmitted infection,

    (b) protecting the physical safety of the child,

    (c) preventing the child from becoming pregnant, or

    (d) promoting the child's emotional well-being by the giving of advice,

and not for the purpose of obtaining sexual gratification or for the purpose of causing or encouraging the activity constituting the offence within subsection (1)(b) or the child's participation in it.

(4) A person guilty of an offence under this section is liable –

    (a) on summary conviction, to imprisonment for a term not exceeding 6 months or a fine not exceeding the statutory maximum or both;

    (b) on conviction on indictment, to imprisonment for a term not exceeding 14 years.

15 Meeting a child following sexual grooming etc.

(1) A person aged 18 or over (A) commits an offence if –

    (a) having met or communicated with another person (B) on at least two earlier occasions, he –

        (i) intentionally meets B, or

        (ii) travels with the intention of meeting B in any part of the world,

    (b) at the time, he intends to do anything to or in respect of B, during or after the meeting and in any part of the world, which if done will involve the commission by A of a relevant offence,

    (c) B is under 16, and

    (d) A does not reasonably believe that B is 16 or over.

(2) In subsection (1) –

    (a) the reference to A having met or communicated with B is a reference to A having met B in any part of the world or having communicated with B by any means from, to or in any part of the world;

    (b) 'relevant offence' means –

        (i) an offence under this Part,

        (ii) an offence within any of paragraphs 61 to 92 of Schedule 3, or

        (iii) anything done outside England and Wales and Northern Ireland which is not an offence within sub-paragraph (i) or (ii) but would be an offence within sub-paragraph (i) if done in England and Wales.

(3) In this section as it applies to Northern Ireland –

    (a) subsection (1) has effect with the substitution of '17' for '16' in both places;

    (b) subsection (2)(b)(iii) has effect with the substitution of 'sub-paragraph (ii) if done in Northern Ireland' for 'sub-paragraph (i) if done in England and Wales'.

(4) A person guilty of an offence under this section is liable –

    (a) on summary conviction, to imprisonment for a term not exceeding 6 months or a fine not exceeding the statutory maximum or both;

    (b) on conviction on indictment, to imprisonment for a term not exceeding 10 years.

Abuse of position of trust

16 Abuse of position of trust: sexual activity with a child

(1) A person aged 18 or over (A) commits an offence if –

    (a) he intentionally touches another person (B),

    (b) the touching is sexual,

   (c) A is in a position of trust in relation to B,

   (d) where subsection (2) applies, A knows or could reasonably be expected to know of the circumstances by virtue of which he is in a position of trust in relation to B, and

   (e) either –

      (i) B is under 18 and A does not reasonably believe that B is 18 or over, or

     (ii) B is under 13.

(2) This subsection applies where A –

   (a) is in a position of trust in relation to B by virtue of circumstances within section 21(2), (3), (4) or (5), and

   (b) is not in such a position of trust by virtue of other circumstances.

(3) Where in proceedings for an offence under this section it is proved that the other person was under 18, the defendant is to be taken not to have reasonably believed that that person was 18 or over unless sufficient evidence is adduced to raise an issue as to whether he reasonably believed it.

(4) Where in proceedings for an offence under this section –

   (a) it is proved that the defendant was in a position of trust in relation to the other person by virtue of circumstances within section 21(2), (3), (4) or (5), and

   (b) it is not proved that he was in such a position of trust by virtue of other circumstances,

it is to be taken that the defendant knew or could reasonably have been expected to know of the circumstances by virtue of which he was in such a position of trust unless sufficient evidence is adduced to raise an issue as to whether he knew or could reasonably have been expected to know of those circumstances.

(5) A person guilty of an offence under this section is liable –

   (a) on summary conviction, to imprisonment for a term not exceeding 6 months or a fine not exceeding the statutory maximum or both;

   (b) on conviction on indictment, to imprisonment for a term not exceeding 5 years.

17 Abuse of position of trust: causing or inciting a child to engage in sexual activity

(1) A person aged 18 or over (A) commits an offence if –

   (a) he intentionally causes or incites another person (B) to engage in an activity,

   (b) the activity is sexual,

   (c) A is in a position of trust in relation to B,

   (d) where subsection (2) applies, A knows or could reasonably be expected to know of the circumstances by virtue of which he is in a position of trust in relation to B, and

   (e) either –

      (i) B is under 18 and A does not reasonably believe that B is 18 or over, or

     (ii) B is under 13.

(2) This subsection applies where A –

   (a) is in a position of trust in relation to B by virtue of circumstances within section 21(2), (3), (4) or (5), and

   (b) is not in such a position of trust by virtue of other circumstances.

(3) Where in proceedings for an offence under this section it is proved that the other person was under 18, the defendant is to be taken not to have reasonably believed that that person was 18 or over unless sufficient evidence is adduced to raise an issue as to whether he reasonably believed it.

(4) Where in proceedings for an offence under this section –

   (a) it is proved that the defendant was in a position of trust in relation to the other person by virtue of circumstances within section 21(2), (3), (4) or (5), and

(b) it is not proved that he was in such a position of trust by virtue of other circumstances,

it is to be taken that the defendant knew or could reasonably have been expected to know of the circumstances by virtue of which he was in such a position of trust unless sufficient evidence is adduced to raise an issue as to whether he knew or could reasonably have been expected to know of those circumstances.

(5) A person guilty of an offence under this section is liable –

(a) on summary conviction, to imprisonment for a term not exceeding 6 months or a fine not exceeding the statutory maximum or both;

(b) on conviction on indictment, to imprisonment for a term not exceeding 5 years.

18 Abuse of position of trust: sexual activity in the presence of a child

(1) A person aged 18 or over (A) commits an offence if –

(a) he intentionally engages in an activity,

(b) the activity is sexual,

(c) for the purpose of obtaining sexual gratification, he engages in it –

(i) when another person (B) is present or is in a place from which A can be observed, and

(ii) knowing or believing that B is aware, or intending that B should be aware, that he is engaging in it,

(d) A is in a position of trust in relation to B,

(e) where subsection (2) applies, A knows or could reasonably be expected to know of the circumstances by virtue of which he is in a position of trust in relation to B, and

(f) either –

(i) B is under 18 and A does not reasonably believe that B is 18 or over, or

(ii) B is under 13.

(2) This subsection applies where A –

(a) is in a position of trust in relation to B by virtue of circumstances within section 21(2), (3), (4) or (5), and

(b) is not in such a position of trust by virtue of other circumstances.

(3) Where in proceedings for an offence under this section it is proved that the other person was under 18, the defendant is to be taken not to have reasonably believed that that person was 18 or over unless sufficient evidence is adduced to raise an issue as to whether he reasonably believed it.

(4) Where in proceedings for an offence under this section –

(a) it is proved that the defendant was in a position of trust in relation to the other person by virtue of circumstances within section 21(2), (3), (4) or (5), and

(b) it is not proved that he was in such a position of trust by virtue of other circumstances,

it is to be taken that the defendant knew or could reasonably have been expected to know of the circumstances by virtue of which he was in such a position of trust unless sufficient evidence is adduced to raise an issue as to whether he knew or could reasonably have been expected to know of those circumstances.

(5) A person guilty of an offence under this section is liable –

(a) on summary conviction, to imprisonment for a term not exceeding 6 months or a fine not exceeding the statutory maximum or both;

(b) on conviction on indictment, to imprisonment for a term not exceeding 5 years.

19 Abuse of position of trust: causing a child to watch a sexual act

(1) A person aged 18 or over (A) commits an offence if –

 (a) for the purpose of obtaining sexual gratification, he intentionally causes another person (B) to watch a third person engaging in an activity, or to look at an image of any person engaging in an activity,

 (b) the activity is sexual,

 (c) A is in a position of trust in relation to B,

 (d) where subsection (2) applies, A knows or could reasonably be expected to know of the circumstances by virtue of which he is in a position of trust in relation to B, and

 (e) either –

  (i)   B is under 18 and A does not reasonably believe that B is 18 or over, or

  (ii) B is under 13.

(2) This subsection applies where A –

 (a) is in a position of trust in relation to B by virtue of circumstances within section 21(2), (3), (4) or (5), and

 (b) is not in such a position of trust by virtue of other circumstances.

(3) Where in proceedings for an offence under this section it is proved that the other person was under 18, the defendant is to be taken not to have reasonably believed that that person was 18 or over unless sufficient evidence is adduced to raise an issue as to whether he reasonably believed it.

(4) Where in proceedings for an offence under this section –

 (a) it is proved that the defendant was in a position of trust in relation to the other person by virtue of circumstances within section 21(2), (3), (4) or (5), and

 (b) it is not proved that he was in such a position of trust by virtue of other circumstances,

it is to be taken that the defendant knew or could reasonably have been expected to know of the circumstances by virtue of which he was in such a position of trust unless sufficient evidence is adduced to raise an issue as to whether he knew or could reasonably have been expected to know of those circumstances.

(5) A person guilty of an offence under this section is liable –

 (a) on summary conviction, to imprisonment for a term not exceeding 6 months or a fine not exceeding the statutory maximum or both;

 (b) on conviction on indictment, to imprisonment for a term not exceeding 5 years.

20 Abuse of position of trust: acts done in Scotland

Anything which, if done in England and Wales or Northern Ireland, would constitute an offence under any of sections 16 to 19 also constitutes that offence if done in Scotland.

21 Positions of trust

(1) For the purposes of sections 16 to 19, a person (A) is in a position of trust in relation to another person (B) if –

 (a) any of the following subsections applies, or

 (b) any condition specified in an order made by the Secretary of State is met.

(2) This subsection applies if A looks after persons under 18 who are detained in an institution by virtue of a court order or under an enactment, and B is so detained in that institution.

(3) This subsection applies if A looks after persons under 18 who are resident in a home or other place in which –

(a) accommodation and maintenance are provided by an authority under section 23(2) of the Children Act 1989 (c. 41) or Article 27(2) of the Children (Northern Ireland) Order 1995 (S.I. 1995/755 (N.I. 2)), or

(b) accommodation is provided by a voluntary organisation under section 59(1) of that Act or Article 75(1) of that Order,

and B is resident, and is so provided with accommodation and maintenance or accommodation, in that place.

(4) This subsection applies if A looks after persons under 18 who are accommodated and cared for in one of the following institutions –

(a) a hospital,

(b) an independent clinic,

(c) a care home, residential care home or private hospital,

(d) a community home, voluntary home or children's home,

(e) a home provided under section 82(5) of the Children Act 1989, or

(f) a residential family centre,

and B is accommodated and cared for in that institution.

(5) This subsection applies if A looks after persons under 18 who are receiving education at an educational institution and B is receiving, and A is not receiving, education at that institution.

(6) This subsection applies if A is appointed to be the guardian of B under Article 159 or 160 of the Children (Northern Ireland) Order 1995 (S.I. 1995/755 (N.I. 2)).

(7) This subsection applies if A is engaged in the provision of services under, or pursuant to anything done under –

(a) sections 8 to 10 of the Employment and Training Act 1973 (c. 50), or

(b) section 114 of the Learning and Skills Act 2000 (c. 21),

and, in that capacity, looks after B on an individual basis.

(8) This subsection applies if A regularly has unsupervised contact with B (whether face to face or by any other means) –

(a) in the exercise of functions of a local authority under section 20 or 21 of the Children Act 1989 (c. 41), or

(b) in the exercise of functions of an authority under Article 21 or 23 of the Children (Northern Ireland) Order 1995.

(9) This subsection applies if A, as a person who is to report to the court under section 7 of the Children Act 1989 or Article 4 of the Children (Northern Ireland) Order 1995 on matters relating to the welfare of B, regularly has unsupervised contact with B (whether face to face or by any other means).

(10) This subsection applies if A is a personal adviser appointed for B under –

(a) section 23B(2) of, or paragraph 19C of Schedule 2 to, the Children Act 1989, or

(b) Article 34A(10) or 34C(2) of the Children (Northern Ireland) Order 1995,

and, in that capacity, looks after B on an individual basis.

(11) This subsection applies if –

(a) B is subject to a care order, a supervision order or an education supervision order, and

(b) in the exercise of functions conferred by virtue of the order on an authorised person or the authority designated by the order, A looks after B on an individual basis.

(12) This subsection applies if A –

(a) is an officer of the Service appointed for B under section 41(1) of the Children Act 1989,

(b) is appointed a children's guardian of B under rule 6 or rule 18 of the Adoption Rules 1984 (S.I. 1984/265), or

(c)   is appointed to be the guardian ad litem of B under rule 9.5 of the Family Proceedings Rules 1991 (S. I. 1991/1247) or under Article 60(1) of the Children (Northern Ireland) Order 1995,

and, in that capacity, regularly has unsupervised contact with B (whether face to face or by any other means).

(13) This subsection applies if –

(a)   B is subject to requirements imposed by or under an enactment on his release from detention for a criminal offence, or is subject to requirements imposed by a court order made in criminal proceedings, and

(b)   A looks after B on an individual basis in pursuance of the requirements.

22 Positions of trust: interpretation

(1)   The following provisions apply for the purposes of section 21.

(2)   Subject to subsection (3), a person looks after persons under 18 if he is regularly involved in caring for, training, supervising or being in sole charge of such persons.

(3)   A person (A) looks after another person (B) on an individual basis if –

(a)   A is regularly involved in caring for, training or supervising B, and

(b)   in the course of his involvement, A regularly has unsupervised contact with B (whether face to face or by any other means).

(4)   A person receives education at an educational institution if –

(a)   he is registered or otherwise enrolled as a pupil or student at the institution, or

(b)   he receives education at the institution under arrangements with another educational institution at which he is so registered or otherwise enrolled.

(5)   In section 21 –

'authority' –

(a)   in relation to England and Wales, means a local authority;

(b)   in relation to Northern Ireland, has the meaning given by Article 2(2) of the Children (Northern Ireland) Order 1995 (S.I. 1995/755 (N.I. 2));

'care home' means an establishment which is a care home for the purposes of the Care Standards Act 2000 (c. 14);

'care order' has –

(a)   in relation to England and Wales, the same meaning as in the Children Act 1989 (c. 41), and

(b)   in relation to Northern Ireland, the same meaning as in the Children (Northern Ireland) Order 1995;

'children's home' has –

(a)   in relation to England and Wales, the meaning given by section 1 of the Care Standards Act 2000, and

(b)   in relation to Northern Ireland, the meaning that would be given by Article 9 of the Health and Personal Social Services (Quality, Improvement and Regulation) (Northern Ireland) Order 2003 (S.I. 2003/431 (N.I. 9)) ('the 2003 Order') if in paragraph (4) of that Article sub-paragraphs (d), (f) and (g) were omitted;

'community home' has the meaning given by section 53 of the Children Act 1989;

'education supervision order' has –

(a)   in relation to England and Wales, the meaning given by section 36 of the Children Act 1989, and

(b)   in relation to Northern Ireland, the meaning given by Article 49(1) of the Children (Northern Ireland) Order 1995;

'hospital' –

(a)   in relation to England and Wales, means a hospital within the meaning given by section 128(1) of the National Health Service Act 1977 (c. 49), or any other establishment which is a hospital within the meaning given by section 2(3) of the Care Standards Act 2000 (c. 14);

(b)   in relation to Northern Ireland, means a hospital within the meaning given by Article 2(2) of the Health and Personal Social Services (Northern Ireland) Order 1972 (S.I. 1972/1265 (N.I. 14)), or any other establishment which is a hospital within the meaning given by Article 2(2) of the 2003 Order;

'independent clinic' has –

(a)   in relation to England and Wales, the meaning given by section 2 of the Care Standards Act 2000;

(b)   in relation to Northern Ireland, the meaning given by Article 2(2) of the 2003 Order;

'private hospital' has the meaning given by Article 90(2) of the Mental Health (Northern Ireland) Order 1986 (S.I. 1986/595 (N.I. 4));

'residential care home' means an establishment which is a residential care home for the purposes of the 2003 Order;

'residential family centre' has the meaning given by section 22 of the Health and Personal Social Services Act (Northern Ireland) 2001 (c. 3);

'supervision order' has –

(a)   in relation to England and Wales, the meaning given by section 31(11) of the Children Act 1989 (c. 41), and

(b)   in relation to Northern Ireland, the meaning given by Article 49(1) of the Children (Northern Ireland) Order 1995 (S.I. 1995/755 (N.I. 2));

'voluntary home' has –

(a)   in relation to England and Wales, the meaning given by section 60(3) of the Children Act 1989, and

(b)   in relation to Northern Ireland, the meaning given by Article 74(1) of the Children (Northern Ireland) Order 1995.

23 Sections 16 to 19: marriage exception

(1)   Conduct by a person (A) which would otherwise be an offence under any of sections 16 to 19 against another person (B) is not an offence under that section if at the time –

(a)   B is 16 or over, and

(b)   A and B are lawfully married.

(2)   In proceedings for such an offence it is for the defendant to prove that A and B were lawfully married at the time.

24 Sections 16 to 19: sexual relationships which pre-date position of trust

(1)   Conduct by a person (A) which would otherwise be an offence under any of sections 16 to 19 against another person (B) is not an offence under that section if, immediately before the position of trust arose, a sexual relationship existed between A and B.

(2)   Subsection (1) does not apply if at that time sexual intercourse between A and B would have been unlawful.

(3)   In proceedings for an offence under any of sections 16 to 19 it is for the defendant to prove that such a relationship existed at that time.

Familial child sex offences

25 Sexual activity with a child family member

(1) A person (A) commits an offence if –

    (a) he intentionally touches another person (B),

    (b) the touching is sexual,

    (c) the relation of A to B is within section 27,

    (d) A knows or could reasonably be expected to know that his relation to B is of a description falling within that section, and

    (e) either –

        (i)   B is under 18 and A does not reasonably believe that B is 18 or over, or

        (ii) B is under 13.

(2) Where in proceedings for an offence under this section it is proved that the other person was under 18, the defendant is to be taken not to have reasonably believed that that person was 18 or over unless sufficient evidence is adduced to raise an issue as to whether he reasonably believed it.

(3) Where in proceedings for an offence under this section it is proved that the relation of the defendant to the other person was of a description falling within section 27, it is to be taken that the defendant knew or could reasonably have been expected to know that his relation to the other person was of that description unless sufficient evidence is adduced to raise an issue as to whether he knew or could reasonably have been expected to know that it was.

(4) A person guilty of an offence under this section, if aged 18 or over at the time of the offence, is liable –

    (a) where subsection (6) applies, on conviction on indictment to imprisonment for a term not exceeding 14 years;

    (b) in any other case –

        (i)   on summary conviction, to imprisonment for a term not exceeding 6 months or a fine not exceeding the statutory maximum or both;

        (ii) on conviction on indictment, to imprisonment for a term not exceeding 14 years.

(5) Unless subsection (4) applies, a person guilty of an offence under this section is liable –

    (a) on summary conviction, to imprisonment for a term not exceeding 6 months or a fine not exceeding the statutory maximum or both;

    (b) on conviction on indictment, to imprisonment for a term not exceeding 5 years.

(6) This subsection applies where the touching involved –

    (a) penetration of B's anus or vagina with a part of A's body or anything else,

    (b) penetration of B's mouth with A's penis,

    (c) penetration of A's anus or vagina with a part of B's body, or

    (d) penetration of A's mouth with B's penis.

26 Inciting a child family member to engage in sexual activity

(1) A person (A) commits an offence if –

    (a) he intentionally incites another person (B) to touch, or allow himself to be touched by, A,

    (b) the touching is sexual,

    (c) the relation of A to B is within section 27,

    (d) A knows or could reasonably be expected to know that his relation to B is of a description falling within that section, and

    (e) either –

(i)   B is under 18 and A does not reasonably believe that B is 18 or over, or

(ii) B is under 13.

(2) Where in proceedings for an offence under this section it is proved that the other person was under 18, the defendant is to be taken not to have reasonably believed that that person was 18 or over unless sufficient evidence is adduced to raise an issue as to whether he reasonably believed it.

(3) Where in proceedings for an offence under this section it is proved that the relation of the defendant to the other person was of a description falling within section 27, it is to be taken that the defendant knew or could reasonably have been expected to know that his relation to the other person was of that description unless sufficient evidence is adduced to raise an issue as to whether he knew or could reasonably have been expected to know that it was.

(4) A person guilty of an offence under this section, if he was aged 18 or over at the time of the offence, is liable –

(a) where subsection (6) applies, on conviction on indictment to imprisonment for a term not exceeding 14 years;

(b) in any other case –

(i)   on summary conviction, to imprisonment for a term not exceeding 6 months or a fine not exceeding the statutory maximum or both;

(ii) on conviction on indictment, to imprisonment for a term not exceeding 14 years.

(5) Unless subsection (4) applies, a person guilty of an offence under this section is liable –

(a) on summary conviction, to imprisonment for a term not exceeding 6 months or a fine not exceeding the statutory maximum or both;

(b) on conviction on indictment, to imprisonment for a term not exceeding 5 years.

(6) This subsection applies where the touching to which the incitement related involved –

(a) penetration of B's anus or vagina with a part of A's body or anything else,

(b) penetration of B's mouth with A's penis,

(c) penetration of A's anus or vagina with a part of B's body, or

(d) penetration of A's mouth with B's penis.

27 Family relationships

(1) The relation of one person (A) to another (B) is within this section if –

(a) it is within any of subsections (2) to (4), or

(b) it would be within one of those subsections but for section 67 of the Adoption and Children Act 2002 (c. 38) (status conferred by adoption).

(2) The relation of A to B is within this subsection if –

(a) one of them is the other's parent, grandparent, brother, sister, half-brother, half-sister, aunt or uncle, or

(b) A is or has been B's foster parent.

(3) The relation of A to B is within this subsection if A and B live or have lived in the same household, or A is or has been regularly involved in caring for, training, supervising or being in sole charge of B, and –

(a) one of them is or has been the other's step-parent,

(b) A and B are cousins,

(c) one of them is or has been the other's stepbrother or stepsister, or

(d) the parent or present or former foster parent of one of them is or has been the other's foster parent.

(4) The relation of A to B is within this subsection if –

(a) A and B live in the same household, and

(b) A is regularly involved in caring for, training, supervising or being in sole charge of B.

(5) For the purposes of this section –

   (a) 'aunt' means the sister or half-sister of a person's parent, and 'uncle' has a corresponding meaning;
   (b) 'cousin' means the child of an aunt or uncle;
   (c) a person is a child's foster parent if –

       (i) he is a person with whom the child has been placed under section 23(2)(a) or 59(1)(a) of the Children Act 1989 (c. 41) (fostering for local authority or voluntary organisation), or
       (ii) he fosters the child privately, within the meaning given by section 66(1)(b) of that Act;

   (d) a person is another's partner (whether they are of different sexes or the same sex) if they live together as partners in an enduring family relationship;
   (e) 'step-parent' includes a parent's partner and 'stepbrother' and 'stepsister' include the child of a parent's partner.

28 Sections 25 and 26: marriage exception

(1) Conduct by a person (A) which would otherwise be an offence under section 25 or 26 against another person (B) is not an offence under that section if at the time –

   (a) B is 16 or over, and
   (b) A and B are lawfully married.

(2) In proceedings for such an offence it is for the defendant to prove that A and B were lawfully married at the time.

29 Sections 25 and 26: sexual relationships which pre-date family relationships

(1) Conduct by a person (A) which would otherwise be an offence under section 25 or 26 against another person (B) is not an offence under that section if –

   (a) the relation of A to B is not within subsection (2) of section 27,
   (b) it would not be within that subsection if section 67 of the Adoption and Children Act 2002 (c. 38) did not apply, and
   (c) immediately before the relation of A to B first became such as to fall within section 27, a sexual relationship existed between A and B.

(2) Subsection (1) does not apply if at the time referred to in subsection (1)(c) sexual intercourse between A and B would have been unlawful.

(3) In proceedings for an offence under section 25 or 26 it is for the defendant to prove the matters mentioned in subsection (1)(a) to (c).

Offences against persons with a mental disorder impeding choice

30 Sexual activity with a person with a mental disorder impeding choice

(1) A person (A) commits an offence if –

   (a) he intentionally touches another person (B),
   (b) the touching is sexual,
   (c) B is unable to refuse because of or for a reason related to a mental disorder, and
   (d) A knows or could reasonably be expected to know that B has a mental disorder and that because of it or for a reason related to it B is likely to be unable to refuse.

(2) B is unable to refuse if –

   (a) he lacks the capacity to choose whether to agree to the touching (whether because he lacks sufficient understanding of the nature or reasonably foreseeable consequences of what is being done, or for any other reason), or

    (b) he is unable to communicate such a choice to A.

(3) A person guilty of an offence under this section, if the touching involved –

    (a) penetration of B's anus or vagina with a part of A's body or anything else,

    (b) penetration of B's mouth with A's penis,

    (c) penetration of A's anus or vagina with a part of B's body, or

    (d) penetration of A's mouth with B's penis,

    is liable, on conviction on indictment, to imprisonment for life.

(4) Unless subsection (3) applies, a person guilty of an offence under this section is liable –

    (a) on summary conviction, to imprisonment for a term not exceeding 6 months or to a fine not exceeding the statutory maximum or both;

    (b) on conviction on indictment, to imprisonment for a term not exceeding 14 years.

31 Causing or inciting a person, with a mental disorder impeding choice, to engage in sexual activity

(1) A person (A) commits an offence if –

    (a) he intentionally causes or incites another person (B) to engage in an activity,

    (b) the activity is sexual,

    (c) B is unable to refuse because of or for a reason related to a mental disorder, and

    (d) A knows or could reasonably be expected to know that B has a mental disorder and that because of it or for a reason related to it B is likely to be unable to refuse.

(2) B is unable to refuse if –

    (a) he lacks the capacity to choose whether to agree to engaging in the activity caused or incited (whether because he lacks sufficient understanding of the nature or reasonably foreseeable consequences of the activity, or for any other reason), or

    (b) he is unable to communicate such a choice to A.

(3) A person guilty of an offence under this section, if the activity caused or incited involved –

    (a) penetration of B's anus or vagina,

    (b) penetration of B's mouth with a person's penis,

    (c) penetration of a person's anus or vagina with a part of B's body or by B with anything else, or

    (d) penetration of a person's mouth with B's penis,

    is liable, on conviction on indictment, to imprisonment for life.

(4) Unless subsection (3) applies, a person guilty of an offence under this section is liable –

    (a) on summary conviction, to imprisonment for a term not exceeding 6 months or to a fine not exceeding the statutory maximum or both;

    (b) on conviction on indictment, to imprisonment for a term not exceeding 14 years.

32 Engaging in sexual activity in the presence of a person with a mental disorder impeding choice

(1) A person (A) commits an offence if –

    (a) he intentionally engages in an activity,

    (b) the activity is sexual,

    (c) for the purpose of obtaining sexual gratification, he engages in it –

        (i) when another person (B) is present or is in a place from which A can be observed, and

        (ii) knowing or believing that B is aware, or intending that B should be aware, that he is engaging in it,

(d) B is unable to refuse because of or for a reason related to a mental disorder, and

(e) A knows or could reasonably be expected to know that B has a mental disorder and that because of it or for a reason related to it B is likely to be unable to refuse.

(2) B is unable to refuse if –

(a) he lacks the capacity to choose whether to agree to being present (whether because he lacks sufficient understanding of the nature of the activity, or for any other reason), or

(b) he is unable to communicate such a choice to A.

(3) A person guilty of an offence under this section is liable –

(a) on summary conviction, to imprisonment for a term not exceeding 6 months or a fine not exceeding the statutory maximum or both;

(b) on conviction on indictment, to imprisonment for a term not exceeding 10 years.

33 Causing a person, with a mental disorder impeding choice, to watch a sexual act

(1) A person (A) commits an offence if –

(a) for the purpose of obtaining sexual gratification, he intentionally causes another person (B) to watch a third person engaging in an activity, or to look at an image of any person engaging in an activity,

(b) the activity is sexual,

(c) B is unable to refuse because of or for a reason related to a mental disorder, and

(d) A knows or could reasonably be expected to know that B has a mental disorder and that because of it or for a reason related to it B is likely to be unable to refuse.

(2) B is unable to refuse if –

(a) he lacks the capacity to choose whether to agree to watching or looking (whether because he lacks sufficient understanding of the nature of the activity, or for any other reason), or

(b) he is unable to communicate such a choice to A.

(3) A person guilty of an offence under this section is liable –

(a) on summary conviction, to imprisonment for a term not exceeding 6 months or a fine not exceeding the statutory maximum or both;

(b) on conviction on indictment, to imprisonment for a term not exceeding 10 years.

Inducements etc. to persons with a mental disorder

34 Inducement, threat or deception to procure sexual activity with a person with a mental disorder

(1) A person (A) commits an offence if –

(a) with the agreement of another person (B) he intentionally touches that person,

(b) the touching is sexual,

(c) A obtains B's agreement by means of an inducement offered or given, a threat made or a deception practised by A for that purpose,

(d) B has a mental disorder, and

(e) A knows or could reasonably be expected to know that B has a mental disorder.

(2) A person guilty of an offence under this section, if the touching involved –

(a) penetration of B's anus or vagina with a part of A's body or anything else,

(b) penetration of B's mouth with A's penis,

(c) penetration of A's anus or vagina with a part of B's body, or

(d) penetration of A's mouth with B's penis,

is liable, on conviction on indictment, to imprisonment for life.

(3)   Unless subsection (2) applies, a person guilty of an offence under this section is liable –

(a)   on summary conviction, to imprisonment for a term not exceeding 6 months or a fine not exceeding the statutory maximum or both;

(b)   on conviction on indictment, to imprisonment for a term not exceeding 14 years.

35 Causing a person with a mental disorder to engage in or agree to engage in sexual activity by inducement, threat or deception

(1)   A person (A) commits an offence if –

(a)   by means of an inducement offered or given, a threat made or a deception practised by him for this purpose, he intentionally causes another person (B) to engage in, or to agree to engage in, an activity,

(b)   the activity is sexual,

(c)   B has a mental disorder, and

(d)   A knows or could reasonably be expected to know that B has a mental disorder.

(2)   A person guilty of an offence under this section, if the activity caused or agreed to involved –

(a)   penetration of B's anus or vagina,

(b)   penetration of B's mouth with a person's penis,

(c)   penetration of a person's anus or vagina with a part of B's body or by B with anything else, or

(d)   penetration of a person's mouth with B's penis,

is liable, on conviction on indictment, to imprisonment for life.

(3)   Unless subsection (2) applies, a person guilty of an offence under this section is liable –

(a)   on summary conviction, to imprisonment for a term not exceeding 6 months or a fine not exceeding the statutory maximum or both;

(b)   on conviction on indictment, to imprisonment for a term not exceeding 14 years.

36 Engaging in sexual activity in the presence, procured by inducement, threat or deception, of a person with a mental disorder

(1)   A person (A) commits an offence if –

(a)   he intentionally engages in an activity,

(b)   the activity is sexual,

(c)   for the purpose of obtaining sexual gratification, he engages in it –

(i)   when another person (B) is present or is in a place from which A can be observed, and

(ii)   knowing or believing that B is aware, or intending that B should be aware, that he is engaging in it,

(d)   B agrees to be present or in the place referred to in paragraph (c)(i) because of an inducement offered or given, a threat made or a deception practised by A for the purpose of obtaining that agreement,

(e)   B has a mental disorder, and

(f)   A knows or could reasonably be expected to know that B has a mental disorder.

(2)   A person guilty of an offence under this section is liable –

(a)   on summary conviction, to imprisonment for a term not exceeding 6 months or a fine not exceeding the statutory maximum or both;

(b)   on conviction on indictment, to imprisonment for a term not exceeding 10 years.

37 Causing a person with a mental disorder to watch a sexual act by inducement, threat or deception

(1) A person (A) commits an offence if –

  (a) for the purpose of obtaining sexual gratification, he intentionally causes another person (B) to watch a third person engaging in an activity, or to look at an image of any person engaging in an activity,

  (b) the activity is sexual,

  (c) B agrees to watch or look because of an inducement offered or given, a threat made or a deception practised by A for the purpose of obtaining that agreement,

  (d) B has a mental disorder, and

  (e) A knows or could reasonably be expected to know that B has a mental disorder.

(2) A person guilty of an offence under this section is liable –

  (a) on summary conviction, to imprisonment for a term not exceeding 6 months or a fine not exceeding the statutory maximum or both;

  (b) on conviction on indictment, to imprisonment for a term not exceeding 10 years.

Care workers for persons with a mental disorder

38 Care workers: sexual activity with a person with a mental disorder

(1) A person (A) commits an offence if –

  (a) he intentionally touches another person (B),

  (b) the touching is sexual,

  (c) B has a mental disorder,

  (d) A knows or could reasonably be expected to know that B has a mental disorder, and

  (e) A is involved in B's care in a way that falls within section 42.

(2) Where in proceedings for an offence under this section it is proved that the other person had a mental disorder, it is to be taken that the defendant knew or could reasonably have been expected to know that that person had a mental disorder unless sufficient evidence is adduced to raise an issue as to whether he knew or could reasonably have been expected to know it.

(3) A person guilty of an offence under this section, if the touching involved –

  (a) penetration of B's anus or vagina with a part of A's body or anything else,

  (b) penetration of B's mouth with A's penis,

  (c) penetration of A's anus or vagina with a part of B's body, or

  (d) penetration of A's mouth with B's penis,

  is liable, on conviction on indictment, to imprisonment for a term not exceeding 14 years.

(4) Unless subsection (3) applies, a person guilty of an offence under this section is liable –

  (a) on summary conviction, to imprisonment for a term not exceeding 6 months or a fine not exceeding the statutory maximum or both;

  (b) on conviction on indictment, to imprisonment for a term not exceeding 10 years.

39 Care workers: causing or inciting sexual activity

(1) A person (A) commits an offence if –

  (a) he intentionally causes or incites another person (B) to engage in an activity,

  (b) the activity is sexual,

  (c) B has a mental disorder,

  (d) A knows or could reasonably be expected to know that B has a mental disorder, and

  (e) A is involved in B's care in a way that falls within section 42.

(2) Where in proceedings for an offence under this section it is proved that the other person had a mental disorder, it is to be taken that the defendant knew or could reasonably have been expected to know that that person had a mental disorder unless sufficient evidence is adduced to raise an issue as to whether he knew or could reasonably have been expected to know it.

(3) A person guilty of an offence under this section, if the activity caused or incited involved –

(a) penetration of B's anus or vagina,

(b) penetration of B's mouth with a person's penis,

(c) penetration of a person's anus or vagina with a part of B's body or by B with anything else, or

(d) penetration of a person's mouth with B's penis,

is liable, on conviction on indictment, to imprisonment for a term not exceeding 14 years.

(4) Unless subsection (3) applies, a person guilty of an offence under this section is liable –

(a) on summary conviction, to imprisonment for a term not exceeding 6 months or a fine not exceeding the statutory maximum or both;

(b) on conviction on indictment, to imprisonment for a term not exceeding 10 years.

40 Care workers: sexual activity in the presence of a person with a mental disorder

(1) A person (A) commits an offence if –

(a) he intentionally engages in an activity,

(b) the activity is sexual,

(c) for the purpose of obtaining sexual gratification, he engages in it –

(i) when another person (B) is present or is in a place from which A can be observed, and

(ii) knowing or believing that B is aware, or intending that B should be aware, that he is engaging in it,

(d) B has a mental disorder,

(e) A knows or could reasonably be expected to know that B has a mental disorder, and

(f) A is involved in B's care in a way that falls within section 42.

(2) Where in proceedings for an offence under this section it is proved that the other person had a mental disorder, it is to be taken that the defendant knew or could reasonably have been expected to know that that person had a mental disorder unless sufficient evidence is adduced to raise an issue as to whether he knew or could reasonably have been expected to know it.

(3) A person guilty of an offence under this section is liable –

(a) on summary conviction, to imprisonment for a term not exceeding 6 months or a fine not exceeding the statutory maximum or both;

(b) on conviction on indictment, to imprisonment for a term not exceeding 7 years.

41 Care workers: causing a person with a mental disorder to watch a sexual act

(1) A person (A) commits an offence if –

(a) for the purpose of obtaining sexual gratification, he intentionally causes another person (B) to watch a third person engaging in an activity, or to look at an image of any person engaging in an activity,

(b) the activity is sexual,

(c) B has a mental disorder,

(d) A knows or could reasonably be expected to know that B has a mental disorder, and

(e) A is involved in B's care in a way that falls within section 42.

(2) Where in proceedings for an offence under this section it is proved that the other person had a mental disorder, it is to be taken that the defendant knew or could reasonably have been expected to know that that person had a mental disorder unless sufficient evidence is adduced to raise an issue as to whether he knew or could reasonably have been expected to know it.

(3) A person guilty of an offence under this section is liable –

(a) on summary conviction, to imprisonment for a term not exceeding 6 months or a fine not exceeding the statutory maximum or both;

(b) on conviction on indictment, to imprisonment for a term not exceeding 7 years.

42 Care workers: interpretation

(1) For the purposes of sections 38 to 41, a person (A) is involved in the care of another person (B) in a way that falls within this section if any of subsections (2) to (4) applies.

(2) This subsection applies if –

(a) B is accommodated and cared for in a care home, community home, voluntary home or children's home, and

(b) A has functions to perform in the home in the course of employment which have brought him or are likely to bring him into regular face to face contact with B.

(3) This subsection applies if B is a patient for whom services are provided –

(a) by a National Health Service body or an independent medical agency, or

(b) in an independent clinic or an independent hospital,

and A has functions to perform for the body or agency or in the clinic or hospital in the course of employment which have brought him or are likely to bring him into regular face to face contact with B.

(4) This subsection applies if A –

(a) is, whether or not in the course of employment, a provider of care, assistance or services to B in connection with B's mental disorder, and

(b) as such, has had or is likely to have regular face to face contact with B.

(5) In this section –

'care home' means an establishment which is a care home for the purposes of the Care Standards Act 2000 (c. 14);

'children's home' has the meaning given by section 1 of that Act;

'community home' has the meaning given by section 53 of the Children Act 1989 (c. 41);

'employment' means any employment, whether paid or unpaid and whether under a contract of service or apprenticeship, under a contract for services, or otherwise than under a contract;

'independent clinic', 'independent hospital' and 'independent medical agency' have the meaning given by section 2 of the Care Standards Act 2000;

'National Health Service body' means –

(a) a Health Authority,

(b) a National Health Service trust,

(c) a Primary Care Trust, or

(d) a Special Health Authority;

'voluntary home' has the meaning given by section 60(3) of the Children Act 1989.

43 Sections 38 to 41: marriage exception

(1) Conduct by a person (A) which would otherwise be an offence under any of sections 38 to 41 against another person (B) is not an offence under that section if at the time –

(a) B is 16 or over, and

(b) A and B are lawfully married.

(2) In proceedings for such an offence it is for the defendant to prove that A and B were lawfully married at the time.

44 Sections 38 to 41: sexual relationships which pre-date care relationships

(1) Conduct by a person (A) which would otherwise be an offence under any of sections 38 to 41 against another person (B) is not an offence under that section if, immediately before A became involved in B's care in a way that falls within section 42, a sexual relationship existed between A and B.

(2) Subsection (1) does not apply if at that time sexual intercourse between A and B would have been unlawful.

(3) In proceedings for an offence under any of sections 38 to 41 it is for the defendant to prove that such a relationship existed at that time.

Indecent photographs of children

45 Indecent photographs of persons aged 16 or 17

(1) The Protection of Children Act 1978 (c. 37) (which makes provision about indecent photographs of persons under 16) is amended as follows.

(2) In section 2(3) (evidence) and section 7(6) (meaning of 'child'), for '16' substitute '18'.

(3) After section 1 insert –

'1A Marriage and other relationships

(1) This section applies where, in proceedings for an offence under section 1(1)(a) of taking or making an indecent photograph of a child, or for an offence under section 1(1)(b) or (c) relating to an indecent photograph of a child, the defendant proves that the photograph was of the child aged 16 or over, and that at the time of the offence charged the child and he –

(a) were married, or

(b) lived together as partners in an enduring family relationship.

(2) Subsections (5) and (6) also apply where, in proceedings for an offence under section 1(1)(b) or (c) relating to an indecent photograph of a child, the defendant proves that the photograph was of the child aged 16 or over, and that at the time when he obtained it the child and he –

(a) were married, or

(b) lived together as partners in an enduring family relationship.

(3) This section applies whether the photograph showed the child alone or with the defendant, but not if it showed any other person.

(4) In the case of an offence under section 1(1)(a), if sufficient evidence is adduced to raise an issue as to whether the child consented to the photograph being taken or made, or as to whether the defendant reasonably believed that the child so consented, the defendant is not guilty of the offence unless it is proved that the child did not so consent and that the defendant did not reasonably believe that the child so consented.

(5) In the case of an offence under section 1(1)(b), the defendant is not guilty of the offence unless it is proved that the showing or distributing was to a person other than the child.

(6) In the case of an offence under section 1(1)(c), if sufficient evidence is adduced to raise an issue both –

(a)   as to whether the child consented to the photograph being in the defendant's possession, or as to whether the defendant reasonably believed that the child so consented, and

(b)   as to whether the defendant had the photograph in his possession with a view to its being distributed or shown to anyone other than the child,

the defendant is not guilty of the offence unless it is proved either that the child did not so consent and that the defendant did not reasonably believe that the child so consented, or that the defendant had the photograph in his possession with a view to its being distributed or shown to a person other than the child.'

(4)   After section 160 of the Criminal Justice Act 1988 (c. 33) (possession of indecent photograph of child) insert –

'160A Marriage and other relationships

(1)   This section applies where, in proceedings for an offence under section 160 relating to an indecent photograph of a child, the defendant proves that the photograph was of the child aged 16 or over, and that at the time of the offence charged the child and he –

(a)   were married, or

(b)   lived together as partners in an enduring family relationship.

(2)   This section also applies where, in proceedings for an offence under section 160 relating to an indecent photograph of a child, the defendant proves that the photograph was of the child aged 16 or over, and that at the time when he obtained it the child and he –

(a)   were married, or

(b)   lived together as partners in an enduring family relationship.

(3)   This section applies whether the photograph showed the child alone or with the defendant, but not if it showed any other person.

(4)   If sufficient evidence is adduced to raise an issue as to whether the child consented to the photograph being in the defendant's possession, or as to whether the defendant reasonably believed that the child so consented, the defendant is not guilty of the offence unless it is proved that the child did not so consent and that the defendant did not reasonably believe that the child so consented.'

46 Criminal proceedings, investigations etc.

(1)   After section 1A of the Protection of Children Act 1978 (c. 37) insert –

'1B Exception for criminal proceedings, investigations etc.

(1)   In proceedings for an offence under section 1(1)(a) of making an indecent photograph or pseudo-photograph of a child, the defendant is not guilty of the offence if he proves that –

(a)   it was necessary for him to make the photograph or pseudo-photograph for the purposes of the prevention, detection or investigation of crime, or for the purposes of criminal proceedings, in any part of the world,

(b)   at the time of the offence charged he was a member of the Security Service, and it was necessary for him to make the photograph or pseudo-photograph for the exercise of any of the functions of the Service, or

(c)   at the time of the offence charged he was a member of GCHQ, and it was necessary for him to make the photograph or pseudo-photograph for the exercise of any of the functions of GCHQ.

(2)   In this section 'GCHQ' has the same meaning as in the Intelligence Services Act 1994.'

(2) After Article 3 of the Protection of Children (Northern Ireland) Order 1978 (S.I. 1978/1047 (N.I. 17)) insert –

'3A. Exception for criminal proceedings, investigations etc.

(1) In proceedings for an offence under Article 3(1)(a) of making an indecent photograph or pseudo-photograph of a child, the defendant is not guilty of the offence if he proves that –

    (a) it was necessary for him to make the photograph or pseudo-photograph for the purposes of the prevention, detection or investigation of crime, or for the purposes of criminal proceedings, in any part of the world,

    (b) at the time of the offence charged he was a member of the Security Service, and it was necessary for him to make the photograph or pseudo-photograph for the exercise of any of the functions of the Service, or

    (c) at the time of the offence charged he was a member of GCHQ, and it was necessary for him to make the photograph or pseudo-photograph for the exercise of any of the functions of GCHQ.

(2) In this Article 'GCHQ' has the same meaning as in the Intelligence Services Act 1994.'

Abuse of children through prostitution and pornography

47 Paying for sexual services of a child

(1) A person (A) commits an offence if –

    (a) he intentionally obtains for himself the sexual services of another person (B),

    (b) before obtaining those services, he has made or promised payment for those services to B or a third person, or knows that another person has made or promised such a payment, and

    (c) either –

        (i) B is under 18, and A does not reasonably believe that B is 18 or over, or

        (ii) B is under 13.

(2) In this section, 'payment' means any financial advantage, including the discharge of an obligation to pay or the provision of goods or services (including sexual services) gratuitously or at a discount.

(3) A person guilty of an offence under this section against a person under 13, where subsection (6) applies, is liable on conviction on indictment to imprisonment for life.

(4) Unless subsection (3) applies, a person guilty of an offence under this section against a person under 16 is liable –

    (a) where subsection (6) applies, on conviction on indictment, to imprisonment for a term not exceeding 14 years;

    (b) in any other case –

        (i) on summary conviction, to imprisonment for a term not exceeding 6 months or a fine not exceeding the statutory maximum or both;

        (ii) on conviction on indictment, to imprisonment for a term not exceeding 14 years.

(5) Unless subsection (3) or (4) applies, a person guilty of an offence under this section is liable –

    (a) on summary conviction, to imprisonment for a term not exceeding 6 months or a fine not exceeding the statutory maximum or both;

    (b) on conviction on indictment, to imprisonment for a term not exceeding 7 years.

(6) This subsection applies where the offence involved –

    (a) penetration of B's anus or vagina with a part of A's body or anything else,

    (b) penetration of B's mouth with A's penis,

    (c) penetration of A's anus or vagina with a part of B's body or by B with anything else, or

    (d) penetration of A's mouth with B's penis.

(7) In the application of this section to Northern Ireland, subsection (4) has effect with the substitution of '17' for '16'.

48 Causing or inciting child prostitution or pornography

(1) A person (A) commits an offence if –

    (a) he intentionally causes or incites another person (B) to become a prostitute, or to be involved in pornography, in any part of the world, and

    (b) either –

        (i)   B is under 18, and A does not reasonably believe that B is 18 or over, or

        (ii) B is under 13.

(2) A person guilty of an offence under this section is liable –

    (a) on summary conviction, to imprisonment for a term not exceeding 6 months or a fine not exceeding the statutory maximum or both;

    (b) on conviction on indictment, to imprisonment for a term not exceeding 14 years.

49 Controlling a child prostitute or a child involved in pornography

(1) A person (A) commits an offence if –

    (a) he intentionally controls any of the activities of another person (B) relating to B's prostitution or involvement in pornography in any part of the world, and

    (b) either –

        (i)   B is under 18, and A does not reasonably believe that B is 18 or over, or

        (ii) B is under 13.

(2) A person guilty of an offence under this section is liable –

    (a) on summary conviction, to imprisonment for a term not exceeding 6 months or a fine not exceeding the statutory maximum or both;

    (b) on conviction on indictment, to imprisonment for a term not exceeding 14 years.

50 Arranging or facilitating child prostitution or pornography

(1) A person (A) commits an offence if –

    (a) he intentionally arranges or facilitates the prostitution or involvement in pornography in any part of the world of another person (B), and

    (b) either –

        (i)   B is under 18, and A does not reasonably believe that B is 18 or over, or

        (ii) B is under 13.

(2) A person guilty of an offence under this section is liable –

    (a) on summary conviction, to imprisonment for a term not exceeding 6 months or a fine not exceeding the statutory maximum or both;

    (b) on conviction on indictment, to imprisonment for a term not exceeding 14 years.

51 Sections 48 to 50: interpretation

(1) For the purposes of sections 48 to 50, a person is involved in pornography if an indecent image of that person is recorded; and similar expressions, and 'pornography', are to be interpreted accordingly.

(2) In those sections 'prostitute' means a person (A) who, on at least one occasion and whether or not compelled to do so, offers or provides sexual services to another person in return for payment or a promise of payment to A or a third person; and 'prostitution' is to be interpreted accordingly.

(3) In subsection (2), 'payment' means any financial advantage, including the discharge of an obligation to pay or the provision of goods or services (including sexual services) gratuitously or at a discount.

Exploitation of prostitution

52 Causing or inciting prostitution for gain

(1) A person commits an offence if –

    (a) he intentionally causes or incites another person to become a prostitute in any part of the world, and

    (b) he does so for or in the expectation of gain for himself or a third person.

(2) A person guilty of an offence under this section is liable –

    (a) on summary conviction, to imprisonment for a term not exceeding 6 months or a fine not exceeding the statutory maximum or both;

    (b) on conviction on indictment, to imprisonment for a term not exceeding 7 years.

53 Controlling prostitution for gain

(1) A person commits an offence if –

    (a) he intentionally controls any of the activities of another person relating to that person's prostitution in any part of the world, and

    (b) he does so for or in the expectation of gain for himself or a third person.

(2) A person guilty of an offence under this section is liable –

    (a) on summary conviction, to imprisonment for a term not exceeding 6 months or a fine not exceeding the statutory maximum or both;

    (b) on conviction on indictment, to imprisonment for a term not exceeding 7 years.

54 Sections 52 and 53: interpretation

(1) In sections 52 and 53, 'gain' means –

    (a) any financial advantage, including the discharge of an obligation to pay or the provision of goods or services (including sexual services) gratuitously or at a discount; or

    (b) the goodwill of any person which is or appears likely, in time, to bring financial advantage.

(2) In those sections 'prostitute' and 'prostitution' have the meaning given by section 51(2).

Amendments relating to prostitution

55 Penalties for keeping a brothel used for prostitution

(1) The Sexual Offences Act 1956 (c. 69) is amended as follows.

(2) After section 33 insert –

    '33A Keeping a brothel used for prostitution

    (1) It is an offence for a person to keep, or to manage, or act or assist in the management of, a brothel to which people resort for practices involving prostitution (whether or not also for other practices).

    (2) In this section 'prostitution' has the meaning given by section 51(2) of the Sexual Offences Act 2003.'

(3) In Schedule 2 (mode of prosecution, punishment etc.), after paragraph 33 insert (as a paragraph with no entry in the fourth column) –

'33A	Keeping a brothel used for prostitution (section 33A).	(i) on indictment (ii) summarily	Seven years Six months, or the statutory maximum, or both.'

56 Extension of gender-specific prostitution offences

Schedule 1 (extension of gender-specific prostitution offences) has effect.

Trafficking

57 Trafficking into the UK for sexual exploitation

(1) A person commits an offence if he intentionally arranges or facilitates the arrival in the United Kingdom of another person (B) and either –

    (a) he intends to do anything to or in respect of B, after B's arrival but in any part of the world, which if done will involve the commission of a relevant offence, or

    (b) he believes that another person is likely to do something to or in respect of B, after B's arrival but in any part of the world, which if done will involve the commission of a relevant offence.

(2) A person guilty of an offence under this section is liable –

    (a) on summary conviction, to imprisonment for a term not exceeding 6 months or a fine not exceeding the statutory maximum or both;

    (b) on conviction on indictment, to imprisonment for a term not exceeding 14 years.

58 Trafficking within the UK for sexual exploitation

(1) A person commits an offence if he intentionally arranges or facilitates travel within the United Kingdom by another person (B) and either –

    (a) he intends to do anything to or in respect of B, during or after the journey and in any part of the world, which if done will involve the commission of a relevant offence, or

    (b) he believes that another person is likely to do something to or in respect of B, during or after the journey and in any part of the world, which if done will involve the commission of a relevant offence.

(2) A person guilty of an offence under this section is liable –

    (a) on summary conviction, to imprisonment for a term not exceeding 6 months or a fine not exceeding the statutory maximum or both;

    (b) on conviction on indictment, to imprisonment for a term not exceeding 14 years.

59 Trafficking out of the UK for sexual exploitation

(1) A person commits an offence if he intentionally arranges or facilitates the departure from the United Kingdom of another person (B) and either –

    (a) he intends to do anything to or in respect of B, after B's departure but in any part of the world, which if done will involve the commission of a relevant offence, or

    (b) he believes that another person is likely to do something to or in respect of B, after B's departure but in any part of the world, which if done will involve the commission of a relevant offence.

(2) A person guilty of an offence under this section is liable –

    (a) on summary conviction, to imprisonment for a term not exceeding 6 months or a fine not exceeding the statutory maximum or both;

    (b) on conviction on indictment, to imprisonment for a term not exceeding 14 years.

60 Sections 57 to 59: interpretation and jurisdiction

(1) In sections 57 to 59, 'relevant offence' means –

   (a) an offence under this Part,
   (b) an offence under section 1(1)(a) of the Protection of Children Act 1978 (c. 37),
   (c) an offence listed in Schedule 1 to the Criminal Justice (Children) (Northern Ireland) Order 1998 (S.I. 1998/1504 (N.I. 9)),
   (d) an offence under Article 3(1)(a) of the Protection of Children (Northern Ireland) Order 1978 (S.I. 1978/1047 (N.I. 17)), or
   (e) anything done outside England and Wales and Northern Ireland which is not an offence within any of paragraphs (a) to (d) but would be if done in England and Wales or Northern Ireland.

(2) Sections 57 to 59 apply to anything done –

   (a) in the United Kingdom, or
   (b) outside the United Kingdom, by a body incorporated under the law of a part of the United Kingdom or by an individual to whom subsection (3) applies.

(3) This subsection applies to –

   (a) a British citizen,
   (b) a British overseas territories citizen,
   (c) a British National (Overseas),
   (d) a British Overseas citizen,
   (e) a person who is a British subject under the British Nationality Act 1981 (c. 61),
   (f) a British protected person within the meaning given by section 50(1) of that Act.

Preparatory offences

61 Administering a substance with intent

(1) A person commits an offence if he intentionally administers a substance to, or causes a substance to be taken by, another person (B) –

   (a) knowing that B does not consent, and
   (b) with the intention of stupefying or overpowering B, so as to enable any person to engage in a sexual activity that involves B.

(2) A person guilty of an offence under this section is liable –

   (a) on summary conviction, to imprisonment for a term not exceeding 6 months or a fine not exceeding the statutory maximum or both;
   (b) on conviction on indictment, to imprisonment for a term not exceeding 10 years.

62 Committing an offence with intent to commit a sexual offence

(1) A person commits an offence under this section if he commits any offence with the intention of committing a relevant sexual offence.

(2) In this section, 'relevant sexual offence' means any offence under this Part (including an offence of aiding, abetting, counselling or procuring such an offence).

(3) A person guilty of an offence under this section is liable on conviction on indictment, where the offence is committed by kidnapping or false imprisonment, to imprisonment for life.

(4) Unless subsection (3) applies, a person guilty of an offence under this section is liable –

   (a) on summary conviction, to imprisonment for a term not exceeding 6 months or a fine not exceeding the statutory maximum or both;
   (b) on conviction on indictment, to imprisonment for a term not exceeding 10 years.

63 Trespass with intent to commit a sexual offence

(1) A person commits an offence if –

    (a) he is a trespasser on any premises,

    (b) he intends to commit a relevant sexual offence on the premises, and

    (c) he knows that, or is reckless as to whether, he is a trespasser.

(2) In this section –

    'premises' includes a structure or part of a structure;

    'relevant sexual offence' has the same meaning as in section 62;

    'structure' includes a tent, vehicle or vessel or other temporary or movable structure.

(3) A person guilty of an offence under this section is liable –

    (a) on summary conviction, to imprisonment for a term not exceeding 6 months or a fine not exceeding the statutory maximum or both;

    (b) on conviction on indictment, to imprisonment for a term not exceeding 10 years.

Sex with an adult relative

64 Sex with an adult relative: penetration

(1) A person aged 16 or over (A) commits an offence if –

    (a) he intentionally penetrates another person's vagina or anus with a part of his body or anything else, or penetrates another person's mouth with his penis,

    (b) the penetration is sexual,

    (c) the other person (B) is aged 18 or over,

    (d) A is related to B in a way mentioned in subsection (2), and

    (e) A knows or could reasonably be expected to know that he is related to B in that way.

(2) The ways that A may be related to B are as parent, grandparent, child, grandchild, brother, sister, half-brother, half-sister, uncle, aunt, nephew or niece.

(3) In subsection (2) –

    (a) 'uncle' means the brother of a person's parent, and 'aunt' has a corresponding meaning;

    (b) 'nephew' means the child of a person's brother or sister, and 'niece' has a corresponding meaning.

(4) Where in proceedings for an offence under this section it is proved that the defendant was related to the other person in any of those ways, it is to be taken that the defendant knew or could reasonably have been expected to know that he was related in that way unless sufficient evidence is adduced to raise an issue as to whether he knew or could reasonably have been expected to know that he was.

(5) A person guilty of an offence under this section is liable –

    (a) on summary conviction, to imprisonment for a term not exceeding 6 months or a fine not exceeding the statutory maximum or both;

    (b) on conviction on indictment, to imprisonment for a term not exceeding 2 years.

65 Sex with an adult relative: consenting to penetration

(1) A person aged 16 or over (A) commits an offence if –

    (a) another person (B) penetrates A's vagina or anus with a part of B's body or anything else, or penetrates A's mouth with B's penis,

    (b) A consents to the penetration,

    (c) the penetration is sexual,

    (d) B is aged 18 or over,

    (e) A is related to B in a way mentioned in subsection (2), and

(f)   A knows or could reasonably be expected to know that he is related to B in that way.

(2)   The ways that A may be related to B are as parent, grandparent, child, grandchild, brother, sister, half-brother, half-sister, uncle, aunt, nephew or niece.

(3)   In subsection (2) –

   (a)   'uncle' means the brother of a person's parent, and 'aunt' has a corresponding meaning;

   (b)   'nephew' means the child of a person's brother or sister, and 'niece' has a corresponding meaning.

(4)   Where in proceedings for an offence under this section it is proved that the defendant was related to the other person in any of those ways, it is to be taken that the defendant knew or could reasonably have been expected to know that he was related in that way unless sufficient evidence is adduced to raise an issue as to whether he knew or could reasonably have been expected to know that he was.

(5)   A person guilty of an offence under this section is liable –

   (a)   on summary conviction, to imprisonment for a term not exceeding 6 months or a fine not exceeding the statutory maximum or both;

   (b)   on conviction on indictment, to imprisonment for a term not exceeding 2 years.

Other offences

66 Exposure

(1)   A person commits an offence if –

   (a)   he intentionally exposes his genitals, and

   (b)   he intends that someone will see them and be caused alarm or distress.

(2)   A person guilty of an offence under this section is liable –

   (a)   on summary conviction, to imprisonment for a term not exceeding 6 months or a fine not exceeding the statutory maximum or both;

   (b)   on conviction on indictment, to imprisonment for a term not exceeding 2 years.

67 Voyeurism

(1)   A person commits an offence if –

   (a)   for the purpose of obtaining sexual gratification, he observes another person doing a private act, and

   (b)   he knows that the other person does not consent to being observed for his sexual gratification.

(2)   A person commits an offence if –

   (a)   he operates equipment with the intention of enabling another person to observe, for the purpose of obtaining sexual gratification, a third person (B) doing a private act, and

   (b)   he knows that B does not consent to his operating equipment with that intention.

(3)   A person commits an offence if –

   (a)   he records another person (B) doing a private act,

   (b)   he does so with the intention that he or a third person will, for the purpose of obtaining sexual gratification, look at an image of B doing the act, and

   (c)   he knows that B does not consent to his recording the act with that intention.

(4)   A person commits an offence if he installs equipment, or constructs or adapts a structure or part of a structure, with the intention of enabling himself or another person to commit an offence under subsection (1).

(5)   A person guilty of an offence under this section is liable –

(a)   on summary conviction, to imprisonment for a term not exceeding 6 months or a fine not exceeding the statutory maximum or both;

(b)   on conviction on indictment, to imprisonment for a term not exceeding 2 years.

68 Voyeurism: interpretation

(1)   For the purposes of section 67, a person is doing a private act if the person is in a place which, in the circumstances, would reasonably be expected to provide privacy, and –

(a)   the person's genitals, buttocks or breasts are exposed or covered only with underwear,

(b)   the person is using a lavatory, or

(c)   the person is doing a sexual act that is not of a kind ordinarily done in public.

(2)   In section 67, 'structure' includes a tent, vehicle or vessel or other temporary or movable structure.

69 Intercourse with an animal

(1)   A person commits an offence if –

(a)   he intentionally performs an act of penetration with his penis,

(b)   what is penetrated is the vagina or anus of a living animal, and

(c)   he knows that, or is reckless as to whether, that is what is penetrated.

(2)   A person (A) commits an offence if –

(a)   A intentionally causes, or allows, A's vagina or anus to be penetrated,

(b)   the penetration is by the penis of a living animal, and

(c)   A knows that, or is reckless as to whether, that is what A is being penetrated by.

(3)   A person guilty of an offence under this section is liable –

(a)   on summary conviction, to imprisonment for a term not exceeding 6 months or a fine not exceeding the statutory maximum or both;

(b)   on conviction on indictment, to imprisonment for a term not exceeding 2 years.

70 Sexual penetration of a corpse

(1)   A person commits an offence if –

(a)   he intentionally performs an act of penetration with a part of his body or anything else,

(b)   what is penetrated is a part of the body of a dead person,

(c)   he knows that, or is reckless as to whether, that is what is penetrated, and

(d)   the penetration is sexual.

(2)   A person guilty of an offence under this section is liable –

(a)   on summary conviction, to imprisonment for a term not exceeding 6 months or a fine not exceeding the statutory maximum or both;

(b)   on conviction on indictment, to imprisonment for a term not exceeding 2 years.

71 Sexual activity in a public lavatory

(1)   A person commits an offence if –

(a)   he is in a lavatory to which the public or a section of the public has or is permitted to have access, whether on payment or otherwise,

(b)   he intentionally engages in an activity, and,

(c)   the activity is sexual.

(2)   For the purposes of this section, an activity is sexual if a reasonable person would, in all the circumstances but regardless of any person's purpose, consider it to be sexual.

(3) A person guilty of an offence under this section is liable on summary conviction, to imprisonment for a term not exceeding 6 months or a fine not exceeding level 5 on the standard scale or both.

Offences outside the United Kingdom

72 Offences outside the United Kingdom

(1) Subject to subsection (2), any act done by a person in a country or territory outside the United Kingdom which –

  (a) constituted an offence under the law in force in that country or territory, and
  (b) would constitute a sexual offence to which this section applies if it had been done in England and Wales or in Northern Ireland,

  constitutes that sexual offence under the law of that part of the United Kingdom.

(2) Proceedings by virtue of this section may be brought only against a person who was on 1st September 1997, or has since become, a British citizen or resident in the United Kingdom.

(3) An act punishable under the law in force in any country or territory constitutes an offence under that law for the purposes of this section, however it is described in that law.

(4) Subject to subsection (5), the condition in subsection (1)(a) is to be taken to be met unless, not later than rules of court may provide, the defendant serves on the prosecution a notice –

  (a) stating that, on the facts as alleged with respect to the act in question, the condition is not in his opinion met,
  (b) showing his grounds for that opinion, and
  (c) requiring the prosecution to prove that it is met.

(5) The court, if it thinks fit, may permit the defendant to require the prosecution to prove that the condition is met without service of a notice under subsection (4).

(6) In the Crown Court the question whether the condition is met is to be decided by the judge alone.

(7) Schedule 2 lists the sexual offences to which this section applies.

Supplementary and general

73 Exceptions to aiding, abetting and counselling

(1) A person is not guilty of aiding, abetting or counselling the commission against a child of an offence to which this section applies if he acts for the purpose of –

  (a) protecting the child from sexually transmitted infection,
  (b) protecting the physical safety of the child,
  (c) preventing the child from becoming pregnant, or
  (d) promoting the child's emotional well-being by the giving of advice,

  and not for the purpose of obtaining sexual gratification or for the purpose of causing or encouraging the activity constituting the offence or the child's participation in it.

(2) This section applies to –

  (a) an offence under any of sections 5 to 7 (offences against children under 13);
  (b) an offence under section 9 (sexual activity with a child);
  (c) an offence under section 13 which would be an offence under section 9 if the offender were aged 18;
  (d) an offence under any of sections 16, 25, 30, 34 and 38 (sexual activity) against a person under 16.

(3) This section does not affect any other enactment or any rule of law restricting the circumstances in which a person is guilty of aiding, abetting or counselling an offence under this Part.

74 'Consent'

For the purposes of this Part, a person consents if he agrees by choice, and has the freedom and capacity to make that choice.

75 Evidential presumptions about consent

(1) If in proceedings for an offence to which this section applies it is proved –

    (a) that the defendant did the relevant act,

    (b) that any of the circumstances specified in subsection (2) existed, and

    (c) that the defendant knew that those circumstances existed,

the complainant is to be taken not to have consented to the relevant act unless sufficient evidence is adduced to raise an issue as to whether he consented, and the defendant is to be taken not to have reasonably believed that the complainant consented unless sufficient evidence is adduced to raise an issue as to whether he reasonably believed it.

(2) The circumstances are that –

    (a) any person was, at the time of the relevant act or immediately before it began, using violence against the complainant or causing the complainant to fear that immediate violence would be used against him;

    (b) any person was, at the time of the relevant act or immediately before it began, causing the complainant to fear that violence was being used, or that immediate violence would be used, against another person;

    (c) the complainant was, and the defendant was not, unlawfully detained at the time of the relevant act;

    (d) the complainant was asleep or otherwise unconscious at the time of the relevant act;

    (e) because of the complainant's physical disability, the complainant would not have been able at the time of the relevant act to communicate to the defendant whether the complainant consented;

    (f) any person had administered to or caused to be taken by the complainant, without the complainant's consent, a substance which, having regard to when it was administered or taken, was capable of causing or enabling the complainant to be stupefied or overpowered at the time of the relevant act.

(3) In subsection (2)(a) and (b), the reference to the time immediately before the relevant act began is, in the case of an act which is one of a continuous series of sexual activities, a reference to the time immediately before the first sexual activity began.

76 Conclusive presumptions about consent

(1) If in proceedings for an offence to which this section applies it is proved that the defendant did the relevant act and that any of the circumstances specified in subsection (2) existed, it is to be conclusively presumed –

    (a) that the complainant did not consent to the relevant act, and

    (b) that the defendant did not believe that the complainant consented to the relevant act.

(2) The circumstances are that –

    (a) the defendant intentionally deceived the complainant as to the nature or purpose of the relevant act;

    (b) the defendant intentionally induced the complainant to consent to the relevant act by impersonating a person known personally to the complainant.

77 Sections 75 and 76: relevant acts

In relation to an offence to which sections 75 and 76 apply, references in those sections to the relevant act and to the complainant are to be read as follows –

Offence	Relevant Act
An offence under section 1 (rape).	The defendant intentionally penetrating, with his penis, the vagina, anus or mouth of another person ('the complainant').
An offence under section 2 (assault by penetration).	The defendant intentionally penetrating, with a part of his body or anything else, the vagina or anus of another person ('the complainant'), where the penetration is sexual.
An offence under section 3 (sexual assault).	The defendant intentionally touching another person ('the complainant'), where the touching is sexual.
An offence under section 4 (causing a person to engage in sexual activity without consent).	The defendant intentionally causing another person ('the complainant') to engage in an activity, where the activity is sexual.

78 'Sexual'

For the purposes of this Part (except section 71), penetration, touching or any other activity is sexual if a reasonable person would consider that –

(a)   whatever its circumstances or any person's purpose in relation to it, it is because of its nature sexual, or

(b)   because of its nature it may be sexual and because of its circumstances or the purpose of any person in relation to it (or both) it is sexual.

79 Part 1: general interpretation

(1) The following apply for the purposes of this Part.

(2) Penetration is a continuing act from entry to withdrawal.

(3) References to a part of the body include references to a part surgically constructed (in particular, through gender reassignment surgery).

(4) 'Image' means a moving or still image and includes an image produced by any means and, where the context permits, a three-dimensional image.

(5) References to an image of a person include references to an image of an imaginary person.

(6) 'Mental disorder' has the meaning given by section 1 of the Mental Health Act 1983 (c. 20).

(7) References to observation (however expressed) are to observation whether direct or by looking at an image.

(8) Touching includes touching –

(a)   with any part of the body,

(b)   with anything else,

(c)   through anything,

and in particular includes touching amounting to penetration.

(9) 'Vagina' includes vulva.

(10) In relation to an animal, references to the vagina or anus include references to any similar part.

PART 2   NOTIFICATION AND ORDERS

Notification requirements

80 Persons becoming subject to notification requirements

(1) A person is subject to the notification requirements of this Part for the period set out in section 82 ('the notification period') if –

    (a) he is convicted of an offence listed in Schedule 3;

    (b) he is found not guilty of such an offence by reason of insanity;

    (c) he is found to be under a disability and to have done the act charged against him in respect of such an offence; or

    (d) in England and Wales or Northern Ireland, he is cautioned in respect of such an offence.

(2) A person for the time being subject to the notification requirements of this Part is referred to in this Part as a 'relevant offender'.

81 Persons formerly subject to Part 1 of the Sex Offenders Act 1997

(1) A person is, from the commencement of this Part until the end of the notification period, subject to the notification requirements of this Part if, before the commencement of this Part –

    (a) he was convicted of an offence listed in Schedule 3;

    (b) he was found not guilty of such an offence by reason of insanity;

    (c) he was found to be under a disability and to have done the act charged against him in respect of such an offence; or

    (d) in England and Wales or Northern Ireland, he was cautioned in respect of such an offence.

(2) Subsection (1) does not apply if the notification period ended before the commencement of this Part.

(3) Subsection (1)(a) does not apply to a conviction before 1st September 1997 unless, at the beginning of that day, the person –

    (a) had not been dealt with in respect of the offence;

    (b) was serving a sentence of imprisonment or a term of service detention, or was subject to a community order, in respect of the offence;

    (c) was subject to supervision, having been released from prison after serving the whole or part of a sentence of imprisonment in respect of the offence; or

    (d) was detained in a hospital or was subject to a guardianship order, following the conviction.

(4) Paragraphs (b) and (c) of subsection (1) do not apply to a finding made before 1st September 1997 unless, at the beginning of that day, the person –

    (a) had not been dealt with in respect of the finding; or

    (b) was detained in a hospital, following the finding.

(5) Subsection (1)(d) does not apply to a caution given before 1st September 1997.

(6) A person who would have been within subsection (3)(b) or (d) or (4)(b) but for the fact that at the beginning of 1st September 1997 he was unlawfully at large or absent without leave, on temporary release or leave of absence, or on bail pending an appeal, is to be treated as being within that provision.

(7) Where, immediately before the commencement of this Part, an order under a provision within subsection (8) was in force in respect of a person, the person is subject to the notification requirements of this Part from that commencement until the order is discharged or otherwise ceases to have effect.

(8) The provisions are –

    (a) section 5A of the Sex Offenders Act 1997 (c. 51) (restraining orders);

    (b) section 2 of the Crime and Disorder Act 1998 (c. 37) (sex offender orders made in England and Wales);

    (c) section 2A of the Crime and Disorder Act 1998 (interim orders made in England and Wales);

    (d) section 20 of the Crime and Disorder Act 1998 (sex offender orders and interim orders made in Scotland);

    (e) Article 6 of the Criminal Justice (Northern Ireland) Order 1998 (S.I. 1998/2839 (N.I. 20)) (sex offender orders made in Northern Ireland);

    (f) Article 6A of the Criminal Justice (Northern Ireland) Order 1998 (interim orders made in Northern Ireland).

82 The notification period

(1) The notification period for a person within section 80(1) or 81(1) is the period in the second column of the following Table opposite the description that applies to him.

TABLE

Description of relevant offender	Notification period
A person who, in respect of the offence, is or has been sentenced to imprisonment for life or for a term of 30 months or more	An indefinite period beginning with the relevant date
A person who, in respect of the offence, has been made the subject of an order under section 210F(1) of the Criminal Procedure (Scotland) Act 1995 (order for lifelong restriction)	An indefinite period beginning with that date
A person who, in respect of the offence or finding, is or has been admitted to a hospital subject to a restriction order	An indefinite period beginning with that date
A person who, in respect of the offence, is or has been sentenced to imprisonment for a term of more than 6 months but less than 30 months	10 years beginning with that date
A person who, in respect of the offence, is or has been sentenced to imprisonment for a term of 6 months or less	7 years beginning with that date
A person who, in respect of the offence or finding, is or has been admitted to a hospital without being subject to a restriction order	7 years beginning with that date
A person within section 80(1)(d)	2 years beginning with that date
A person in whose case an order for conditional discharge or, in Scotland, a probation order, is made in respect of the offence	The period of conditional discharge or, in Scotland, the probation period
A person of any other description	5 years beginning with the relevant date

(2) Where a person is under 18 on the relevant date, subsection (1) has effect as if for any reference to a period of 10 years, 7 years, 5 years or 2 years there were substituted a reference to one-half of that period.

(3) Subsection (4) applies where a relevant offender within section 80(1)(a) or 81(1)(a) is or has been sentenced, in respect of two or more offences listed in Schedule 3 –

    (a) to consecutive terms of imprisonment; or

    (b) to terms of imprisonment which are partly concurrent.

(4) Where this subsection applies, subsection (1) has effect as if the relevant offender were or had been sentenced, in respect of each of the offences, to a term of imprisonment which –

    (a) in the case of consecutive terms, is equal to the aggregate of those terms;

    (b) in the case of partly concurrent terms (X and Y, which overlap for a period Z), is equal to X plus Y minus Z.

(5) Where a relevant offender the subject of a finding within section 80(1)(c) or 81(1)(c) is subsequently tried for the offence, the notification period relating to the finding ends at the conclusion of the trial.

(6) In this Part, 'relevant date' means –

    (a) in the case of a person within section 80(1)(a) or 81(1)(a), the date of the conviction;

    (b) in the case of a person within section 80(1)(b) or (c) or 81(1)(b) or (c), the date of the finding;

    (c) in the case of a person within section 80(1)(d) or 81(1)(d), the date of the caution;

    (d) in the case of a person within section 81(7), the date which, for the purposes of Part 1 of the Sex Offenders Act 1997 (c. 51), was the relevant date in relation to that person.

83 Notification requirements: initial notification

(1) A relevant offender must, within the period of 3 days beginning with the relevant date (or, if later, the commencement of this Part), notify to the police the information set out in subsection (5).

(2) Subsection (1) does not apply to a relevant offender in respect of a conviction, finding or caution within section 80(1) if –

    (a) immediately before the conviction, finding or caution, he was subject to the notification requirements of this Part as a result of another conviction, finding or caution or an order of a court ('the earlier event'),

    (b) at that time, he had made a notification under subsection (1) in respect of the earlier event, and

    (c) throughout the period referred to in subsection (1), he remains subject to the notification requirements as a result of the earlier event.

(3) Subsection (1) does not apply to a relevant offender in respect of a conviction, finding or caution within section 81(1) or an order within section 81(7) if the offender complied with section 2(1) of the Sex Offenders Act 1997 in respect of the conviction, finding, caution or order.

(4) Where a notification order is made in respect of a conviction, finding or caution, subsection (1) does not apply to the relevant offender in respect of the conviction, finding or caution if –

    (a) immediately before the order was made, he was subject to the notification requirements of this Part as a result of another conviction, finding or caution or an order of a court ('the earlier event'),

    (b) at that time, he had made a notification under subsection (1) in respect of the earlier event, and

    (c) throughout the period referred to in subsection (1), he remains subject to the notification requirements as a result of the earlier event.

(5) The information is –

    (a) the relevant offender's date of birth;

    (b) his national insurance number;

    (c) his name on the relevant date and, where he used one or more other names on that date, each of those names;

    (d) his home address on the relevant date;

    (e) his name on the date on which notification is given and, where he uses one or more other names on that date, each of those names;

    (f) his home address on the date on which notification is given;

    (g) the address of any other premises in the United Kingdom at which, at the time the notification is given, he regularly resides or stays.

(6) When determining the period for the purpose of subsection (1), there is to be disregarded any time when the relevant offender is –

    (a) remanded in or committed to custody by an order of a court;

    (b) serving a sentence of imprisonment or a term of service detention;

    (c) detained in a hospital; or

    (d) outside the United Kingdom.

(7) In this Part, 'home address' means, in relation to any person –

    (a) the address of his sole or main residence in the United Kingdom, or

    (b) where he has no such residence, the address or location of a place in the United Kingdom where he can regularly be found and, if there is more than one such place, such one of those places as the person may select.

84 Notification requirements: changes

(1) A relevant offender must, within the period of 3 days beginning with –

    (a) his using a name which has not been notified to the police under section 83(1), this subsection, or section 2 of the Sex Offenders Act 1997 (c. 51),

    (b) any change of his home address,

    (c) his having resided or stayed, for a qualifying period, at any premises in the United Kingdom the address of which has not been notified to the police under section 83(1), this subsection, or section 2 of the Sex Offenders Act 1997, or

    (d) his release from custody pursuant to an order of a court or from imprisonment, service detention or detention in a hospital,

notify to the police that name, the new home address, the address of those premises or (as the case may be) the fact that he has been released, and (in addition) the information set out in section 83(5).

(2) A notification under subsection (1) may be given before the name is used, the change of home address occurs or the qualifying period ends, but in that case the relevant offender must also specify the date when the event is expected to occur.

(3) If a notification is given in accordance with subsection (2) and the event to which it relates occurs more than 2 days before the date specified, the notification does not affect the duty imposed by subsection (1).

(4) If a notification is given in accordance with subsection (2) and the event to which it relates has not occurred by the end of the period of 3 days beginning with the date specified –

    (a) the notification does not affect the duty imposed by subsection (1), and

    (b) the relevant offender must, within the period of 6 days beginning with the date specified, notify to the police the fact that the event did not occur within the period of 3 days beginning with the date specified.

(5) Section 83(6) applies to the determination of the period of 3 days mentioned in subsection (1) and the period of 6 days mentioned in subsection (4)(b), as it applies to the determination of the period mentioned in section 83(1).

(6) In this section, 'qualifying period' means –

(a) a period of 7 days, or

(b) two or more periods, in any period of 12 months, which taken together amount to 7 days.

85 Notification requirements: periodic notification

(1) A relevant offender must, within the period of one year after each event within subsection (2), notify to the police the information set out in section 83(5), unless within that period he has given a notification under section 84(1).

(2) The events are –

(a) the commencement of this Part (but only in the case of a person who is a relevant offender from that commencement);

(b) any notification given by the relevant offender under section 83(1) or 84(1); and

(c) any notification given by him under subsection (1).

(3) Where the period referred to in subsection (1) would (apart from this subsection) end whilst subsection (4) applies to the relevant offender, that period is to be treated as continuing until the end of the period of 3 days beginning when subsection (4) first ceases to apply to him.

(4) This subsection applies to the relevant offender if he is –

(a) remanded in or committed to custody by an order of a court,

(b) serving a sentence of imprisonment or a term of service detention,

(c) detained in a hospital, or

(d) outside the United Kingdom.

86 Notification requirements: travel outside the United Kingdom

(1) The Secretary of State may by regulations make provision requiring relevant offenders who leave the United Kingdom, or any description of such offenders –

(a) to give in accordance with the regulations, before they leave, a notification under subsection (2);

(b) if they subsequently return to the United Kingdom, to give in accordance with the regulations a notification under subsection (3).

(2) A notification under this subsection must disclose –

(a) the date on which the offender will leave the United Kingdom;

(b) the country (or, if there is more than one, the first country) to which he will travel and his point of arrival (determined in accordance with the regulations) in that country;

(c) any other information prescribed by the regulations which the offender holds about his departure from or return to the United Kingdom or his movements while outside the United Kingdom.

(3) A notification under this subsection must disclose any information prescribed by the regulations about the offender's return to the United Kingdom.

(4) Regulations under subsection (1) may make different provision for different categories of person.

87 Method of notification and related matters

(1) A person gives a notification under section 83(1), 84(1) or 85(1) by –

(a) attending at such police station in his local police area as the Secretary of State may by regulations prescribe or, if there is more than one, at any of them, and

(b) giving an oral notification to any police officer, or to any person authorised for the purpose by the officer in charge of the station.

(2) A person giving a notification under section 84(1) –

(a) in relation to a prospective change of home address, or

(b) in relation to premises referred to in subsection (1)(c) of that section,

may give the notification at a police station that would fall within subsection (1) above if the change in home address had already occurred or (as the case may be) if the address of those premises were his home address.

(3) Any notification under this section must be acknowledged; and an acknowledgement under this subsection must be in writing, and in such form as the Secretary of State may direct.

(4) Where a notification is given under section 83(1), 84(1) or 85(1), the relevant offender must, if requested to do so by the police officer or person referred to in subsection (1)(b), allow the officer or person to –

(a) take his fingerprints,

(b) photograph any part of him, or

(c) do both these things.

(5) The power in subsection (4) is exercisable for the purpose of verifying the identity of the relevant offender.

(6) Regulations under subsection (1) may make different provision for different categories of person.

88 Section 87: interpretation

(1) Subsections (2) to (4) apply for the purposes of section 87.

(2) 'Photograph' includes any process by means of which an image may be produced.

(3) 'Local police area' means, in relation to a person –

(a) the police area in which his home address is situated;

(b) in the absence of a home address, the police area in which the home address last notified is situated;

(c) in the absence of a home address and of any such notification, the police area in which the court which last dealt with the person in a way mentioned in subsection (4) is situated.

(4) The ways are –

(a) dealing with a person in respect of an offence listed in Schedule 3 or a finding in relation to such an offence;

(b) dealing with a person in respect of an offence under section 128 or a finding in relation to such an offence;

(c) making, in respect of a person, a notification order, interim notification order, sexual offences prevention order or interim sexual offences prevention order;

(d) making, in respect of a person, an order under section 2, 2A or 20 of the Crime and Disorder Act 1998 (c. 37) (sex offender orders and interim orders made in England and Wales or Scotland) or Article 6 or 6A of the Criminal Justice (Northern Ireland) Order 1998 (S.I. 1998/2839 (N.I. 20)) (sex offender orders and interim orders made in Northern Ireland); and in paragraphs (a) and (b), 'finding' in relation to an offence means a finding of not guilty of the offence by reason of insanity or a finding that the person was under a disability and did the act or omission charged against him in respect of the offence.

(5) Subsection (3) applies as if Northern Ireland were a police area.

89 Young offenders: parental directions

(1) Where a person within the first column of the following Table ('the young offender') is under 18 (or, in Scotland, 16) when he is before the court referred to in the second column of the Table opposite the description that applies to him, that court may direct that subsection (2) applies in respect of an individual ('the parent') having parental responsibility for (or, in Scotland, parental responsibilities in relation to) the young offender.

TABLE

Description of person	Court which may make the direction
A relevant offender within section 80(1)(a) to (c) or 81(1)(a) to (c)	The court which deals with the offender in respect of the offence or finding
A relevant offender within section 129(1)(a) to (c)	The court which deals with the offender in respect of the offence or finding
A person who is the subject of a notification order, interim notification order, sexual offences prevention order or interim sexual offences prevention order	The court which makes the order
A relevant offender who is the defendant to an application under subsection (4) (or, in Scotland, the subject of an application under subsection (5))	The court which hears the application

(2) Where this subsection applies –

    (a) the obligations that would (apart from this subsection) be imposed by or under sections 83 to 86 on the young offender are to be treated instead as obligations on the parent, and

    (b) the parent must ensure that the young offender attends at the police station with him, when a notification is being given.

(3) A direction under subsection (1) takes immediate effect and applies –

    (a) until the young offender attains the age of 18 (or, where a court in Scotland gives the direction, 16); or

    (b) for such shorter period as the court may, at the time the direction is given, direct.

(4) A chief officer of police may, by complaint to any magistrates' court whose commission area includes any part of his police area, apply for a direction under subsection (1) in respect of a relevant offender ('the defendant') –

    (a) who resides in his police area, or who the chief officer believes is in or is intending to come to his police area, and

    (b) who the chief officer believes is under 18.

(5) In Scotland, a chief constable may, by summary application to any sheriff within whose sheriffdom lies any part of the area of his police force, apply for a direction under subsection (1) in respect of a relevant offender ('the subject') –

    (a) who resides in that area, or who the chief constable believes is in or is intending to come to that area, and

    (b) who the chief constable believes is under 16.

90 Parental directions: variations, renewals and discharges

(1) A person within subsection (2) may apply to the appropriate court for an order varying, renewing or discharging a direction under section 89(1).

(2) The persons are –

    (a) the young offender;

    (b) the parent;

    (c) the chief officer of police for the area in which the young offender resides;

    (d) a chief officer of police who believes that the young offender is in, or is intending to come to, his police area;

    (e) in Scotland, where the appropriate court is a civil court –

        (i) the chief constable of the police force within the area of which the young offender resides;

   (ii)   a chief constable who believes that the young offender is in, or is intending
           to come to, the area of his police force,and in any other case, the prosecutor;
   (f)   where the direction was made on an application under section 89(4), the chief
         officer of police who made the application;
   (g)   where the direction was made on an application under section 89(5), the chief
         constable who made the application.
(3)   An application under subsection (1) may be made –
   (a)   where the appropriate court is the Crown Court (or in Scotland a criminal
         court), in accordance with rules of court;
   (b)   in any other case, by complaint (or, in Scotland, by summary application).
(4)   On the application the court, after hearing the person making the application and (if
      they wish to be heard) the other persons mentioned in subsection (2), may make
      any order, varying, renewing or discharging the direction, that the court considers
      appropriate.
(5)   In this section, the 'appropriate court' means –
   (a)   where the Court of Appeal made the order, the Crown Court;
   (b)   in any other case, the court that made the direction under section 89(1).

91 Offences relating to notification

(1)   A person commits an offence if he –
   (a)   fails, without reasonable excuse, to comply with section 83(1), 84(1), 84(4)(b),
         85(1), 87(4) or 89(2)(b) or any requirement imposed by regulations made under
         section 86(1); or
   (b)   notifies to the police, in purported compliance with section 83(1), 84(1) or
         85(1) or any requirement imposed by regulations made under section 86(1), any
         information which he knows to be false.
(2)   A person guilty of an offence under this section is liable –
   (a)   on summary conviction, to imprisonment for a term not exceeding 6 months or
         a fine not exceeding the statutory maximum or both;
   (b)   on conviction on indictment, to imprisonment for a term not exceeding 5 years.
(3)   A person commits an offence under paragraph (a) of subsection (1) on the day on
      which he first fails, without reasonable excuse, to comply with section 83(1), 84(1)
      or 85(1) or a requirement imposed by regulations made under section 86(1), and con-
      tinues to commit it throughout any period during which the failure continues; but a
      person must not be prosecuted under subsection (1) more than once in respect of the
      same failure.
(4)   Proceedings for an offence under this section may be commenced in any court having
      jurisdiction in any place where the person charged with the offence resides or is
      found.

92 Certificates for purposes of Part 2

(1)   Subsection (2) applies where on any date a person is –
   (a)   convicted of an offence listed in Schedule 3;
   (b)   found not guilty of such an offence by reason of insanity; or
   (c)   found to be under a disability and to have done the act charged against him in
         respect of such an offence.
(2)   If the court by or before which the person is so convicted or found –
   (a)   states in open court –
      (i)   that on that date he has been convicted, found not guilty by reason of
            insanity or found to be under a disability and to have done the act charged
            against him, and

      (ii)   that the offence in question is an offence listed in Schedule 3, and

    (b) certifies those facts, whether at the time or subsequently, the certificate is, for the purposes of this Part, evidence (or, in Scotland, sufficient evidence) of those facts.

(3) Subsection (4) applies where on any date a person is, in England and Wales or Northern Ireland, cautioned in respect of an offence listed in Schedule 3.

(4) If the constable –

    (a) informs the person that he has been cautioned on that date and that the offence in question is an offence listed in Schedule 3, and

    (b) certifies those facts, whether at the time or subsequently, in such form as the Secretary of State may by order prescribe, the certificate is, for the purposes of this Part, evidence (or, in Scotland, sufficient evidence) of those facts.

93 Abolished homosexual offences

Schedule 4 (procedure for ending notification requirements for abolished homosexual offences) has effect.

Information for verification

94 Part 2: supply of information to Secretary of State etc. for verification

(1) This section applies to information notified to the police under –

    (a) section 83, 84 or 85, or

    (b) section 2(1) to (3) of the Sex Offenders Act 1997 (c. 51).

(2) A person within subsection (3) may, for the purposes of the prevention, detection, investigation or prosecution of offences under this Part, supply information to which this section applies to –

    (a) the Secretary of State,

    (b) a Northern Ireland Department, or

    (c) a person providing services to the Secretary of State or a Northern Ireland Department in connection with a relevant function, for use for the purpose of verifying the information.

(3) The persons are –

    (a) a chief officer of police (in Scotland, a chief constable),

    (b) the Police Information Technology Organisation,

    (c) the Director General of the National Criminal Intelligence Service,

    (d) the Director General of the National Crime Squad.

(4) In relation to information supplied under subsection (2) to any person, the reference to verifying the information is a reference to –

    (a) checking its accuracy by comparing it with information held –

        (i)   where the person is the Secretary of State or a Northern Ireland Department, by him or it in connection with the exercise of a relevant function, or

        (ii) where the person is within subsection (2)(c), by that person in connection with the provision of services referred to there, and

    (b) compiling a report of that comparison.

(5) Subject to subsection (6), the supply of information under this section is to be taken not to breach any restriction on the disclosure of information (however arising or imposed).

(6) This section does not authorise the doing of anything that contravenes the Data Protection Act 1998 (c. 29).

(7) This section does not affect any power existing apart from this section to supply information.

(8) In this section –

'Northern Ireland Department' means the Department for Employment and Learning, the Department of the Environment or the Department for Social Development;

'relevant function' means –

(a) a function relating to social security, child support, employment or training,

(b) a function relating to passports,

(c) a function under Part 3 of the Road Traffic Act 1988 (c. 52) or Part 2 of the Road Traffic (Northern Ireland) Order 1981 (S.I. 1981/154 (N.I. 1)).

95 Part 2: supply of information by Secretary of State etc.

(1) A report compiled under section 94 may be supplied by –

(a) the Secretary of State,

(b) a Northern Ireland Department, or

(c) a person within section 94(2)(c),

to a person within subsection (2).

(2) The persons are –

(a) a chief officer of police (in Scotland, a chief constable),

(b) the Director General of the National Criminal Intelligence Service,

(c) the Director General of the National Crime Squad.

(3) Such a report may contain any information held –

(a) by the Secretary of State or a Northern Ireland Department in connection with the exercise of a relevant function, or

(b) by a person within section 94(2)(c) in connection with the provision of services referred to there.

(4) Where such a report contains information within subsection (3), the person within subsection (2) to whom it is supplied –

(a) may retain the information, whether or not used for the purposes of the prevention, detection, investigation or prosecution of an offence under this Part, and

(b) may use the information for any purpose related to the prevention, detection, investigation or prosecution of offences (whether or not under this Part), but for no other purpose.

(5) Subsections (5) to (8) of section 94 apply in relation to this section as they apply in relation to section 94.

Information about release or transfer

96 Information about release or transfer

(1) This section applies to a relevant offender who is serving a sentence of imprisonment or a term of service detention, or is detained in a hospital.

(2) The Secretary of State may by regulations make provision requiring notice to be given by the person who is responsible for that offender to persons prescribed by the regulations, of any occasion when the offender is released or a different person becomes responsible for him.

(3) The regulations may make provision for determining who is to be treated for the purposes of this section as responsible for an offender.

Notification orders

97 Notification orders: applications and grounds

(1) A chief officer of police may, by complaint to any magistrates' court whose commission area includes any part of his police area, apply for an order under this section (a 'notification order') in respect of a person ('the defendant') if –

    (a) it appears to him that the following three conditions are met with respect to the defendant, and

    (b) the defendant resides in his police area or the chief officer believes that the defendant is in, or is intending to come to, his police area.

(2) The first condition is that under the law in force in a country outside the United Kingdom –

    (a) he has been convicted of a relevant offence (whether or not he has been punished for it),

    (b) a court exercising jurisdiction under that law has made in respect of a relevant offence a finding equivalent to a finding that he is not guilty by reason of insanity,

    (c) such a court has made in respect of a relevant offence a finding equivalent to a finding that he is under a disability and did the act charged against him in respect of the offence, or

    (d) he has been cautioned in respect of a relevant offence.

(3) The second condition is that –

    (a) the first condition is met because of a conviction, finding or caution which occurred on or after 1st September 1997,

    (b) the first condition is met because of a conviction or finding which occurred before that date, but the person was dealt with in respect of the offence or finding on or after that date, or has yet to be dealt with in respect of it, or

    (c) the first condition is met because of a conviction or finding which occurred before that date, but on that date the person was, in respect of the offence or finding, subject under the law in force in the country concerned to detention, supervision or any other disposal equivalent to any of those mentioned in section 81(3) (read with sections 81(6) and 131).

(4) The third condition is that the period set out in section 82 (as modified by subsections (2) and (3) of section 98) in respect of the relevant offence has not expired.

(5) If on the application it is proved that the conditions in subsections (2) to (4) are met, the court must make a notification order.

(6) In this section and section 98, 'relevant offence' has the meaning given by section 99.

98 Notification orders: effect

(1) Where a notification order is made –

    (a) the application of this Part to the defendant in respect of the conviction, finding or caution to which the order relates is subject to the modifications set out below, and

    (b) subject to those modifications, the defendant becomes or (as the case may be) remains subject to the notification requirements of this Part for the notification period set out in section 82.

(2) The 'relevant date' means –

    (a) in the case of a person within section 97(2)(a), the date of the conviction;

    (b) in the case of a person within section 97(2)(b) or (c), the date of the finding;

    (c) in the case of a person within section 97(2)(d), the date of the caution.

(3) In section 82 –

        (a) references, except in the Table, to a person (or relevant offender) within any provision of section 80 are to be read as references to the defendant;

(b) the reference in the Table to section 80(1)(d) is to be read as a reference to section 97(2)(d);

(c) references to an order of any description are to be read as references to any corresponding disposal made in relation to the defendant in respect of an offence or finding by reference to which the notification order was made;

(d) the reference to offences listed in Schedule 3 is to be read as a reference to relevant offences.

(4) In sections 83 and 85, references to the commencement of this Part are to be read as references to the date of service of the notification order.

99 Sections 97 and 98: relevant offences

(1) 'Relevant offence' in sections 97 and 98 means an act which –

(a) constituted an offence under the law in force in the country concerned, and

(b) would have constituted an offence listed in Schedule 3 (other than at paragraph 60) if it had been done in any part of the United Kingdom.

(2) An act punishable under the law in force in a country outside the United Kingdom constitutes an offence under that law for the purposes of subsection (1) however it is described in that law.

(3) Subject to subsection (4), on an application for a notification order the condition in subsection (1)(b) is to be taken as met unless, not later than rules of court may provide, the defendant serves on the applicant a notice –

(a) stating that, on the facts as alleged with respect to the act concerned, the condition is not in his opinion met,

(b) showing his grounds for that opinion, and

(c) requiring the applicant to prove that the condition is met.

(4) The court, if it thinks fit, may permit the defendant to require the applicant to prove that the condition is met without service of a notice under subsection (3).

100 Interim notification orders

(1) This section applies where an application for a notification order ('the main application') has not been determined.

(2) An application for an order under this section ('an interim notification order') –

(a) may be made in the complaint containing the main application, or

(b) if the main application has been made, may be made by the person who has made that application, by complaint to the court to which that application has been made.

(3) The court may, if it considers it just to do so, make an interim notification order.

(4) Such an order –

(a) has effect only for a fixed period, specified in the order;

(b) ceases to have effect, if it has not already done so, on the determination of the main application.

(5) While such an order has effect –

(a) the defendant is subject to the notification requirements of this Part;

(b) this Part applies to the defendant, subject to the modification set out in subsection (6).

(6) The 'relevant date' means the date of service of the order.

(7) The applicant or the defendant may by complaint apply to the court that made the interim notification order for the order to be varied, renewed or discharged.

101 Notification orders and interim notification orders: appeals

A defendant may appeal to the Crown Court against the making of a notification order or interim notification order.

102 Appeals in relation to notification orders and interim notification orders: Scotland

In Scotland –

    (a) an interlocutor granting or refusing a notification order or interim notification order is an appealable interlocutor; and

    (b) where an appeal is taken against an interlocutor so granting such an order the order shall, without prejudice to any power of the court to vary or recall it, continue to have effect pending the disposal of the appeal.

103 Sections 97 to 100: Scotland

(1) Sections 97 to 100 apply to Scotland with the following modifications –

    (a) references to a chief officer of police and to his police area are to be read, respectively, as references to a chief constable and to the area of his police force;

    (b) references to the defendant are to be read as references to the person in respect of whom the order is sought or has effect;

    (c) an application for a notification order or interim notification order is made by summary application to any sheriff within whose sheriffdom lies any part of the area of the applicant's police force (references to 'the court' being construed accordingly).

(2) A record of evidence shall be kept on any summary application made by virtue of subsection (1)(c) above.

(3) The clerk of the court by which, by virtue of that subsection, a notification order or interim notification order is made, varied, renewed or discharged shall cause a copy of, as the case may be –

    (a) the order as so made, varied or renewed; or

    (b) the interlocutor by which discharge is effected,

to be given to the person named in the order or sent to him by registered post or by the recorded delivery service (an acknowledgement or certificate of delivery of a copy so sent, issued by the Post Office, being sufficient evidence of the delivery of the copy on the day specified in the acknowledgement or certificate).

Sexual offences prevention orders

104 Sexual offences prevention orders: applications and grounds

(1) A court may make an order under this section in respect of a person ('the defendant') where any of subsections (2) to (4) applies to the defendant and –

    (a) where subsection (4) applies, it is satisfied that the defendant's behaviour since the appropriate date makes it necessary to make such an order, for the purpose of protecting the public or any particular members of the public from serious sexual harm from the defendant;

    (b) in any other case, it is satisfied that it is necessary to make such an order, for the purpose of protecting the public or any particular members of the public from serious sexual harm from the defendant.

(2) This subsection applies to the defendant where the court deals with him in respect of an offence listed in Schedule 3 or 5.

(3) This subsection applies to the defendant where the court deals with him in respect of a finding –

(a) that he is not guilty of an offence listed in Schedule 3 or 5 by reason of insanity, or

(b) that he is under a disability and has done the act charged against him in respect of such an offence.

(4) This subsection applies to the defendant where –

(a) an application under subsection (5) has been made to the court in respect of him, and

(b) on the application, it is proved that he is a qualifying offender.

(5) A chief officer of police may by complaint to a magistrates' court apply for an order under this section in respect of a person who resides in his police area or who the chief officer believes is in, or is intending to come to, his police area if it appears to the chief officer that –

(a) the person is a qualifying offender, and

(b) the person has since the appropriate date acted in such a way as to give reasonable cause to believe that it is necessary for such an order to be made.

(6) An application under subsection (5) may be made to any magistrates' court whose commission area includes –

(a) any part of the applicant's police area, or

(b) any place where it is alleged that the person acted in a way mentioned in subsection (5)(b).

105 SOPOs: further provision as respects Scotland

(1) A chief constable may apply for an order under this section in respect of a person who he believes is in, or is intending to come to, the area of his police force if it appears to the chief constable that –

(a) the person has been convicted of, found not guilty by reason of insanity of or found to be under a disability and to have done the act charged against him in respect of –

   (i) an offence listed in paragraph 60 of Schedule 3; or

   (ii) before the commencement of this Part, an offence in Scotland other than is mentioned in paragraphs 36 to 59 of that Schedule if the chief constable considers that had the conviction or finding been after such commencement it is likely that a determination such as is mentioned in paragraph 60 would have been made in relation to the offence; and

(b) the person has since the conviction or finding acted in such a way as to give reasonable cause to believe that it is necessary for such an order to be made.

(2) An application under subsection (1) may be made by summary application to a sheriff within whose sheriffdom lies –

(a) any part of the area of the applicant's police force; or

(b) any place where it is alleged that the person acted in a way mentioned in subsection (1)(b).

(3) The sheriff may make the order where satisfied –

(a) that the person's behaviour since the conviction or finding makes it necessary to make such an order, for the purposes of protecting the public or any particular members of the public from serious sexual harm from the person; and

(b) where the application is by virtue of subsection (1)(a)(ii), that there was a significant sexual aspect to the person's behaviour in committing the offence.

(4) Subsection (3) of section 106 applies for the purposes of this section as it applies for the purposes of section 104 and subsections (2) and (3) of section 112 apply in relation to a summary application made by virtue of subsection (1) as they apply in relation to one made by virtue of subsection (1)(g) of that section.

106 Section 104: supplemental

(1) In this Part, 'sexual offences prevention order' means an order under section 104 or 105.

(2) Subsections (3) to (8) apply for the purposes of section 104.

(3) 'Protecting the public or any particular members of the public from serious sexual harm from the defendant' means protecting the public in the United Kingdom or any particular members of that public from serious physical or psychological harm, caused by the defendant committing one or more offences listed in Schedule 3.

(4) Acts, behaviour, convictions and findings include those occurring before the commencement of this Part.

(5) 'Qualifying offender' means a person within subsection (6) or (7).

(6) A person is within this subsection if, whether before or after the commencement of this Part, he –

    (a) has been convicted of an offence listed in Schedule 3 (other than at paragraph 60) or in Schedule 5,

    (b) has been found not guilty of such an offence by reason of insanity,

    (c) has been found to be under a disability and to have done the act charged against him in respect of such an offence, or

    (d) in England and Wales or Northern Ireland, has been cautioned in respect of such an offence.

(7) A person is within this subsection if, under the law in force in a country outside the United Kingdom and whether before or after the commencement of this Part –

    (a) he has been convicted of a relevant offence (whether or not he has been punished for it),

    (b) a court exercising jurisdiction under that law has made in respect of a relevant offence a finding equivalent to a finding that he is not guilty by reason of insanity,

    (c) such a court has made in respect of a relevant offence a finding equivalent to a finding that he is under a disability and did the act charged against him in respect of the offence, or

    (d) he has been cautioned in respect of a relevant offence.

(8) 'Appropriate date', in relation to a qualifying offender, means the date or (as the case may be) the first date on which he was convicted, found or cautioned as mentioned in subsection (6) or (7).

(9) In subsection (7), 'relevant offence' means an act which –

    (a) constituted an offence under the law in force in the country concerned, and

    (b) would have constituted an offence listed in Schedule 3 (other than at paragraph 60) or in Schedule 5 if it had been done in any part of the United Kingdom.

(10) An act punishable under the law in force in a country outside the United Kingdom constitutes an offence under that law for the purposes of subsection (9), however it is described in that law.

(11) Subject to subsection (12), on an application under section 104(5) the condition in subsection (9)(b) (where relevant) is to be taken as met unless, not later than rules of court may provide, the defendant serves on the applicant a notice –

    (a) stating that, on the facts as alleged with respect to the act concerned, the condition is not in his opinion met,

    (b) showing his grounds for that opinion, and

    (c) requiring the applicant to prove that the condition is met.

(12) The court, if it thinks fit, may permit the defendant to require the applicant to prove that the condition is met without service of a notice under subsection (11).

107 SOPOs: effect

(1) A sexual offences prevention order –

    (a) prohibits the defendant from doing anything described in the order, and

    (b) has effect for a fixed period (not less than 5 years) specified in the order or until further order.

(2) The only prohibitions that may be included in the order are those necessary for the purpose of protecting the public or any particular members of the public from serious sexual harm from the defendant.

(3) Where –

    (a) an order is made in respect of a defendant who was a relevant offender immediately before the making of the order, and

    (b) the defendant would (apart from this subsection) cease to be subject to the notification requirements of this Part while the order (as renewed from time to time) has effect, the defendant remains subject to the notification requirements.

(4) Where an order is made in respect of a defendant who was not a relevant offender immediately before the making of the order –

    (a) the order causes the defendant to become subject to the notification requirements of this Part from the making of the order until the order (as renewed from time to time) ceases to have effect, and

    (b) this Part applies to the defendant, subject to the modification set out in subsection (5).

(5) The 'relevant date' is the date of service of the order.

(6) Where a court makes a sexual offences prevention order in relation to a person already subject to such an order (whether made by that court or another), the earlier order ceases to have effect.

(7) Section 106(3) applies for the purposes of this section and section 108.

108 SOPOs: variations, renewals and discharges

(1) A person within subsection (2) may apply to the appropriate court for an order varying, renewing or discharging a sexual offences prevention order.

(2) The persons are –

    (a) the defendant;

    (b) the chief officer of police for the area in which the defendant resides;

    (c) a chief officer of police who believes that the defendant is in, or is intending to come to, his police area;

    (d) where the order was made on an application under section 104(5), the chief officer of police who made the application.

(3) An application under subsection (1) may be made –

    (a) where the appropriate court is the Crown Court, in accordance with rules of court;

    (b) in any other case, by complaint.

(4) Subject to subsections (5) and (6), on the application the court, after hearing the person making the application and (if they wish to be heard) the other persons mentioned in subsection (2), may make any order, varying, renewing or discharging the sexual offences prevention order, that the court considers appropriate.

(5) An order may be renewed, or varied so as to impose additional prohibitions on the defendant, only if it is necessary to do so for the purpose of protecting the public or any particular members of the public from serious sexual harm from the defendant (and any renewed or varied order may contain only such prohibitions as are necessary for this purpose).

(6) The court must not discharge an order before the end of 5 years beginning with the day on which the order was made, without the consent of the defendant and –

(a) where the application is made by a chief officer of police, that chief officer, or

(b) in any other case, the chief officer of police for the area in which the defendant resides.

(7) In this section 'the appropriate court' means –

(a) where the Crown Court or the Court of Appeal made the sexual offences prevention order, the Crown Court;

(b) where a magistrates' court made the order, that court, a magistrates' court for the area in which the defendant resides or, where the application is made by a chief officer of police, any magistrates' court whose commission area includes any part of the chief officer's police area;

(c) where a youth court made the order, that court, a youth court for the area in which the defendant resides or, where the application is made by a chief officer of police, any youth court whose commission area includes any part of the chief officer's police area.

(8) This section applies to orders under –

(a) section 5A of the Sex Offenders Act 1997 (c. 51) (restraining orders),

(b) section 2 or 20 of the Crime and Disorder Act 1998 (c. 37) (sex offender orders made in England and Wales or Scotland), and

(c) Article 6 of the Criminal Justice (Northern Ireland) Order 1998 (S.I. 1998/2839 (N.I. 20)) (sex offender orders made in Northern Ireland), as it applies to sexual offences prevention orders.

109 Interim SOPOs

(1) This section applies where an application under section 104(5) or 105(1) ('the main application') has not been determined.

(2) An application for an order under this section ('an interim sexual offences prevention order') –

(a) may be made by the complaint by which the main application is made, or

(b) if the main application has been made, may be made by the person who has made that application, by complaint to the court to which that application has been made.

(3) The court may, if it considers it just to do so, make an interim sexual offences prevention order, prohibiting the defendant from doing anything described in the order.

(4) Such an order –

(a) has effect only for a fixed period, specified in the order;

(b) ceases to have effect, if it has not already done so, on the determination of the main application.

(5) Section 107(3) to (5) apply to an interim sexual offences prevention order as if references to an order were references to such an order, and with the omission of 'as renewed from time to time' in both places.

(6) The applicant or the defendant may by complaint apply to the court that made the interim sexual offences prevention order for the order to be varied, renewed or discharged

(7) Subsection (6) applies to orders under –

(a) section 2A or 20(4)(a) of the Crime and Disorder Act 1998 (c. 37) (interim orders made in England and Wales or Scotland), and

(b) Article 6A of the Criminal Justice (Northern Ireland) Order 1998 (S.I. 1998/2839 (N.I. 20)) (interim orders made in Northern Ireland), as it applies to interim sexual offences prevention orders.

110 SOPOs and interim SOPOs: appeals

(1) A defendant may appeal against the making of a sexual offences prevention order –

    (a) where section 104(2) applied to him, as if the order were a sentence passed on him for the offence;

    (b) where section 104(3) (but not section 104(2)) applied to him, as if he had been convicted of the offence and the order were a sentence passed on him for that offence;

    (c) where the order was made on an application under section 104(5), to the Crown Court.

(2) A defendant may appeal to the Crown Court against the making of an interim sexual offences prevention order.

(3) A defendant may appeal against the making of an order under section 108, or the refusal to make such an order –

    (a) where the application for such an order was made to the Crown Court, to the Court of Appeal;

    (b) in any other case, to the Crown Court.

(4) On an appeal under subsection (1)(c), (2) or (3)(b), the Crown Court may make such orders as may be necessary to give effect to its determination of the appeal, and may also make such incidental or consequential orders as appear to it to be just.

(5) Any order made by the Crown Court on an appeal under subsection (1)(c) or (2) (other than an order directing that an application be re-heard by a magistrates' court) is for the purpose of section 108(7) or 109(7) (respectively) to be treated as if it were an order of the court from which the appeal was brought (and not an order of the Crown Court).

111 Appeals in relation to SOPOs and interim SOPOs: Scotland

In Scotland –

    (a) an interlocutor granting, refusing, varying, renewing or discharging a sexual offences prevention order or interim sexual offences prevention order is an appealable interlocutor; and

    (b) where an appeal is taken against an interlocutor so granting, varying or renewing such an order the order shall, without prejudice to any power of the court to vary or recall it, continue to have effect pending the disposal of the appeal.

112 Sections 104 and 106 to 109: Scotland

(1) Sections 104 and 106 to 109 apply to Scotland with the following modifications –

    (a) subsections (1)(b), (2) and (3) of section 104 shall be disregarded;

    (b) an application under subsection (5) of section 104 shall not be competent in respect of a person who is a qualifying offender by virtue only of a conviction or finding which relates to any offence listed at paragraphs 64 to 111 of Schedule 5;

    (c) references to a chief officer of police and to his police area are to be read, respectively, as references to a chief constable and to the area of his police force;

    (d) references to the defendant are to be read as references to the person in respect of whom the order is sought or has effect;

    (e) an application for a sexual offences prevention order or interim sexual offences prevention order is made by summary application to any sheriff within whose sheriffdom lies –

        (i)   any part of the area of the applicant's police force; or

        (ii) any place where it is alleged that the person in respect of whom the order is sought or has effect acted in a way mentioned in subsection (5)(b) of section 104, (references to 'the court' being construed accordingly);

(f) an application for the variation, renewal or discharge of either such order is made
     by summary application to the sheriff who made the order or to a sheriff –

     (i)   within whose sheriffdom the person subject to the order resides; or
     (ii) where the application is made by a chief constable, within whose sheriff-
           dom lies any part of the area of the applicant's police force, (references to
           'the court' being construed accordingly).

(2) A record of evidence shall be kept on any summary application made by virtue of
     subsection (1)(e) or (f) above.
(3) The clerk of the court by which, by virtue of that subsection, a sexual offences
     prevention order or interim sexual offences prevention order is made, varied, renewed
     or discharged shall cause a copy of, as the case may be –

     (a) the order as so made, varied or renewed; or
     (b) the interlocutor by which discharge is effected,

     to be given to the person named in the order or sent to him by registered post or by
     the recorded delivery service (an acknowledgement or certificate of delivery of a copy
     so sent, issued by the Post Office, being sufficient evidence of the delivery of the
     copy on the day specified in the acknowledgement or certificate).

113 Offence: breach of SOPO or interim SOPO

(1) A person commits an offence if, without reasonable excuse, he does anything which
     he is prohibited from doing by –
     (a) a sexual offences prevention order;
     (b) an interim sexual offences prevention order;
     (c) an order under section 5A of the Sex Offenders Act 1997 (c. 51) (restraining
          orders);
     (d) an order under section 2, 2A or 20 of the Crime and Disorder Act 1998 (c. 37)
          (sex offender orders and interim orders made in England and Wales and in
          Scotland);
     (e) an order under Article 6 or 6A of the Criminal Justice (Northern Ireland) Order
          1998 (S.I. 1998/2839 (N.I. 20)) (sex offender orders and interim orders made in
          Northern Ireland).
(2) A person guilty of an offence under this section is liable –
     (a) on summary conviction, to imprisonment for a term not exceeding 6 months or
          a fine not exceeding the statutory maximum or both;
     (b) on conviction on indictment, to imprisonment for a term not exceeding 5 years.
(3) Where a person is convicted of an offence under this section, it is not open to the
     court by or before which he is convicted to make, in respect of the offence, an order
     for conditional discharge or, in Scotland, a probation order.

Foreign travel orders

114 Foreign travel orders: applications and grounds

(1) A chief officer of police may by complaint to a magistrates' court apply for an order
     under this section (a 'foreign travel order') in respect of a person ('the defendant') who
     resides in his police area or who the chief officer believes is in or is intending to come
     to his police area if it appears to the chief officer that –
     (a) the defendant is a qualifying offender, and
     (b) the defendant has since the appropriate date acted in such a way as to give
          reasonable cause to believe that it is necessary for such an order to be made.
(2) An application under subsection (1) may be made to any magistrates' court whose
     commission area includes any part of the applicant's police area.

(3) On the application, the court may make a foreign travel order if it is satisfied that –

    (a) the defendant is a qualifying offender, and

    (b) the defendant's behaviour since the appropriate date makes it necessary to make such an order, for the purpose of protecting children generally or any child from serious sexual harm from the defendant outside the United Kingdom.

115 Section 114: interpretation

(1) Subsections (2) to (5) apply for the purposes of section 114.

(2) 'Protecting children generally or any child from serious sexual harm from the defendant outside the United Kingdom' means protecting persons under 16 generally or any particular person under 16 from serious physical or psychological harm caused by the defendant doing, outside the United Kingdom, anything which would constitute an offence listed in Schedule 3 if done in any part of the United Kingdom.

(3) Acts and behaviour include those occurring before the commencement of this Part.

(4) 'Qualifying offender' has the meaning given by section 116.

(5) 'Appropriate date', in relation to a qualifying offender, means the date or (as the case may be) the first date on which he was convicted, found or cautioned as mentioned in subsection (1) or (3) of section 116.

(6) In this section and section 116 as they apply to Northern Ireland, references to persons, or to a person, under 16 are to be read as references to persons, or to a person, under 17.

116 Section 114: qualifying offenders

(1) A person is a qualifying offender for the purposes of section 114 if, whether before or after the commencement of this Part, he –

    (a) has been convicted of an offence within subsection (2),

    (b) has been found not guilty of such an offence by reason of insanity,

    (c) has been found to be under a disability and to have done the act charged against him in respect of such an offence, or

    (d) in England and Wales or Northern Ireland, has been cautioned in respect of such an offence.

(2) The offences are –

    (a) an offence within any of paragraphs 13 to 15, 44 to 46, 77, 78 and 82 of Schedule 3;

    (b) an offence within paragraph 31 of that Schedule, if the intended offence was an offence against a person under 16;

    (c) an offence within paragraph 93 of that Schedule, if –

        (i) the corresponding civil offence is an offence within any of paragraphs 13 to 15 of that Schedule;

        (ii) the corresponding civil offence is an offence within paragraph 31 of that Schedule, and the intended offence was an offence against a person under 16; or

        (iii) the corresponding civil offence is an offence within any of paragraphs 1 to 12, 16 to 30 and 32 to 35 of that Schedule, and the victim of the offence was under 16 at the time of the offence.

    (d) an offence within any other paragraph of that Schedule, if the victim of the offence was under 16 at the time of the offence.

(3) A person is also a qualifying offender for the purposes of section 114 if, under the law in force in a country outside the United Kingdom and whether before or after the commencement of this Part –

    (a) he has been convicted of a relevant offence (whether or not he has been punished for it),

(b)   a court exercising jurisdiction under that law has made in respect of a relevant offence a finding equivalent to a finding that he is not guilty by reason of insanity,

(c)   such a court has made in respect of a relevant offence a finding equivalent to a finding that he is under a disability and did the act charged against him in respect of the offence, or

(d)   he has been cautioned in respect of a relevant offence.

(4)   In subsection (3), 'relevant offence' means an act which –

(a)   constituted an offence under the law in force in the country concerned, and

(b)   would have constituted an offence within subsection (2) if it had been done in any part of the United Kingdom.

(5)   An act punishable under the law in force in a country outside the United Kingdom constitutes an offence under that law for the purposes of subsection (4), however it is described in that law.

(6)   Subject to subsection (7), on an application under section 114 the condition in subsection (4)(b) above (where relevant) is to be taken as met unless, not later than rules of court may provide, the defendant serves on the applicant a notice –

(a)   stating that, on the facts as alleged with respect to the act concerned, the condition is not in his opinion met,

(b)   showing his grounds for that opinion, and

(c)   requiring the applicant to prove that the condition is met.

(7)   The court, if it thinks fit, may permit the defendant to require the applicant to prove that the condition is met without service of a notice under subsection (6).

117 Foreign travel orders: effect

(1)   A foreign travel order has effect for a fixed period of not more than 6 months, specified in the order.

(2)   The order prohibits the defendant from doing whichever of the following is specified in the order –

(a)   travelling to any country outside the United Kingdom named or described in the order,

(b)   travelling to any country outside the United Kingdom other than a country named or described in the order, or

(c)   travelling to any country outside the United Kingdom.

(3)   The only prohibitions that may be included in the order are those necessary for the purpose of protecting children generally or any child from serious sexual harm from the defendant outside the United Kingdom.

(4)   If at any time while an order (as renewed from time to time) has effect a defendant is not a relevant offender, the order causes him to be subject to the requirements imposed by regulations made under section 86(1) (and for these purposes the defendant is to be treated as if he were a relevant offender).

(5)   Where a court makes a foreign travel order in relation to a person already subject to such an order (whether made by that court or another), the earlier order ceases to have effect.

(6)   Section 115(2) applies for the purposes of this section and section 118.

118 Foreign travel orders: variations, renewals and discharges

(1)   A person within subsection (2) may by complaint to the appropriate court apply for an order varying, renewing or discharging a foreign travel order.

(2)   The persons are –

(a)   the defendant;

(b)   the chief officer of police on whose application the foreign travel order was made;

(c)   the chief officer of police for the area in which the defendant resides;

(d) a chief officer of police who believes that the defendant is in, or is intending to come to, his police area.

(3) Subject to subsection (4), on the application the court, after hearing the person making the application and (if they wish to be heard) the other persons mentioned in subsection (2), may make any order, varying, renewing or discharging the foreign travel order, that the court considers appropriate.

(4) An order may be renewed, or varied so as to impose additional prohibitions on the defendant, only if it is necessary to do so for the purpose of protecting children generally or any child from serious sexual harm from the defendant outside the United Kingdom (and any renewed or varied order may contain only such prohibitions as are necessary for this purpose).

(5) In this section 'the appropriate court' means –

(a) the court which made the foreign travel order;
(b) a magistrates' court for the area in which the defendant resides; or
(c) where the application is made by a chief officer of police, any magistrates' court whose commission area includes any part of his police area.

119 Foreign travel orders: appeals

(1) A defendant may appeal to the Crown Court –

(a) against the making of a foreign travel order;
(b) against the making of an order under section 118, or the refusal to make such an order.

(2) On any such appeal, the Crown Court may make such orders as may be necessary to give effect to its determination of the appeal, and may also make such incidental or consequential orders as appear to it to be just.

(3) Any order made by the Crown Court on an appeal under subsection (1)(a) (other than an order directing that an application be re-heard by a magistrates' court) is for the purposes of section 118(5) to be treated as if it were an order of the court from which the appeal was brought (and not an order of the Crown Court).

120 Appeals in relation to foreign travel orders: Scotland

In Scotland –

(a) an interlocutor granting, refusing, varying, renewing or discharging a foreign travel order is an appealable interlocutor; and
(b) where an appeal is taken against an interlocutor so granting, varying or renewing such an order the order shall, without prejudice to any power of the court to vary or recall it, continue to have effect pending the disposal of the appeal.

121 Sections 114 to 118: Scotland

(1) Sections 114 to 118 apply to Scotland with the following modifications –

(a) references to a chief officer of police and to his police area are to be read, respectively, as references to a chief constable and to the area of his police force;
(b) references to the defendant are to be read as references to the person in respect of whom the order is sought or has effect;
(c) an application for a foreign travel order is made by summary application to any sheriff within whose sheriffdom lies any part of the area of the applicant's police force (references to 'the court' being construed accordingly);
(d) for paragraphs (a) to (c) of section 118(5) there is substituted –

'(a) the sheriff who made the foreign travel order; or (b) where the application is made by a chief constable, a sheriff whose sheriffdom includes any part of the area of the applicant's police force.'

(2) A record of evidence shall be kept on any summary application made by virtue of sub-section (1)(c) above.

(3) The clerk of the court by which, by virtue of that subsection, a foreign travel order is made, varied, renewed or discharged shall cause a copy of, as the case may be –

(a) the order as so made, varied or renewed; or

(b) the interlocutor by which discharge is effected,

to be given to the person named in the order or sent to him by registered post or by the recorded delivery service (an acknowledgement or certificate of delivery of a copy so sent, issued by the Post Office, being sufficient evidence of the delivery of the copy on the day specified in the acknowledgement or certificate).

122 Offence: breach of foreign travel order

(1) A person commits an offence if, without reasonable excuse, he does anything which he is prohibited from doing by a foreign travel order.

(2) A person guilty of an offence under this section is liable –

(a) on summary conviction, to imprisonment for a term not exceeding 6 months or a fine not exceeding the statutory maximum or both;

(b) on conviction on indictment, to imprisonment for a term not exceeding 5 years.

(3) Where a person is convicted of an offence under this section, it is not open to the court by or before which he is convicted to make, in respect of the offence, an order for conditional discharge (or, in Scotland, a probation order).

Risk of sexual harm orders

123 Risk of sexual harm orders: applications, grounds and effect

(1) A chief officer of police may by complaint to a magistrates' court apply for an order under this section (a 'risk of sexual harm order') in respect of a person aged 18 or over ('the defendant') who resides in his police area or who the chief officer believes is in, or is intending to come to, his police area if it appears to the chief officer that –

(a) the defendant has on at least two occasions, whether before or after the commencement of this Part, done an act within subsection (3), and

(b) as a result of those acts, there is reasonable cause to believe that it is necessary for such an order to be made.

(2) An application under subsection (1) may be made to any magistrates' court whose commission area includes –

(a) any part of the applicant's police area, or

(b) any place where it is alleged that the defendant acted in a way mentioned in subsection (1)(a).

(3) The acts are –

(a) engaging in sexual activity involving a child or in the presence of a child;

(b) causing or inciting a child to watch a person engaging in sexual activity or to look at a moving or still image that is sexual;

(c) giving a child anything that relates to sexual activity or contains a reference to such activity;

(d) communicating with a child, where any part of the communication is sexual.

(4) On the application, the court may make a risk of sexual harm order if it is satisfied that –

(a) the defendant has on at least two occasions, whether before or after the commencement of this section, done an act within subsection (3); and

(b) it is necessary to make such an order, for the purpose of protecting children generally or any child from harm from the defendant.

(5) Such an order –

(a) prohibits the defendant from doing anything described in the order;

(b) has effect for a fixed period (not less than 2 years) specified in the order or until further order.

(6) The only prohibitions that may be imposed are those necessary for the purpose of protecting children generally or any child from harm from the defendant.

(7) Where a court makes a risk of sexual harm order in relation to a person already subject to such an order (whether made by that court or another), the earlier order ceases to have effect.

124 Section 123: interpretation

(1) Subsections (2) to (7) apply for the purposes of section 123.

(2) 'Protecting children generally or any child from harm from the defendant' means protecting children generally or any child from physical or psychological harm, caused by the defendant doing acts within section 123(3).

(3) 'Child' means a person under 16.

(4) 'Image' means an image produced by any means, whether of a real or imaginary subject.

(5) 'Sexual activity' means an activity that a reasonable person would, in all the circumstances but regardless of any person's purpose, consider to be sexual.

(6) A communication is sexual if –

(a) any part of it relates to sexual activity, or

(b) a reasonable person would, in all the circumstances but regardless of any person's purpose, consider that any part of the communication is sexual.

(7) An image is sexual if –

(a) any part of it relates to sexual activity, or

(b) a reasonable person would, in all the circumstances but regardless of any person's purpose, consider that any part of the image is sexual.

(8) In this section, as it applies to Northern Ireland, subsection (3) has effect with the substitution of '17' for '16'.

125 RSHOs: variations, renewals and discharges

(1) A person within subsection (2) may by complaint to the appropriate court apply for an order varying, renewing or discharging a risk of sexual harm order.

(2) The persons are –

(a) the defendant;

(b) the chief officer of police on whose application the risk of sexual harm order was made;

(c) the chief officer of police for the area in which the defendant resides;

(d) a chief officer of police who believes that the defendant is in, or is intending to come to, his police area.

(3) Subject to subsections (4) and (5), on the application the court, after hearing the person making the application and (if they wish to be heard) the other persons mentioned in subsection (2), may make any order, varying, renewing or discharging the risk of sexual harm order, that the court considers appropriate.

(4) An order may be renewed, or varied so as to impose additional prohibitions on the defendant, only if it is necessary to do so for the purpose of protecting children generally or any child from harm from the defendant (and any renewed or varied order may contain only such prohibitions as are necessary for this purpose).

(5) The court must not discharge an order before the end of 2 years beginning with the day on which the order was made, without the consent of the defendant and –

(a) where the application is made by a chief officer of police, that chief officer, or

(b) in any other case, the chief officer of police for the area in which the defendant resides.

(6) Section 124(2) applies for the purposes of this section.

(7) In this section 'the appropriate court' means –

(a) the court which made the risk of sexual harm order;

(b) a magistrates' court for the area in which the defendant resides; or

(c) where the application is made by a chief officer of police, any magistrates' court whose commission area includes any part of his police area.

126 Interim RSHOs

(1) This section applies where an application for a risk of sexual harm order ('the main application') has not been determined.

(2) An application for an order under this section ('an interim risk of sexual harm order') –

(a) may be made by the complaint by which the main application is made, or

(b) if the main application has been made, may be made by the person who has made that application, by complaint to the court to which that application has been made.

(3) The court may, if it considers it just to do so, make an interim risk of sexual harm order, prohibiting the defendant from doing anything described in the order.

(4) Such an order –

(a) has effect only for a fixed period, specified in the order;

(b) ceases to have effect, if it has not already done so, on the determination of the main application.

(5) The applicant or the defendant may by complaint apply to the court that made the interim risk of sexual harm order for the order to be varied, renewed or discharged.

127 RSHOs and interim RSHOs: appeals

(1) A defendant may appeal to the Crown Court –

(a) against the making of a risk of sexual harm order;

(b) against the making of an interim risk of sexual harm order; or

(c) against the making of an order under section 125, or the refusal to make such an order.

(2) On any such appeal, the Crown Court may make such orders as may be necessary to give effect to its determination of the appeal, and may also make such incidental or consequential orders as appear to it to be just.

(3) Any order made by the Crown Court on an appeal under subsection (1)(a) or (b) (other than an order directing that an application be re-heard by a magistrates' court) is for the purpose of section 125(7) or 126(5) (respectively) to be treated as if it were an order of the court from which the appeal was brought (and not an order of the Crown Court).

128 Offence: breach of RSHO or interim RSHO

(1) A person commits an offence if, without reasonable excuse, he does anything which he is prohibited from doing by –

(a) a risk of sexual harm order; or

(b) an interim risk of sexual harm order.

(2) A person guilty of an offence under this section is liable –

(a) on summary conviction, to imprisonment for a term not exceeding 6 months or a fine not exceeding the statutory maximum or both;

(b) on conviction on indictment, to imprisonment for a term not exceeding 5 years.

(3)   Where a person is convicted of an offence under this section, it is not open to the court by or before which he is convicted to make, in respect of the offence, an order for conditional discharge.

129 Effect of conviction etc. of an offence under section 128

(1)   This section applies to a person ('the defendant') who –

   (a)   is convicted of an offence under section 128;
   (b)   is found not guilty of such an offence by reason of insanity;
   (c)   is found to be under a disability and to have done the act charged against him in respect of such an offence; or
   (d)   is cautioned in respect of such an offence.

(2)   Where –

   (a)   a defendant was a relevant offender immediately before this section applied to him, and
   (b)   the defendant would (apart from this subsection) cease to be subject to the notification requirements of this Part while the relevant order (as renewed from time to time) has effect, the defendant remains subject to the notification requirements.

(3)   Where the defendant was not a relevant offender immediately before this section applied to him –

   (a)   this section causes the defendant to become subject to the notification requirements of this Part from the time the section first applies to him until the relevant order (as renewed from time to time) ceases to have effect, and
   (b)   this Part applies to the defendant, subject to the modification set out in subsection (4).

(4)   The 'relevant date' is the date on which this section first applies to the defendant.

(5)   In this section 'relevant order' means –

   (a)   where the conviction, finding or caution within subsection (1) is in respect of a breach of a risk of sexual harm order, that order;
   (b)   where the conviction, finding or caution within subsection (1) is in respect of a breach of an interim risk of sexual harm order, any risk of sexual harm order made on the hearing of the application to which the interim risk of sexual harm order relates or, if no such order is made, the interim risk of sexual harm order.

Power to amend Schedules 3 and 5

130 Power to amend Schedules 3 and 5

(1)   The Secretary of State may by order amend Schedule 3 or 5.

(2)   Subject to subsection (3), an amendment within subsection (4) does not apply to convictions, findings and cautions before the amendment takes effect.

(3)   For the purposes of sections 106 and 116, an amendment within subsection (4) applies to convictions, findings and cautions before as well as after the amendment takes effect.

(4)   An amendment is within this subsection if it –

   (a)   adds an offence,
   (b)   removes a threshold relating to an offence, or
   (c)   changes a threshold in such a way as to cause an offence committed by or against a person of a particular age or in certain circumstances, or resulting in a particular disposal, to be within a Schedule when it would not otherwise be.

General

131 Young offenders: application

This Part applies to –

(a) a period of detention which a person is liable to serve under a detention and training order, or a secure training order,

(b) a period for which a person is ordered to be detained in residential accommodation under section 44(1) of the Criminal Procedure (Scotland) Act 1995 (c. 46),

(c) a period of training in a training school, or of custody in a remand centre, which a person is liable to undergo or serve by virtue of an order under section 74(1)(a) or (e) of the Children and Young Persons Act (Northern Ireland) 1968 (c. 34 (N.I.)),

(d) a period for which a person is ordered to be detained in a juvenile justice centre under Article 39 of the Criminal Justice (Children) (Northern Ireland) Order 1998 (S.I. 1998/1504 (N.I. 9)),

(e) a period for which a person is ordered to be kept in secure accommodation under Article 44A of the Order referred to in paragraph (d),

(f) a sentence of detention in a young offender institution, a young offenders institution or a young offenders centre,

(g) a sentence under a custodial order within the meaning of section 71AA of, or paragraph 10(1) of Schedule 5A to, the Army Act 1955 (3 & 4 Eliz. 2 c. 18) or the Air Force Act 1955 (3 & 4 Eliz. 2 c. 19) or section 43AA of, or paragraph 10(1) of Schedule 4A to, the Naval Discipline Act 1957 (c. 53),

(h) a sentence of detention under section 90 or 91 of the Powers of Criminal Courts (Sentencing) Act 2000 (c. 6), section 208 of the Criminal Procedure (Scotland) Act 1995 or Article 45 of the Criminal Justice (Children) (Northern Ireland) Order 1998,

(i) a sentence of custody for life under section 93 or 94 of the Powers of Criminal Courts (Sentencing) Act 2000 (c. 6),

(j) a sentence of detention, or custody for life, under section 71A of the Army Act 1955 (3 & 4 Eliz. 2 c. 18) or the Air Force Act 1955 (3 & 4 Eliz. 2 c. 19) or section 43A of the Naval Discipline Act 1957 (c. 53),

as it applies to an equivalent sentence of imprisonment; and references in this Part to prison or imprisonment are to be interpreted accordingly.

132 Offences with thresholds

(1) This section applies to an offence which in Schedule 3 is listed subject to a condition relating to the way in which the defendant is dealt with in respect of the offence or (where a relevant finding has been made in respect of him) in respect of the finding (a 'sentencing condition').

(2) Where an offence is listed if either a sentencing condition or a condition of another description is met, this section applies only to the offence as listed subject to the sentencing condition.

(3) For the purposes of this Part (including in particular section 82(6)) –

(a) a person is to be regarded as convicted of an offence to which this section applies, or

(b) (as the case may be) a relevant finding in relation to such an offence is to be regarded as made, at the time when the sentencing condition is met.

(4) In the following subsections, references to a foreign offence are references to an act which –

(a) constituted an offence under the law in force in a country outside the United Kingdom ('the relevant foreign law'), and

(b) would have constituted an offence to which this section applies (but not an offence, listed in Schedule 3, to which this section does not apply) if it had been done in any part of the United Kingdom.

(5) In relation to a foreign offence, references to the corresponding UK offence are references to the offence (or any offence) to which subsection (3)(b) applies in the case of that foreign offence.

(6) For the purposes of this Part, a person is to be regarded as convicted under the relevant foreign law of a foreign offence at the time when he is, in respect of the offence, dealt with under that law in a way equivalent to that mentioned in Schedule 3 as it applies to the corresponding UK offence.

(7) Where in the case of any person a court exercising jurisdiction under the relevant foreign law makes in respect of a foreign offence a finding equivalent to a relevant finding, the court's finding is, for the purposes of this Part, to be regarded as made at the time when the person is, in respect of the finding, dealt with under that law in a way equivalent to that mentioned in Schedule 3 as it applies to the corresponding UK offence.

(8) Where (by virtue of an order under section 130 or otherwise) an offence is listed in Schedule 5 subject to a sentencing condition, this section applies to that offence as if references to Schedule 3 were references to Schedule 5.

(9) In this section, 'relevant finding', in relation to an offence, means –

(a) a finding that a person is not guilty of the offence by reason of insanity, or
(b) a finding that a person is under a disability and did the act charged against him in respect of the offence.

133 Part 2: general interpretation

(1) In this Part –

'admitted to a hospital' means admitted to a hospital under –

(a) section 37 of the Mental Health Act 1983 (c. 20), section 57(2)(a) or 58 of the Criminal Procedure (Scotland) Act 1995 (c. 46) or Article 44 or 50A(2) of the Mental Health (Northern Ireland) Order 1986 (S.I. 1986/595 (N.I. 4));

(b) Schedule 1 to the Criminal Procedure (Insanity and Unfitness to Plead) Act 1991 (c. 25); or

(c) regulations under subsection (3) of section 116B of the Army Act 1955 (3 & 4 Eliz. 2 c. 18) or the Air Force Act 1955 (3 & 4 Eliz. 2 c. 19) or section 63B of the Naval Discipline Act 1957 (c. 53);

'cautioned' means –

(a) cautioned by a police officer after the person concerned has admitted the offence, or

(b) reprimanded or warned within the meaning given by section 65 of the Crime and Disorder Act 1998 (c. 37), and 'caution' is to be interpreted accordingly;

'community order' means –

(a) a community order within the meaning of the Powers of Criminal Courts (Sentencing) Act 2000 (c. 6);

(b) a probation order or community service order under the Criminal Procedure (Scotland) Act 1995 or a supervised attendance order made in pursuance of section 235 of that Act;

(c) a community order within the meaning of the Criminal Justice (Northern Ireland) Order 1996 (S.I. 1996/3160 (N.I. 24)), a probation order under section 1 of the Probation Act (Northern Ireland) 1950 (c. 7 (N.I.)) or a community service order under Article 7 of the Treatment of Offenders (Northern Ireland) Order 1976 (S.I. 1976/226 (N.I. 40)); or

(d)   a community supervision order;

'community supervision order' means an order under paragraph 4 of Schedule 5A to the Army Act 1955 or the Air Force Act 1955 or Schedule 4A to the Naval Discipline Act 1957;

'country' includes territory;

'detained in a hospital' means detained in a hospital under –

(a)   Part 3 of the Mental Health Act 1983, section 71 of the Mental Health (Scotland) Act 1984 (c. 36), Part 6 of the Criminal Procedure (Scotland) Act 1995 or Part III of the Mental Health (Northern Ireland) Order 1986;

(b)   Schedule 1 to the Criminal Procedure (Insanity and Unfitness to Plead) Act 1991; or

(c)   regulations under subsection (3) of section 116B of the Army Act 1955 or the Air Force Act 1955 or section 63B of the Naval Discipline Act 1957;

'guardianship order' means a guardianship order under section 37 of the Mental Health Act 1983 (c. 20), section 58 of the Criminal Procedure (Scotland) Act 1995 (c. 46) or Article 44 of the Mental Health (Northern Ireland) Order 1986 (S.I. 1986/595 (N.I. 4));

'home address' has the meaning given by section 83(7);

'interim notification order' has the meaning given by section 100(2);

'interim risk of sexual harm order' has the meaning given by section 126(2);

'interim sexual offences prevention order' has the meaning given by section 109(2);

'local police area' has the meaning given by section 88(3);

'local probation board' has the same meaning as in the Criminal Justice and Court Services Act 2000 (c. 43);

'notification order' has the meaning given by section 97(1);

'notification period' has the meaning given by section 80(1);

'order for conditional discharge' has the meaning given by each of the following –

(a)   section 12(3) of the Powers of Criminal Courts (Sentencing) Act 2000 (c. 6);

(b)   Article 2(2) of the Criminal Justice (Northern Ireland) Order 1996 (S.I. 1996/3160 (N.I. 24));

(c)   paragraph 2(1) of Schedule 5A to the Army Act 1955 (3 & 4 Eliz. 2 c. 18);

(d)   paragraph 2(1) of Schedule 5A to the Air Force Act 1955 (3 & 4 Eliz. 2 c. 19);

(e)   paragraph 2(1) of Schedule 4A to the Naval Discipline Act 1957 (c. 53);

'parental responsibility' has the same meaning as in the Children Act 1989 (c. 41) or the Children (Northern Ireland) Order 1995 (S.I. 1995/ 755 (N.I. 2)), and 'parental responsibilities' has the same meaning as in Part 1 of the Children (Scotland) Act 1995 (c. 36);

'the period of conditional discharge' has the meaning given by each of the following –

(a)   section 12(3) of the Powers of Criminal Courts (Sentencing) Act 2000;

(b)   Article 2(2) of the Criminal Justice (Northern Ireland) Order 1996;

(c)   paragraph 2(1) of Schedule 5A to the Army Act 1955;

(d)   paragraph 2(1) of Schedule 5A to the Air Force Act 1955;

(e)   paragraph 2(1) of Schedule 4A to the Naval Discipline Act 1957;

'probation order' has the meaning given by section 228(1) of the Criminal Procedure (Scotland) Act 1995;

'probation period' has the meaning given by section 307(1) of the Criminal Procedure (Scotland) Act 1995;

'relevant date' has the meaning given by section 82(6) (save in the circumstances mentioned in sections 98, 100, 107, 109 and 129);

'relevant offender' has the meaning given by section 80(2);

'restriction order' means –

(a)   an order under section 41 of the Mental Health Act 1983, section 57(2)(b) or 59 of the Criminal Procedure (Scotland) Act 1995 or Article 47(1) of the Mental Health (Northern Ireland) Order 1986;

(b)   a direction under paragraph 2(1)(b) of Schedule 1 to the Criminal Procedure (Insanity and Unfitness to Plead) Act 1991 (c. 25) or Article 50A(3)(b) of the Mental Health (Northern Ireland) Order 1986 (S.I. 1986/595 (N.I. 4)); or

(c)   a direction under subsection (2) of section 116B of the Army Act 1955 (3 & 4 Eliz. 2 c. 18) or the Air Force Act 1955 (3 & 4 Eliz. 2 c. 19) or section 63B of the Naval Discipline Act 1957 (c. 53);

'risk of sexual harm order' has the meaning given by section 123(1);

'sexual offences prevention order' has the meaning given by section 106(1);

'supervision' means supervision in pursuance of an order made for the purpose or, in the case of a person released from prison on licence, in pursuance of a condition contained in his licence;

'term of service detention' means a term of detention awarded under section 71(1)(e) of the Army Act 1955 or the Air Force Act 1955 or section 43(1)(e) of the Naval Discipline Act 1957.

(2) Where under section 141 different days are appointed for the commencement of different provisions of this Part, a reference in any such provision to the commencement of this Part is to be read (subject to section 98(4)) as a reference to the commencement of that provision.

134 Conditional discharges and probation orders

(1) The following provisions do not apply for the purposes of this Part to a conviction for an offence in respect of which an order for conditional discharge or, in Scotland, a probation order is made –

(a)   section 14(1) of the Powers of Criminal Courts (Sentencing) Act 2000 (c. 6) (conviction with absolute or conditional discharge deemed not to be a conviction);

(b)   Article 6(1) of the Criminal Justice (Northern Ireland) Order 1996 (S.I. 1996/3160 (N.I. 24)) (conviction with absolute or conditional discharge deemed not to be a conviction);

(c)   section 247(1) of the Criminal Procedure (Scotland) Act 1995 (c. 46) (conviction with probation order or absolute discharge deemed not to be a conviction);

(d)   paragraph 5(1) of Schedule 5A to the Army Act 1955 (3 & 4 Eliz. 2 c. 18) or the Air Force Act 1955 (3 & 4 Eliz. 2 c. 19) or Schedule 4A to the Naval Discipline Act 1957 (c. 53) (conviction with absolute or conditional discharge or community supervision order deemed not to be a conviction).

(2) Subsection (1) applies only to convictions after the commencement of this Part.

(3) The provisions listed in subsection (1)(d) do not apply for the purposes of this Part to a conviction for an offence in respect of which a community supervision order is or has (before or after the commencement of this Part) been made.

135 Interpretation: mentally disordered offenders

(1) In this Part, a reference to a conviction includes a reference to a finding of a court in summary proceedings, where the court makes an order under an enactment within subsection (2), that the accused did the act charged; and similar references are to be interpreted accordingly.

(2) The enactments are –

(a)   section 37(3) of the Mental Health Act 1983 (c. 20);

(b)   section 58(3) of the Criminal Procedure (Scotland) Act 1995 (c. 46);

(c) Article 44(4) of the Mental Health (Northern Ireland) Order 1986 (S.I. 1986/595 (N.I. 4)).

(3) In this Part, a reference to a person being or having been found to be under a disability and to have done the act charged against him in respect of an offence includes a reference to his being or having been found –

(a) unfit to be tried for the offence;

(b) to be insane so that his trial for the offence cannot or could not proceed; or

(c) unfit to be tried and to have done the act charged against him in respect of the offence.

(4) In section 133 –

(a) a reference to admission or detention under Schedule 1 to the Criminal Procedure (Insanity and Unfitness to Plead) Act 1991 (c. 25), and the reference to a direction under paragraph 2(1)(b) of that Schedule, include respectively –

 (i) a reference to admission or detention under Schedule 1 to the Criminal Procedure (Insanity) Act 1964 (c. 84); and

 (ii) a reference to a restriction order treated as made by paragraph 2(1) of that Schedule;

(b) a reference to admission or detention under any provision of Part 6 of the Criminal Procedure (Scotland) Act 1995, and the reference to an order under section 57(2)(b) or 59 of that Act, include respectively –

 (i) a reference to admission or detention under section 174(3) or 376(2) of the Criminal Procedure (Scotland) Act 1975 (c. 21); and

 (ii) a reference to a restriction order made under section 178(1) or 379(1) of that Act;

(c) a reference to admission or detention under regulations made under subsection (3), and the reference to a direction under subsection (2), of section 116B of the Army Act 1955 (3 & 4 Eliz. 2 c. 18) or the Air Force Act 1955 (3 & 4 Eliz. 2 c. 19) or section 63B of the Naval Discipline Act 1957 (c. 53) include respectively –

 (i) a reference to admission or detention, and

 (ii) a reference to a direction, under section 46 of the Mental Health Act 1983, section 69 of the Mental Health (Scotland) Act 1984 (c. 36) or Article 52 of the Mental Health (Northern Ireland) Order 1986.

136 Part 2: Northern Ireland

(1) This Part applies to Northern Ireland with the following modifications.

(2) References to a chief officer of police are to be read as references to the Chief Constable of the Police Service of Northern Ireland.

(3) References to police areas are to be read as references to Northern Ireland.

(4) References to a complaint are to be read as references to a complaint under Part VIII of the Magistrates' Courts (Northern Ireland) Order 1981 (S.I. 1981/1675 (N.I. 26)) to a court of summary jurisdiction.

(5) Subject to subsection (6), references to a magistrates' court are to be read as references to a court of summary jurisdiction.

(6) References to a magistrates' court for the area in which the defendant resides are to be read as references to a court of summary jurisdiction for the petty sessions district which includes the area where the defendant resides.

(7) References to a youth court for the area in which the defendant resides are to be read as references to a youth court for the petty sessions district which includes the area where the defendant resides.

(8) References in sections 101, 110(1), (2), (3)(b), (4) and (5), 119 and 127 to the Crown Court are to be read as references to a county court.

(9) Any direction of the county court made under section 89(1) on an appeal under Article 143 of the Magistrates' Courts (Northern Ireland) Order 1981 (appeals in other cases) (other than one directing that an application be re-heard by a court of summary jurisdiction) is, for the purposes of section 90, to be treated as if it were made by the court from which the appeal was brought and not by the county court.

(10) Any order of the county court made on an appeal under Article 143 of the Magistrates' Courts (Northern Ireland) Order 1981 (other than one directing that an application be re-heard by a court of summary jurisdiction) is, for the purposes of section 108, to be treated as if it were an order of the court from which the appeal was brought and not an order of the county court.

PART 3   GENERAL

137 Service courts

(1) In this Act –

(a) a reference to a court order or a conviction or finding includes a reference to an order of or a conviction or finding by a service court,

(b) a reference to an offence includes a reference to an offence triable by a service court,

(c) 'proceedings' includes proceedings before a service court, and

(d) a reference to proceedings for an offence under this Act includes a reference to proceedings for the offence under section 70 of the Army Act 1955 (3 & 4 Eliz. 2 c. 18) or the Air Force Act 1955 (3 & 4 Eliz. 2 c. 19) or section 42 of the Naval Discipline Act 1957 (c. 53) for which the offence under this Act is the corresponding civil offence.

(2) In sections 92 and 104(1), 'court' includes a service court.

(3) Where the court making a sexual offences prevention order is a service court –

(a) sections 104(1)(a) and (4) to (6), 105, 109, 111 and 112 do not apply,

(b) in section 108, 'the appropriate court' means the Crown Court in England and Wales, and

(c) in section 110(3)(a), the references to the Crown Court and Court of Appeal are references to the Crown Court and Court of Appeal in England and Wales.

(4) In this section 'service court' means a court-martial or Standing Civilian Court.

138 Orders and regulations

(1) Any power to make orders or regulations conferred by this Act on the Secretary of State is exercisable by statutory instrument.

(2) A statutory instrument containing an order or regulations under section 21, 86 or 130 may not be made unless a draft of the instrument has been laid before, and approved by resolution of, each House of Parliament.

(3) Any other statutory instrument, except one containing an order under section 141, is to be subject to annulment in pursuance of a resolution of either House of Parliament.

139 Minor and consequential amendments

Schedule 6 contains minor and consequential amendments.

140 Repeals and revocations

The provisions listed in Schedule 7 are repealed or revoked to the extent specified.

141 Commencement

(1) This Act, except this section and sections 138, 142 and 143, comes into force in accordance with provision made by the Secretary of State by order.

(2) An order under subsection (1) may –

    (a) make different provision for different purposes;

    (b) include supplementary, incidental, saving or transitional provisions.

142 Extent, saving etc.

(1) Subject to section 137 and to subsections (2) to (4), this Act extends to England and Wales only.

(2) The following provisions also extend to Northern Ireland –

    (a) sections 15 to 24, 46 to 54, 57 to 60, 66 to 72, 78 and 79,

    (b) Schedule 2,

    (c) Part 2, and

    (d) sections 138, 141, 143 and this section.

(3) The following provisions also extend to Scotland –

    (a) Part 2 except sections 93 and 123 to 129 and Schedule 4, and

    (b) sections 138, 141, 143 and this section.

(4) Unless otherwise provided, any amendment, repeal or revocation made by this Act has the same extent as the provision to which it relates.

(5) Section 16B of the Criminal Law (Consolidation) (Scotland) Act 1995 (c. 39) continues to have effect despite the repeal by this Act of section 8 of the Sex Offenders Act 1997 (c. 51).

(6) For the purposes of the Scotland Act 1998 (c. 46), this Act is to be taken to be a pre–commencement enactment.

143 Short title

This Act may be cited as the Sexual Offences Act 2003.

SCHEDULES

SCHEDULE 1   EXTENSION OF GENDER-SPECIFIC PROSTITUTION OFFENCES   Section 56

Sexual Offences Act 1956 (c. 69)

1   In section 36 of the Sexual Offences Act 1956 (permitting premises to be used for prostitution), at the end insert '(whether any prostitute involved is male or female)'.

Street Offences Act 1959 (c. 57)

2   In section 1(1) of the Street Offences Act 1959 (loitering or soliciting for purposes of prostitution), after 'prostitute' insert '(whether male or female)'.

3   (1)   Section 2 of that Act (application to court by woman cautioned for loitering or soliciting) is amended as follows.

(2)   In the heading of the section, for 'woman' substitute 'person'.

(3)   In subsection (1) –

    (a)   for 'woman' substitute 'person',
    (b)   for 'her' in each place substitute 'his', and
    (c)   for 'she' in each place substitute 'he'.

(4)   In subsection (2) –

    (a)   for 'woman' in the first place substitute 'person',
    (b)   for 'he' substitute 'the chief officer', and
    (c)   for 'woman' in the second place substitute 'person cautioned'.

(5)   In subsection (3), for 'woman' substitute 'person cautioned'.

Sexual Offences Act 1985 (c. 44)

4   (1)   The Sexual Offences Act 1985 is amended as follows.

(2)   For the heading 'Soliciting of women by men' substitute 'Soliciting for the purpose of prostitution'.

(3)   In section 1 (kerb-crawling) –

    (a)   for 'man' substitute 'person',
    (b)   for 'a woman' substitute 'another person',
    (c)   for 'women' in each place substitute 'persons', and
    (d)   for 'the woman' substitute 'the person'.

(4)   In section 2 (persistent soliciting of women for the purpose of prostitution) –

    (a)   for the heading of the section substitute 'Persistent soliciting',
    (b)   for 'man' substitute 'person',
    (c)   for 'a woman' substitute 'another person', and
    (d)   for 'women' substitute 'persons'.

(5)   In section 4 (interpretation) –

    (a)   omit subsections (2) and (3),
    (b)   for 'man' substitute 'person',
    (c)   for 'a woman' substitute 'another person',
    (d)   for 'her' in the first place substitute 'that person', and
    (e)   for 'her' in the second place substitute 'that person's'.

SCHEDULE 2   SEXUAL OFFENCES TO WHICH SECTION 72 APPLIES

Section 72(7)

England and Wales

1   In relation to England and Wales, the following are sexual offences to which section 72 applies –

(a)   an offence under any of sections 5 to 15 (offences against children under 13 or under 16);

(b)   an offence under any of sections 1 to 4, 16 to 41, 47 to 50 and 61 where the victim of the offence was under 16 at the time of the offence;

(c)   an offence under section 62 or 63 where the intended offence was an offence against a person under 16;

(d)   an offence under –

(i)   section 1 of the Protection of Children Act 1978 (c. 37) (indecent photographs of children), or

(ii)   section 160 of the Criminal Justice Act 1988 (c. 33) (possession of indecent photograph of child), in relation to a photograph or pseudo-photograph showing a child under 16.

Northern Ireland

2   (1)   In relation to Northern Ireland, the following are sexual offences to which section 72 applies –

(a)   rape;

(b)   an offence under –

(i)   section 52 of the Offences against the Person Act 1861 (c. 100) (indecent assault upon a female person), or

(ii)   section 53 or 54 of that Act (abduction of woman);

(c)   an offence under –

(i)   section 2 of the Criminal Law Amendment Act 1885 (c. 69) (procuration of girl under 21),

(ii)   section 3 of that Act (procuring defilement of woman using threats, etc.),

(iii)   section 4 of that Act of unlawful carnal knowledge of a girl under 14,

(iv)   section 5 of that Act of unlawful carnal knowledge of a girl under 17, or

(v)   section 7 of that Act (abduction of girl under 18);

(d)   an offence under –

(i)   section 1 of the Punishment of Incest Act 1908 (c. 45) (incest by males), or

(ii)   section 2 of that Act (incest by females);

(e)   an offence under –

(i)   section 21 of the Children and Young Persons Act (Northern Ireland) 1968 (c. 34 (N.I.)) (causing or encouraging seduction, etc. of girl under 17), or

(ii)   section 22 of that Act (indecent conduct towards a child);

(f)   an offence under Article 3 of the Protection of Children (Northern Ireland) Order 1978 (S.I. 1978/1047 (N.I. 17)) (indecent photographs of children);

(g) an offence under Article 9 of the Criminal Justice (Northern Ireland) Order 1980 (S.I. 1980/704 (N.I. 6)) (inciting girl under 16 to have incestuous sexual intercourse);

(h) an offence under Article 15 of the Criminal Justice (Evidence, Etc.) (Northern Ireland) Order 1988 (S.I. 1988/1847 (N.I. 17)) (indecent photographs of children);

(i) an offence under –

   (i) Article 19 of the Criminal Justice (Northern Ireland) Order 2003 (S.I. 2003/1247 (N.I. 13)) (buggery),

   (ii) Article 20 of that Order (assault with intent to commit buggery), or

   (iii) Article 21 of that Order (indecent assault on a male);

(j) an offence under –

   (i) section 15 of this Act (meeting a child following sexual grooming etc.), or

   (ii) any of sections 16 to 19 or 47 to 50 of this Act (abuse of trust, prostitution, child pornography).

(2) Sub-paragraph (1), apart from paragraphs (f) and (h), does not apply where the victim of the offence was 17 or over at the time of the offence.

General

3   A reference in paragraph 1 or 2(1) to an offence includes –

(a) a reference to an attempt, conspiracy or incitement to commit that offence; and

(b) a reference to aiding and abetting, counselling or procuring the commission of that offence.

SCHEDULE 3   SEXUAL OFFENCES FOR PURPOSES OF PART 2

Section 80

England and Wales

1   An offence under section 1 of the Sexual Offences Act 1956 (c. 69) (rape).

2   An offence under section 5 of that Act (intercourse with girl under 13).

3   An offence under section 6 of that Act (intercourse with girl under 16), if the offender was 20 or over.

4   An offence under section 10 of that Act (incest by a man), if the victim or (as the case may be) other party was under 18.

5   An offence under section 12 of that Act (buggery) if –

(a) the offender was 20 or over, and

(b) the victim or (as the case may be) other party was under 18.

6   An offence under section 13 of that Act (indecency between men) if –

(a) the offender was 20 or over, and

(b) the victim or (as the case may be) other party was under 18.

7   An offence under section 14 of that Act (indecent assault on a woman) if –

(a) the victim or (as the case may be) other party was under 18, or

(b) the offender, in respect of the offence or finding, is or has been –

   (i) sentenced to imprisonment for a term of at least 30 months; or

   (ii) admitted to a hospital subject to a restriction order.

8   An offence under section 15 of that Act (indecent assault on a man) if –

   (a)   the victim or (as the case may be) other party was under 18, or

   (b)   the offender, in respect of the offence or finding, is or has been –

      (i)   sentenced to imprisonment for a term of at least 30 months; or

      (ii)   admitted to a hospital subject to a restriction order.

9   An offence under section 16 of that Act (assault with intent to commit buggery), if the victim or (as the case may be) other party was under 18.

10   An offence under section 28 of that Act (causing or encouraging the prostitution of, intercourse with or indecent assault on girl under 16).

11   An offence under section 1 of the Indecency with Children Act 1960 (c. 33) (indecent conduct towards young child).

12   An offence under section 54 of the Criminal Law Act 1977 (c. 45) (inciting girl under 16 to have incestuous sexual intercourse).

13   An offence under section 1 of the Protection of Children Act 1978 (c. 37) (indecent photographs of children), if the indecent photographs or pseudo-photographs showed persons under 16 and –

   (a)   the conviction, finding or caution was before the commencement of this Part, or

   (b)   the offender –

      (i)   was 18 or over, or

      (ii)   is sentenced in respect of the offence to imprisonment for a term of at least 12 months.

14   An offence under section 170 of the Customs and Excise Management Act 1979 (c. 2) (penalty for fraudulent evasion of duty etc.) in relation to goods prohibited to be imported under section 42 of the Customs Consolidation Act 1876 (c. 36) (indecent or obscene articles), if the prohibited goods included indecent photographs of persons under 16 and –

   (a)   the conviction, finding or caution was before the commencement of this Part, or

   (b)   the offender –

      (i)   was 18 or over, or

      (ii)   is sentenced in respect of the offence to imprisonment for a term of at least 12 months.

15   An offence under section 160 of the Criminal Justice Act 1988 (c. 33) (possession of indecent photograph of a child), if the indecent photographs or pseudo-photographs showed persons under 16 and –

   (a)   the conviction, finding or caution was before the commencement of this Part, or

   (b)   the offender –

      (i)   was 18 or over, or

      (ii)   is sentenced in respect of the offence to imprisonment for a term of at least 12 months.

16   An offence under section 3 of the Sexual Offences (Amendment) Act 2000 (c. 44) (abuse of position of trust), if the offender was 20 or over.

17   An offence under section 1 or 2 of this Act (rape, assault by penetration).

18   An offence under section 3 of this Act (sexual assault) if –

   (a)   where the offender was under 18, he is or has been sentenced, in respect of the offence, to imprisonment for a term of at least 12 months;

   (b)   in any other case –

      (i)   the victim was under 18, or

      (ii)   the offender, in respect of the offence or finding, is or has been –

         (a)   sentenced to a term of imprisonment,

         (b)   detained in a hospital, or

         (c)   made the subject of a community sentence of at least 12 months.

19   An offence under any of sections 4 to 6 of this Act (causing sexual activity without consent, rape of a child under 13, assault of a child under 13 by penetration).

20   An offence under section 7 of this Act (sexual assault of a child under 13) if the offender –

    (a)   was 18 or over, or
    (b)   is or has been sentenced in respect of the offence to imprisonment for a term of at least 12 months.

21   An offence under any of sections 8 to 12 of this Act (causing or inciting a child under 13 to engage in sexual activity, child sex offences committed by adults).

22   An offence under section 13 of this Act (child sex offences committed by children or young persons), if the offender is or has been sentenced, in respect of the offence, to imprisonment for a term of at least 12 months.

23   An offence under section 14 of this Act (arranging or facilitating the commission of a child sex offence) if the offender –

    (a)   was 18 or over, or
    (b)   is or has been sentenced, in respect of the offence, to imprisonment for a term of at least 12 months.

24   An offence under section 15 of this Act (meeting a child following sexual grooming etc).

25   An offence under any of sections 16 to 19 of this Act (abuse of a position of trust) if the offender, in respect of the offence, is or has been –

    (a)   sentenced to a term of imprisonment,
    (b)   detained in a hospital, or
    (c)   made the subject of a community sentence of at least 12 months.

26   An offence under section 25 or 26 of this Act (familial child sex offences) if the offender –

    (a)   was 18 or over, or
    (b)   is or has been sentenced in respect of the offence to imprisonment for a term of at least 12 months.

27   An offence under any of sections 30 to 37 of this Act (offences against persons with a mental disorder impeding choice, inducements etc. to persons with mental disorder).

28   An offence under any of sections 38 to 41 of this Act (care workers for persons with mental disorder) if –

    (a)   where the offender was under 18, he is or has been sentenced in respect of the offence to imprisonment for a term of at least 12 months;
    (b)   in any other case, the offender, in respect of the offence or finding, is or has been –

        (i)   sentenced to a term of imprisonment,
        (ii)   detained in a hospital, or
        (iii)   made the subject of a community sentence of at least 12 months.

29 An offence under section 47 of this Act (paying for sexual services of a child) if the victim or (as the case may be) other party was under 16, and the offender –

    (a)   was 18 or over, or
    (b)   is or has been sentenced in respect of the offence to imprisonment for a term of at least 12 months.

30   An offence under section 61 of this Act (administering a substance with intent).

31   An offence under section 62 or 63 of this Act (committing an offence or trespassing, with intent to commit a sexual offence) if –

    (a)   where the offender was under 18, he is or has been sentenced in respect of the offence to imprisonment for a term of at least 12 months;
    (b)   in any other case –

      (i)   the intended offence was an offence against a person under 18, or

     (ii)   the offender, in respect of the offence or finding, is or has been –

         (a)   sentenced to a term of imprisonment,

         (b)   detained in a hospital, or

         (c)   made the subject of a community sentence of at least 12 months.

32   An offence under section 64 or 65 of this Act (sex with an adult relative) if –

   (a) where the offender was under 18, he is or has been sentenced in respect of the offence to imprisonment for a term of at least 12 months;

   (b) in any other case, the offender, in respect of the offence or finding, is or has been –

      (i)   sentenced to a term of imprisonment, or

     (ii)   detained in a hospital.

33   An offence under section 66 of this Act (exposure) if –

   (a) where the offender was under 18, he is or has been sentenced in respect of the offence to imprisonment for a term of at least 12 months;

   (b) in any other case –

      (i)   the victim was under 18, or

     (ii)   the offender, in respect of the offence or finding, is or has been –

         (a)   sentenced to a term of imprisonment,

         (b)   detained in a hospital, or

         (c)   made the subject of a community sentence of at least 12 months.

34   An offence under section 67 of this Act (voyeurism) if –

   (a) where the offender was under 18, he is or has been sentenced in respect of the offence to imprisonment for a term of at least 12 months;

   (b) in any other case –

      (i)   the victim was under 18, or

     (ii)   the offender, in respect of the offence or finding, is or has been –

         (a)   sentenced to a term of imprisonment,

         (b)   detained in a hospital, or

         (c)   made the subject of a community sentence of at least 12 months.

35   An offence under section 69 or 70 of this Act (intercourse with an animal, sexual penetration of a corpse) if –

   (a) where the offender was under 18, he is or has been sentenced in respect of the offence to imprisonment for a term of at least 12 months;

   (b) in any other case, the offender, in respect of the offence or finding, is or has been –

      (i)   sentenced to a term of imprisonment, or

     (ii)   detained in a hospital.

Scotland

36   Rape.

37   Clandestine injury to women.

38   Abduction of woman or girl with intent to rape.

39   Assault with intent to rape or ravish.

40   Indecent assault.

41   Lewd, indecent or libidinous behaviour or practices.

42   Shameless indecency, if a person (other than the offender) involved in the offence was under 18.

43   Sodomy, unless every person involved in the offence was 16 or over and was a willing participant.

44   An offence under section 170 of the Customs and Excise Management Act 1979 (c. 2) (penalty for fraudulent evasion of duty etc.) in relation to goods prohibited to be imported under section 42 of the Customs Consolidation Act 1876 (c. 36) (indecent or obscene articles), if the prohibited goods included indecent photographs of persons under 16.

45   An offence under section 52 of the Civic Government (Scotland) Act 1982 (c. 45) (taking and distribution of indecent images of children).

46   An offence under section 52A of that Act (possession of indecent images of children).

47   An offence under section 106 of the Mental Health (Scotland) Act 1984 (c. 36) (protection of mentally handicapped females).

48   An offence under section 107 of that Act (protection of patients).

49   An offence under section 1 of the Criminal Law (Consolidation) (Scotland) Act 1995 (c. 39) (incest), if a person (other than the offender) involved in the offence was under 18.

50   An offence under section 2 of that Act (intercourse with a stepchild), if a person (other than the offender) involved in the offence was under 18.

51   An offence under section 3 of that Act (intercourse with child under 16 by person in position of trust).

52   An offence under section 5 of that Act (unlawful intercourse with girl under 16), save in the case of an offence in contravention of subsection (3) of that section where the offender was under 20.

53   An offence under section 6 of that Act (indecent behaviour towards girl between 12 and 16).

54   An offence under section 8 of that Act (abduction of girl under 18 for purposes of unlawful intercourse).

55   An offence under section 10 of that Act (person having parental responsibilities causing or encouraging sexual activity in relation to a girl under 16).

56   An offence under section 13(5) of that Act (homosexual offences) unless every person involved (whether in the offence or in the homosexual act) was 16 or over and was a willing participant.

57   An offence under section 3 of the Sexual Offences (Amendment) Act 2000 (c. 44) (abuse of position of trust), where the offender was 20 or over.

58   An offence under section 311(1) of the Mental Health (Care and Treatment) (Scotland) Act 2003 (asp 13) (non-consensual sexual acts).

59   An offence under section 313(1) of that Act (persons providing care services: sexual offences).

60   An offence in Scotland other than is mentioned in paragraphs 36 to 59 if the court, in imposing sentence or otherwise disposing of the case, determines for the purposes of this paragraph that there was a significant sexual aspect to the offender's behaviour in committing the offence.

Northern Ireland

61   Rape.

62   An offence under section 52 of the Offences against the Person Act 1861 (c. 100) (indecent assault upon a female) if –

(a)   where the offender was under 18, he is or has been sentenced, in respect of the offence, to imprisonment for a term of at least 12 months;

(b)   in any other case –

(i)   the victim was under 18, or

(ii)   the offender, in respect of the offence or finding, is or has been –

    (a)   sentenced to a term of imprisonment,

    (b)   detained in a hospital, or

    (c)   made the subject of a community sentence of at least 12 months.

63   An offence under section 53 or 54 of that Act (abduction of woman by force for unlawful sexual intercourse) if the offender –

    (a)   was 18 or over, or

    (b)   is or has been sentenced in respect of the offence to imprisonment for a term of at least 12 months.

64   An offence under section 61 of that Act (buggery) if –

    (a)   the offender was 20 or over, and

    (b)   the victim or (as the case may be) other party was under 18.

65   An offence under section 62 of that Act of assault with intent to commit buggery if the victim or (as the case may be) other party was under 18, and the offender –

    (a)   was 18 or over, or

    (b)   is or has been sentenced in respect of the offence to imprisonment for a term of at least 12 months.

66   An offence under section 62 of that Act of indecent assault upon a male person if –

    (a)   where the offender was under 18, he is or has been sentenced, in respect of the offence, to imprisonment for a term of at least 12 months;

    (b)   in any other case –

        (i)   the victim was under 18, or

        (ii) the offender, in respect of the offence or finding, is or has been –

            (a)   sentenced to a term of imprisonment,

            (b)   detained in a hospital, or

            (c)   made the subject of a community sentence of at least 12 months.

67   An offence under section 2 of the Criminal Law Amendment Act 1885 (c. 69) (procuration) if the offender –

    (a)   was 18 or over, or

    (b)   is or has been sentenced in respect of the offence to imprisonment for a term of at least 12 months.

68   An offence under section 3 of that Act (procuring defilement of woman by threats or fraud, etc.) if the offender –

    (a)   was 18 or over, or

    (b)   is or has been sentenced in respect of the offence to imprisonment for a term of at least 12 months.

69   An offence under section 4 of that Act of unlawful carnal knowledge of a girl under 14 if the offender –

    (a)   was 18 or over, or

    (b)   is or has been sentenced in respect of the offence to imprisonment for a term of at least 12 months.

70   An offence under section 5 of that Act of unlawful carnal knowledge of a girl under 17, if the offender was 20 or over.

71   An offence under section 7 of that Act (abduction of girl under 18) if the offender –

    (a)   was 18 or over, or

    (b)   is or has been sentenced in respect of the offence to imprisonment for a term of at least 12 months.

72   An offence under section 11 of that Act (homosexual offences) if –

    (a)   the offender was 20 or over, and

    (b)   the victim or (as the case may be) other party was under 18.

73   An offence under section 1 of the Punishment of Incest Act 1908 (c. 45) (incest by males), if –

  (a)   where the offender was under 18, he is or has been sentenced in respect of the offence to imprisonment for a term of at least 12 months;

  (b)   in any other case –

    (i)   the victim or (as the case may be) other party was under 18, or

    (ii)   the offender, in respect of the offence or finding, is or has been –

      (a)   sentenced to a term of imprisonment, or

      (b)   detained in a hospital.

74   An offence under section 2 of that Act (incest by females), if –

  (a)   where the offender was under 18, he is or has been sentenced in respect of the offence to imprisonment for a term of at least 12 months;

  (b)   in any other case –

    (i)   the victim or (as the case may be) other party was under 18, or

    (ii)   the offender, in respect of the offence or finding, is or has been –

      (a)   sentenced to a term of imprisonment, or

      (b)   detained in a hospital.

75   An offence under section 21 of the Children and Young Persons Act (Northern Ireland) 1968 (c. 34) (causing or encouraging seduction or prostitution of a girl under 17) if the offender –

  (a)   was 18 or over, or

  (b)   is or has been sentenced in respect of the offence to imprisonment for a term of at least 12 months.

76   An offence under section 22 of that Act (indecent conduct towards a child) if the offender –

  (a)   was 18 or over, or

  (b)   is or has been sentenced in respect of the offence to imprisonment for a term of at least 12 months.

77   An offence under Article 3 of the Protection of Children (Northern Ireland) Order 1978 (S.I. 1978/1047 (N.I. 17)) (indecent photographs of children) if the offender –

  (a)   was 18 or over, or

  (b)   is or has been sentenced in respect of the offence to imprisonment for a term of at least 12 months.

78   An offence under section 170 of the Customs and Excise Management Act 1979 (c. 2) (penalty for fraudulent evasion of duty etc.) in relation to goods prohibited to be imported under section 42 of the Customs Consolidation Act 1876 (c. 36) (indecent or obscene articles), if the prohibited goods included indecent photographs of persons under 16, and the offender –

  (a)   was 18 or over, or

  (b)   is or has been sentenced in respect of the offence to imprisonment for a term of at least 12 months.

79   An offence under Article 9 of the Criminal Justice (Northern Ireland) Order 1980 (S.I. 1980/704 (N.I. 6)) (inciting girl under 16 to have incestuous sexual intercourse) if the offender –

  (a)   was 18 or over, or

  (b)   is or has been sentenced in respect of the offence to imprisonment for a term of at least 12 months.

80   An offence under Article 122 of the Mental Health (Northern Ireland) Order 1986 (S.I. 1986/595 (N.I. 4)) (offences against women suffering from severe mental handicap).

81   An offence under Article 123 of that Order (offences against patients) if –

   (a)   where the offender was under 18, he is or has been sentenced in respect of the offence to imprisonment for a term of at least 12 months;

   (b)   in any other case, the offender, in respect of the offence or finding, is or has been –

      (i)   sentenced to a term of imprisonment,

      (ii)   detained in a hospital, or

      (iii)   made the subject of a community sentence of at least 12 months.

82   An offence under Article 15 of the Criminal Justice (Evidence, etc.) (Northern Ireland) Order 1988 (S.I. 1988/1847 (N.I. 17) (possession of indecent photographs of children) if the offender –

   (a)   was 18 or over, or

   (b)   is or has been sentenced in respect of the offence to imprisonment for a term of at least 12 months.

83   An offence under section 3 of the Sexual Offences (Amendment) Act 2000 (c. 44) (abuse of position of trust), if the offender, in respect of the offence or finding, is or has been –

   (a)   sentenced to a term of imprisonment,

   (b)   detained in a hospital, or

   (c)   made the subject of a community sentence of at least 12 months.

84   An offence under Article 19 of the Criminal Justice (Northern Ireland) Order 2003 (S.I. 2003/1247 (N.I. 13)) (buggery) if –

   (a)   the offender was 20 or over, and

   (b)   the victim or (as the case may be) other party was under 17.

85   An offence under Article 20 of that Order (assault with intent to commit buggery) if the victim was under 18 and the offender –

   (a)   was 18 or over, or

   (b)   is or has been sentenced in respect of the offence to imprisonment for a term of at least 12 months.

86   An offence under Article 21 of that Order (indecent assault upon a male) if –

   (a)   where the offender was under 18, he is or has been sentenced, in respect of the offence, to imprisonment for a term of at least 12 months;

   (b)   in any other case –

      (i)   the victim was under 18, or

      (ii)   the offender, in respect of the offence or finding, is or has been –

         (a)   sentenced to a term of imprisonment,

         (b)   detained in a hospital, or

         (c)   made the subject of a community sentence of at least 12 months.

87   An offence under section 15 of this Act (meeting a child following sexual grooming etc.).

88   An offence under any of sections 16 to 19 of this Act (abuse of trust) if the offender, in respect of the offence or finding, is or has been –

   (a)   sentenced to a term of imprisonment,

   (b)   detained in a hospital, or

   (c)   made the subject of a community sentence of at least 12 months.

89   An offence under section 47 of this Act (paying for sexual services of a child) if the victim or (as the case may be) other party was under 17 and the offender –

   (a)   was 18 or over, or

   (b)   is or has been sentenced in respect of the offence to a term of imprisonment of at least 12 months.

90   An offence under section 66 of this Act (exposure) if –

(a)   where the offender was under 18, he is or has been sentenced in respect of the offence to imprisonment for a term of at least 12 months;

(b)   in any other case –

    (i)   the victim was under 18, or

    (ii)   the offender, in respect of the offence or finding, is or has been –

        (a)   sentenced to a term of imprisonment,

        (b)   detained in a hospital, or

        (c)   made the subject of a community sentence of at least 12 months.

91   An offence under section 67 of this Act (voyeurism) if –

(a)   where the offender was under 18, he is or has been sentenced in respect of the offence to imprisonment for a term of at least 12 months;

(b)   in any other case –

    (i)   the victim was under 18, or

    (ii)   the offender, in respect of the offence or finding, is or has been –

        (a)   sentenced to a term of imprisonment,

        (b)   detained in a hospital, or

        (c)   made the subject of a community sentence of at least 12 months.

92   An offence under section 69 or 70 of this Act (intercourse with an animal, sexual penetration of a corpse) if –

(a)   where the offender was under 18, he is or has been sentenced in respect of the offence to imprisonment for a term of at least 12 months;

(b)   in any other case, the offender, in respect of the offence or finding, is or has been –

    (i)   sentenced to a term of imprisonment, or

    (ii)   detained in a hospital.

Service offences

93   (1)   An offence under –

(a)   section 70 of the Army Act 1955 (3 & 4 Eliz. 2 c. 18),

(b)   section 70 of the Air Force Act 1955 (3 & 4 Eliz. 2 c. 19), or

(c)   section 42 of the Naval Discipline Act 1957 (c. 53), of which the corresponding civil offence (within the meaning of that Act) is an offence listed in any of paragraphs 1 to 35.

(2)   A reference in any of those paragraphs to being made the subject of a community sentence of at least 12 months is to be read, in relation to an offence under an enactment referred to in sub-paragraph (1), as a reference to being sentenced to a term of service detention of at least 112 days.

General

94   A reference in a preceding paragraph to an offence includes –

(a)   a reference to an attempt, conspiracy or incitement to commit that offence, and

(b)   except in paragraphs 36 to 43, a reference to aiding, abetting, counselling or procuring the commission of that offence.

95   A reference in a preceding paragraph to a person's age is –

(a)   in the case of an indecent photograph, a reference to the person's age when the photograph was taken;

(b)   in any other case, a reference to his age at the time of the offence.

96   In this Schedule 'community sentence' has –

(a)   in relation to England and Wales, the same meaning as in the Powers of Criminal Courts (Sentencing) Act 2000 (c. 6), and

(b)   in relation to Northern Ireland, the same meaning as in the Criminal Justice (Northern Ireland) Order 1996 (S.I. 1996/3160 (N.I. 24)).

97   For the purposes of paragraphs 14, 44 and 78 –

(a)   a person is to be taken to have been under 16 at any time if it appears from the evidence as a whole that he was under that age at that time;

(b)   section 7 of the Protection of Children Act 1978 (c. 37) (interpretation), subsections (2) to (2C) and (8) of section 52 of the Civic Government (Scotland) Act 1982 (c. 45), and Article 2(2) and (3) of the Protection of Children (Northern Ireland) Order 1978 (S.I. 1978/1047 (N.I. 17)) (interpretation) (respectively) apply as each provision applies for the purposes of the Act or Order of which it forms part.

98   A determination under paragraph 60 constitutes part of a person's sentence, within the meaning of the Criminal Procedure (Scotland) Act 1995 (c. 46), for the purposes of any appeal or review.

SCHEDULE 4   PROCEDURE FOR ENDING NOTIFICATION REQUIREMENTS FOR ABOLISHED HOMOSEXUAL OFFENCES   Section 93

Scope of Schedule

1   This Schedule applies where a relevant offender is subject to the notification requirements of this Part as a result of a conviction, finding or caution in respect of an offence under –

(a)   section 12 or 13 of the Sexual Offences Act 1956 (c. 69) (buggery or indecency between men), or

(b)   section 61 of the Offences against the Person Act 1861 (c. 100) or section 11 of the Criminal Law Amendment Act 1885 (c. 69) (corresponding Northern Ireland offences).

Application for decision

2   (1)   The relevant offender may apply to the Secretary of State for a decision as to whether it appears that, at the time of the offence, the other party to the act of buggery or gross indecency –

(a)   where paragraph 1(a) applies, was aged 16 or over,

(b)   where paragraph 1(b) applies, was aged 17 or over, and consented to the act.

(2)   An application must be in writing and state –

(a)   the name, address and date of birth of the relevant offender,

(b)   his name and address at the time of the conviction, finding or caution,

(c)   so far as known to him, the time when and the place where the conviction or finding was made or the caution given and, for a conviction or finding, the case number,

(d)   such other information as the Secretary of State may require.

(3)   An application may include representations by the relevant offender about the matters mentioned in sub-paragraph (1).

Decision by Secretary of State

3   (1)   In making the decision applied for, the Secretary of State must consider –

(a)   any representations included in the application, and

(b)   any available record of the investigation of the offence and of any proceedings relating to it that appears to him to be relevant, but is not to seek evidence from any witness.

(2)   On making the decision the Secretary of State must –

(a)   record it in writing, and

(b)   give notice in writing to the relevant offender.

Effect of decision

4   (1)   If the Secretary of State decides that it appears as mentioned in paragraph 2(1), the relevant offender ceases, from the beginning of the day on which the decision is recorded under paragraph 3(2)(a), to be subject to the notification requirements of this Part as a result of the conviction, finding or caution in respect of the offence.

(2)   Sub-paragraph (1) does not affect the operation of this Part as a result of any other conviction, finding or caution or any court order.

Right of appeal

5   (1)   If the Secretary of State decides that it does not appear as mentioned in paragraph 2(1), and if the High Court gives permission, the relevant offender may appeal to that court.

(2)   On an appeal the court may not receive oral evidence.

(3)   The court –

(a)   if it decides that it appears as mentioned in paragraph 2(1), must make an order to that effect,

(b)   otherwise, must dismiss the appeal.

(4)   An order under sub-paragraph (3)(a) has the same effect as a decision of the Secretary of State recorded under paragraph 3(2)(a) has under paragraph 4.

(5)   There is no appeal from the decision of the High Court.

Interpretation

6   (1)   In this Schedule a reference to an offence includes –

(a)   a reference to an attempt, conspiracy or incitement to commit that offence, and

(b)   a reference to aiding, abetting, counselling or procuring the commission of that offence.

(2)   In the case of an attempt, conspiracy or incitement, references in paragraph 2 to the act of buggery or gross indecency are references to the act of buggery or gross indecency to which the attempt, conspiracy or incitement related (whether or not that act occurred).

Transitional provision

7   Until the coming into force of the repeal by this Act of Part 1 of the Sex Offenders Act 1997 (c. 51), this Schedule has effect as if references to this Part of this Act were references to Part 1 of that Act.

SCHEDULE 5   OTHER OFFENCES FOR PURPOSES OF PART 2

Section 104

England and Wales

1   Murder.
2   Manslaughter.
3   Kidnapping.
4   False imprisonment.
5   An offence under section 4 of the Offences against the Person Act 1861 (c. 100) (soliciting murder).
6   An offence under section 16 of that Act (threats to kill).
7   An offence under section 18 of that Act (wounding with intent to cause grievous bodily harm).
8   An offence under section 20 of that Act (malicious wounding).
9   An offence under section 21 of that Act (attempting to choke, suffocate or strangle in order to commit or assist in committing an indictable offence).
10   An offence under section 22 of that Act (using chloroform etc. to commit or assist in the committing of any indictable offence).
11   An offence under section 23 of that Act (maliciously administering poison etc. so as to endanger life or inflict grievous bodily harm).
12   An offence under section 27 of that Act (abandoning children).
13   An offence under section 28 of that Act (causing bodily injury by explosives).
14   An offence under section 29 of that Act (using explosives etc. with intent to do grievous bodily harm).
15   An offence under section 30 of that Act (placing explosives with intent to do bodily injury).
16   An offence under section 31 of that Act (setting spring guns etc. with intent to do grievous bodily harm).
17   An offence under section 32 of that Act (endangering the safety of railway passengers).
18   An offence under section 35 of that Act (injuring persons by furious driving).
19   An offence under section 37 of that Act (assaulting officer preserving wreck).
20   An offence under section 38 of that Act (assault with intent to resist arrest).
21   An offence under section 47 of that Act (assault occasioning actual bodily harm).
22   An offence under section 2 of the Explosive Substances Act 1883 (c. 3) (causing explosion likely to endanger life or property).
23   An offence under section 3 of that Act (attempt to cause explosion, or making or keeping explosive with intent to endanger life or property)
24   An offence under section 1 of the Infant Life (Preservation) Act 1929 (c. 34) (child destruction).
25   An offence under section 1 of the Children and Young Persons Act 1933 (c. 12) (cruelty to children).
26   An offence under section 1 of the Infanticide Act 1938 (c. 36) (infanticide).
27   An offence under section 16 of the Firearms Act 1968 (c. 27) (possession of firearm with intent to endanger life).
28   An offence under section 16A of that Act (possession of firearm with intent to cause fear of violence).

29   An offence under section 17(1) of that Act (use of firearm to resist arrest).

30   An offence under section 17(2) of that Act (possession of firearm at time of committing or being arrested for offence specified in Schedule 1 to that Act).

31   An offence under section 18 of that Act (carrying a firearm with criminal intent).

32   An offence under section 8 of the Theft Act 1968 (c. 60) (robbery or assault with intent to rob).

33   An offence under section 9 of that Act of burglary with intent to –

(a)   inflict grievous bodily harm on a person, or
(b)   do unlawful damage to a building or anything in it.

34   An offence under section 10 of that Act (aggravated burglary).

35   An offence under section 12A of that Act (aggravated vehicle-taking) involving an accident which caused the death of any person.

36   An offence of arson under section 1 of the Criminal Damage Act 1971 (c. 48).

37   An offence under section 1(2) of that Act (destroying or damaging property) other than an offence of arson.

38.   An offence under section 1 of the Taking of Hostages Act 1982 (c. 28) (hostage-taking).

39   An offence under section 1 of the Aviation Security Act 1982 (c. 36) (hijacking).

40   An offence under section 2 of that Act (destroying, damaging or endangering safety of aircraft).

41   An offence under section 3 of that Act (other acts endangering or likely to endanger safety of aircraft).

42   An offence under section 4 of that Act (offences in relation to certain dangerous articles).

43   An offence under section 127 of the Mental Health Act 1983 (c. 20) (ill-treatment of patients).

44   An offence under section 1 of the Prohibition of Female Circumcision Act 1985 (c. 38) (prohibition of female circumcision).

45   An offence under section 1 of the Public Order Act 1986 (c. 64) (riot).

46   An offence under section 2 of that Act (violent disorder).

47   An offence under section 3 of that Act (affray).

48   An offence under section 134 of the Criminal Justice Act 1988 (c. 33) (torture).

49   An offence under section 1 of the Road Traffic Act 1988 (c. 52) (causing death by dangerous driving).

50   An offence under section 3A of that Act (causing death by careless driving when under influence of drink or drugs).

51   An offence under section 1 of the Aviation and Maritime Security Act 1990 (c. 31) (endangering safety at aerodromes).

52   An offence under section 9 of that Act (hijacking of ships).

53   An offence under section 10 of that Act (seizing or exercising control of fixed platforms).

54   An offence under section 11 of that Act (destroying fixed platforms or endangering their safety).

55   An offence under section 12 of that Act (other acts endangering or likely to endanger safe navigation).

56   An offence under section 13 of that Act (offences involving threats).

57   An offence under section 4 of the Protection from Harassment Act 1997 (c. 40) (putting people in fear of violence).

58   An offence under section 29 of the Crime and Disorder Act 1998 (c. 37) (racially or religiously aggravated assaults).

59   An offence falling within section 31(1)(a) or (b) of that Act (racially or religiously aggravated offences under section 4 or 4A of the Public Order Act 1986 (c. 64)).

60   An offence under Part II of the Channel Tunnel (Security) Order 1994 (S.I. 1994/570) (offences relating to Channel Tunnel trains and the tunnel system).

61   An offence under section 51 or 52 of the International Criminal Court Act 2001 (c. 17) (genocide, crimes against humanity, war crimes and related offences), other than one involving murder.

62   An offence under section 47 of this Act, where the victim or (as the case may be) other party was 16 or over.

63   An offence under any of sections 48 to 53 or 57 to 59 of this Act.

Scotland

64   Murder.

65   Culpable homicide.

66   Assault.

67   Assault and robbery.

68   Abduction.

69   Plagium.

70   Wrongful imprisonment.

71   Threatening personal violence.

72   Breach of the peace inferring personal violence.

73   Wilful fireraising.

74   Culpable and reckless fireraising.

75   Mobbing and rioting.

76   An offence under section 2 of the Explosive Substances Act 1883 (c. 3) (causing explosion likely to endanger life or property).

77   An offence under section 3 of that Act (attempt to cause explosion, or making or keeping explosives with intent to endanger life or property).

78   An offence under section 12 of the Children and Young Persons (Scotland) Act 1937 (c. 37) (cruelty to persons under 16).

79   An offence under section 16 of the Firearms Act 1968 (c. 27) (possession of firearm with intent to endanger life).

80   An offence under section 16A of that Act (possession of firearm with intent to cause fear of violence).

81   An offence under section 17(1) of that Act (use of firearm to resist arrest).

82   An offence under section 17(2) of that Act (possession of firearm at time of committing or being arrested for offence specified in Schedule 1 to that Act).

83   An offence under section 18 of that Act (carrying a firearm with criminal intent).

84   An offence under section 1 of the Taking of Hostages Act 1982 (c. 28) (hostage-taking).

85   An offence under section 1 of the Aviation Security Act 1982 (c. 36) (hijacking).

86   An offence under section 2 of that Act (destroying, damaging or endangering safety of aircraft).

87   An offence under section 3 of that Act (other acts endangering or likely to endanger safety of aircraft).

88   An offence under section 4 of that Act (offences in relation to certain dangerous articles).

89   An offence under section 105 of the Mental Health (Scotland) Act 1984 (c. 36) (ill-treatment of patients).

90   An offence under section 1 of the Prohibition of Female Circumcision Act 1985 (c. 38) (prohibition of female circumcision).

91   An offence under section 134 of the Criminal Justice Act 1988 (c. 33) (torture).

92   An offence under section 1 of the Road Traffic Act 1988 (c. 52) (causing death by dangerous driving).

93   An offence under section 3A of that Act (causing death by careless driving when under influence of drink or drugs).

94 An offence under section 1 of the Aviation and Maritime Security Act 1990 (c. 31) (endangering safety at aerodromes).

95 An offence under section 9 of that Act (hijacking of ships).

96 An offence under section 10 of that Act (seizing or exercising control of fixed platforms).

97 An offence under section 11 of that Act (destroying fixed platforms or endangering their safety).

98 An offence under section 12 of that Act (other acts endangering or likely to endanger safe navigation).

99 An offence under section 13 of that Act (offences involving threats).

100 An offence under Part II of the Channel Tunnel (Security) Order 1994 (S.I. 1994/570) (offences relating to Channel Tunnel trains and the tunnel system).

101 An offence under section 7 of the Criminal Law (Consolidation) (Scotland) Act 1995 (c. 39) (procuring).

102 An offence under section 9 of that Act (permitting girl to use premises for intercourse).

103 An offence under section 11 of that Act (trading in prostitution and brothel-keeping).

104 An offence under section 12 of that Act (allowing child to be in brothel).

105 An offence under section 13(9) of that Act (living on earnings of male prostitution etc.).

106 An offence under section 50A of that Act (racially-aggravated harassment).

107 An offence under section 51 or 52 of the International Criminal Court Act 2001 (c. 17) (genocide, crimes against humanity, war crimes and related offences), other than one involving murder.

108 An offence under section 1 of the International Criminal Court (Scotland) Act 2001 (asp 13) (genocide, crimes against humanity, war crimes and related offences as specified in Schedule 1 to that Act).

109 An offence under section 22 of the Criminal Justice (Scotland) Act 2003 (asp 7) (traffic in prostitution etc.).

110 An offence to which section 74 of that Act applies (offences aggravated by religious prejudice).

111 An offence under section 315 of the Mental Health (Care and Treatment) (Scotland) Act 2003 (asp 13) (ill-treatment and wilful neglect of mentally disordered person).

Northern Ireland

112 Murder.

113 Manslaughter.

114 Kidnapping.

115 Riot.

116 Affray.

117 False imprisonment.

118 An offence under section 4 of the Offences against the Person Act 1861 (c. 100) (soliciting murder).

119 An offence under section 16 of that Act (threats to kill).

120 An offence under section 18 of that Act (wounding with intent to cause grievous bodily harm).

121 An offence under section 20 of that Act (malicious wounding).

122 An offence under section 21 of that Act (attempting to choke, suffocate or strangle in order to commit or assist in committing an indictable offence).

123 An offence under section 22 of that Act (using chloroform etc. to commit or assist in the committing of any indictable offence).

124 An offence under section 23 of that Act (maliciously administering poison etc. so as to endanger life or inflict grievous bodily harm).

125 An offence under section 27 of that Act (abandoning children).

126 An offence under section 28 of that Act (causing bodily injury by explosives).

127 An offence under section 29 of that Act (using explosives etc. with intent to do grievous bodily harm).

128 An offence under section 30 of that Act (placing explosives with intent to do bodily injury).

129 An offence under section 31 of that Act (setting spring guns etc. with intent to do grievous bodily harm).

130 An offence under section 32 of that Act (endangering the safety of railway passengers).

131 An offence under section 35 of that Act (injuring persons by furious driving).

132 An offence under section 37 of that Act (assaulting officer preserving wreck).

133 An offence under section 47 of that Act of assault occasioning actual bodily harm.

134 An offence under section 2 of the Explosive Substances Act 1883 (c. 3) (causing explosion likely to endanger life or property).

135 An offence under section 3 of that Act (attempt to cause explosion, or making or keeping explosive with intent to endanger life or property).

136 An offence under section 25 of the Criminal Justice (Northern Ireland) Act 1945 (c. 15) (child destruction).

137 An offence under section 1 of the Infanticide Act (Northern Ireland) 1939 (c. 5) (infanticide).

138 An offence under section 7(1)(b) of the Criminal Justice (Miscellaneous Provisions) Act (Northern Ireland) 1968 (c. 28) (assault with intent to resist arrest).

139 An offence under section 20 of the Children and Young Persons Act (Northern Ireland) 1968 (c. 34) (cruelty to children).

140 An offence under section 8 of the Theft Act (Northern Ireland) 1969 (c. 16) (robbery or assault with intent to rob).

141 An offence under section 9 of that Act of burglary with intent to –

   (a)   inflict grievous bodily harm on a person, or
   (b)   do unlawful damage to a building or anything in it.

142 An offence under section 10 of that Act (aggravated burglary).

143 An offence of arson under Article 3 of the Criminal Damage (Northern Ireland) Order 1977 (S.I. 1977/426 (N.I. 4)).

144 An offence under Article 3(2) of that Order (destroying or damaging property) other than an offence of arson.

145 An offence under Article 17 of the Firearms (Northern Ireland) Order 1981 (S.I. 1981/155 (N.I. 2)) (possession of firearm with intent to endanger life).

146 An offence under Article 17A of that Order (possession of firearm with intent to cause fear of violence).

147 An offence under Article 18(1) of that Order (use of firearm to resist arrest).

148 An offence under Article 18(2) of that Order (possession of firearm at time of committing or being arrested for an offence specified in Schedule 1 to that Order).

149 An offence under Article 19 of that Order (carrying a firearm with criminal intent).

150 An offence under section 1 of the Taking of Hostages Act 1982 (c. 28) (hostage-taking).

151 An offence under section 1 of the Aviation Security Act 1982 (c. 36) (hijacking).

152 An offence under section 2 of that Act (destroying, damaging or endangering safety of aircraft).

153 An offence under section 3 of that Act (other acts endangering or likely to endanger safety of aircraft).

154 An offence under section 4 of that Act (offences in relation to certain dangerous articles).

155 An offence under section 1 of the Prohibition of Female Circumcision Act 1985 (c. 38) (prohibition of female circumcision).

156 An offence under Article 121 of the Mental Health (Northern Ireland) Order 1986 (S.I. 1986/595 (N.I. 4) (ill-treatment of patients).

157 An offence under section 134 of the Criminal Justice Act 1988 (c. 33) (torture).

158 An offence under section 1 of the Aviation and Maritime Security Act 1990 (c. 31) (endangering safety at aerodromes).

159 An offence under section 9 of that Act (hijacking of ships).

160 An offence under section 10 of that Act (seizing or exercising control of fixed platforms).

161 An offence under section 11 of that Act (destroying fixed platforms or endangering their safety).

162 An offence under section 12 of that Act (other acts endangering or likely to endanger safe navigation).

163 An offence under section 13 of that Act (offences involving threats).

164 An offence under Article 9 of the Road Traffic (Northern Ireland) Order 1995 (S.I. 1995/2994 (N.I. 18)) (causing death or grievous bodily injury by dangerous driving).

165 An offence under Article 14 of that Order (causing death or grievous bodily injury by careless driving when under the influence of drink or drugs).

166 An offence under Article 6 of the Protection from Harassment (Northern Ireland) Order 1997 (S.I. 1997/1180 (N.I. 9) (putting people in fear of violence).

167 An offence under section 66 of the Police (Northern Ireland) Act 1998 (c. 32) (assaulting or obstructing a constable etc.).

168 An offence under Part II of the Channel Tunnel (Security) Order 1994 (S.I. 1994/570) (offences relating to Channel Tunnel trains and the tunnel system).

169 An offence under section 51 or 52 of the International Criminal Court Act 2001 (c. 17) (genocide, crimes against humanity, war crimes and related offences), other than one involving murder.

170 An offence under section 47 of this Act, where the victim or (as the case may be) other party was 17 or over.

171 An offence under any of sections 48 to 53 or 57 to 59 of this Act.

Service offences

172 An offence under –

    (a)   section 70 of the Army Act 1955 (3 & 4 Eliz. 2 c. 18),

    (b)   section 70 of the Air Force Act 1955 (3 & 4 Eliz. 2 c. 19), or

    (c)   section 42 of the Naval Discipline Act 1957 (c. 53), of which the corresponding civil offence (within the meaning of that Act) is an offence under a provision listed in any of paragraphs 1 to 63.

General

173 A reference in a preceding paragraph to an offence includes –

    (a)   a reference to an attempt, conspiracy or incitement to commit that offence, and

    (b)   a reference to aiding, abetting, counselling or procuring the commission of that offence.

174 A reference in a preceding paragraph to a person's age is a reference to his age at the time of the offence.

SCHEDULE 6   MINOR AND CONSEQUENTIAL AMENDMENTS

Section 139

Vagrancy Act 1824 (c. 83)

1   In section 4 of the Vagrancy Act 1824 (rogues and vagabonds) except so far as extending to Northern Ireland, omit the words from 'every person wilfully' to 'female'.

2   In section 4 of the Vagrancy Act 1824 as it extends to Northern Ireland, omit the words from 'wilfully, openly, lewdly' to 'any female; or'.

Town Police Clauses Act 1847 (c. 89)

3   In section 28 of the Town Police Clauses Act 1847 (penalty for committing certain acts), omit 'Every person who wilfully and indecently exposes his person:'.

Offences against the Person Act 1861 (c. 100)

4   In the Offences against the Person Act 1861, omit sections 61 and 62.

Criminal Law Amendment Act 1885 (c. 69)

5   In the Criminal Law Amendment Act 1885, omit –
   (a)   in section 2, subsections (2) to (4), and
   (b)   section 11.

Vagrancy Act 1898 (c. 39)

6   The Vagrancy Act 1898 ceases to have effect.

Children and Young Persons Act 1933 (c. 12)

7   In Schedule 1 to the Children and Young Persons Act 1933 (offences to which special provisions of that Act apply), for the entry relating to offences under the Sexual Offences Act 1956 (c. 69) substitute –

'Any offence against a child or young person under any of sections 1 to 41, 47 to 53, 57 to 61, 66 and 67 of the Sexual Offences Act 2003, or any attempt to commit such an offence.
Any offence under section 62 or 63 of the Sexual Offences Act 2003 where the intended offence was an offence against a child or young person, or any attempt to commit such an offence.'

Visiting Forces Act 1952 (c. 67)

8   (1)   Paragraph 1 of the Schedule to the Visiting Forces Act 1952 (offences referred to in section 3 of that Act) is amended as follows.
   (2)   Before sub-paragraph (a) insert –
'(za) rape and buggery (offences under the law of Northern Ireland);'.
   (3)   In sub-paragraph (a), omit 'rape' and 'buggery'.

(4) In sub-paragraph (b), after paragraph (xii) insert –

'(xiii) Part 1 of the Sexual Offences Act 2003.'

Army Act 1955 (3 & 4 Eliz. 2 c. 18)

9   In section 70(4) of the Army Act 1955 (person not to be charged with an offence committed in the United Kingdom where corresponding civil offence is within the
subsection) –

(a) omit 'or rape', and

(b) after 'International Criminal Court Act 2001' insert 'or an offence under section
1 of the Sexual Offences Act 2003 (rape)'.

Air Force Act 1955 (3 & 4 Eliz. 2.c. 19)

10   In section 70(4) of the Air Force Act 1955 (person not to be charged with an offence
committed in the United Kingdom where corresponding civil offence is within the
subsection) –

(a) omit 'or rape', and

(b) after 'International Criminal Court Act 2001' insert 'or an offence under section
1 of the Sexual Offences Act 2003 (rape)'.

Sexual Offences Act 1956 (c. 37)

11   In the Sexual Offences Act 1956, omit –

(a) sections 1 to 7, 9 to 17, 19 to 32 and 41 to 47 (offences), and

(b) in Schedule 2 (prosecution, punishment etc.), paragraphs 1 to 32.

Naval Discipline Act 1957 (c. 53)

12 In section 48(2) of the Naval Discipline Act 1957 (courts-martial not to have
jurisdiction as regards certain offences committed in the United Kingdom) –

(a) omit 'or rape', and

(b) before 'committed on shore' insert 'or an offence under section 1 of the Sexual
Offences Act 2003 (rape)'.

Mental Health Act 1959 (c. 72)

13   In the Mental Health Act 1959, omit sections 127 (amendment of Sexual Offences Act
1956) and 128 (sexual intercourse with patients).

Indecency with Children Act 1960 (c. 33)

14   The Indecency with Children Act 1960 ceases to have effect.

Sexual Offences Act 1967 (c. 60)

15   In the Sexual Offences Act 1967, omit the following –

(a) section 1 (amendment of law relating to homosexual acts in private),

(b) section 4 (procuring others to commit homosexual acts),

(c) section 5 (living on earnings of male prostitution),

(d) section 7 (time limit on prosecutions),

(e) section 8 (restriction on prosecutions), and

(f) section 10 (past offences).

Firearms Act 1968 (c. 27)

16 In Schedule 1 to the Firearms Act 1968 (offences to which section 17(2) of that Act applies), for paragraph 6 substitute –

'6. Offences under any of the following provisions of the Sexual Offences Act 2003 –

(a) section 1 (rape);

(b) section 2 (assault by penetration);

(c) section 4 (causing a person to engage in sexual activity without consent), where the activity caused involved penetration within subsection (4)(a) to (d) of that section;

(d) section 5 (rape of a child under 13);

(e) section 6 (assault of a child under 13 by penetration);

(f) section 8 (causing or inciting a child under 13 to engage in sexual activity), where an activity involving penetration within subsection (3)(a) to (d) of that section was caused;

(g) section 30 (sexual activity with a person with a mental disorder impeding choice), where the touching involved penetration within subsection (3)(a) to (d) of that section;

(h) section 31 (causing or inciting a person, with a mental disorder impeding choice, to engage in sexual activity), where an activity involving penetration within subsection (3)(a) to (d) of that section was caused.'

Theft Act 1968 (c. 60)

17 In section 9 of the Theft Act 1968 (burglary), in subsection (2) omit 'or raping any person'.

Children and Young Persons Act (Northern Ireland) 1968 (c. 34 (N.I.))

18 (1) The Children and Young Persons Act (Northern Ireland) 1968 is amended as follows.

(2) In section 21 (causing or encouraging seduction or prostitution of girl under 17), omit –

(a) in subsection (1), 'or the prostitution of,', and

(b) in subsection (2), 'or the prostitution of,' and 'or who has become a prostitute,'.

(3) In Schedule 1 (offences against children and young persons to which special provisions of that Act apply), at the end insert –

'Any offence against a child or young person under any of sections 15 to 19, 47 to 59, 66 and 67 of the Sexual Offences Act 2003 or any attempt to commit such an offence.'

Rehabilitation of Offenders Act 1974 (c. 53)

19   In section 7 of the Rehabilitation of Offenders Act 1974 (limitations on rehabilitation under that Act), in subsection (2), for paragraph (bb) substitute –
'(bb) in any proceedings under Part 2 of the Sexual Offences Act 2003, or on appeal from any such proceedings;'.

Sexual Offences (Amendment) Act 1976 (c. 82)

20   (1)   The Sexual Offences (Amendment) Act 1976 is amended as follows
(2)   In section 1 (meaning of 'rape'), omit subsection (2).
(3)   In section 7 (citation, interpretation etc.) –

(a)   for subsection (2) substitute –

'(2)   In this Act –

(a)   'a rape offence' means any of the following –

(i) an offence under section 1 of the Sexual Offences Act 2003 (rape);

(ii) an offence under section 2 of that Act (assault by penetration);

(iii) an offence under section 4 of that Act (causing a person to engage in sexual activity without consent), where the activity caused involved penetration within subsection (4)(a) to (d) of that section;

(iv) an offence under section 5 of that Act (rape of a child under 13);

(v) an offence under section 6 of that Act (assault of a child under 13 by penetration);

(vi) an offence under section 8 of that Act (causing or inciting a child under 13 to engage in sexual activity), where an activity involving penetration within subsection (3)(a) to (d) of that section was caused;

(vii) an offence under section 30 of that Act (sexual activity with a person with a mental disorder impeding choice), where the touching involved penetration within subsection (3)(a) to (d) of that section;

(viii) an offence under section 31 of that Act (causing or inciting a person, with a mental disorder impeding choice, to engage in sexual activity), where an activity involving penetration within subsection (3)(a) to (d) of that section was caused;

(ix) an attempt, conspiracy or incitement to commit an offence within any of paragraphs (i) to (vii);

(x) aiding, abetting, counselling or procuring the commission of such an offence or an attempt to commit such an offence.

(b)   the use in any provision of the word 'man' without the addition of the word 'boy' does not prevent the provision applying to any person to whom it would have applied if both words had been used, and similarly with the words 'woman' and 'girl'.';

(b)   omit subsection (3).

Criminal Law Act 1977 (c. 45)

21   In the Criminal Law Act 1977, omit section 54 (inciting girl under 16 to have incestuous sexual intercourse).

Internationally Protected Persons Act 1978 (c. 17)

22   In section 1 of the Internationally Protected Persons Act 1978 (attacks and threats of attacks on protected persons) –

(a)   in subsection (1)(a) –

   (i)   omit 'rape,';
   (ii)   after 'Explosive Substances Act 1883' insert 'or an offence listed in subsection (1A)';

(b)   after subsection (1) insert –

'(1A) The offences mentioned in subsection (1)(a) are –

   (a)   in Scotland or Northern Ireland, rape;
   (b)   an offence under section 1 or 2 of the Sexual Offences Act 2003;
   (c)   an offence under section 4 of that Act, where the activity caused involved penetration within subsection (4)(a) to (d) of that section;
   (d)   an offence under section 5 or 6 of that Act;
   (e)   an offence under section 8 of that Act, where an activity involving penetration within subsection (3)(a) to (d) of that section was caused;
   (f)   an offence under section 30 of that Act, where the touching involved penetration within subsection (3)(a) to (d) of that section;
   (g)   an offence under section 31 of that Act, where an activity involving penetration within subsection (3)(a) to (d) of that section was caused.'

Suppression of Terrorism Act 1978 (c. 26)

23   (1)   Schedule 1 to the Suppression of Terrorism Act 1978 (offences for the purposes of that Act) is amended as follows.
      (2)   In paragraph 3, after 'Rape' insert 'under the law of Scotland or Northern Ireland'.
      (3)   For paragraph 9 substitute –

'9. An offence under any of the following provisions of the Sexual Offences Act 2003 –
   (a)   sections 1 or 2 (rape, assault by penetration);
   (b)   section 4 (causing a person to engage in sexual activity without consent), where the activity caused involved penetration within subsection (4)(a) to (d) of that section;
   (c)   section 5 or 6 (rape of a child under 13, assault of a child under 13 by penetration);
   (d)   section 8 (causing or inciting a child under 13 to engage in sexual activity), where an activity involving penetration within subsection (3)(a) to (d) of that section was caused;
   (e)   section 30 (sexual activity with a person with a mental disorder impeding choice), where the touching involved penetration within subsection (3)(a) to (d) of that section;
   (f)   section 31 (causing or inciting a person, with a mental disorder impeding choice, to engage in sexual activity), where an activity involving penetration within subsection (3)(a) to (d) of that section was caused.'.

Protection of Children Act 1978 (c. 37)

24   In section 1(1) of the Protection of Children Act 1978 (indecent photographs of children), at the beginning insert 'Subject to sections 1A and 1B,'.

Rehabilitation of Offenders (Northern Ireland) Order 1978 (S.I. 1978/1908 (N.I. 27))

25   In Article 8 of the Rehabilitation of Offenders (Northern Ireland) Order 1978 (limitations on rehabilitation under that Order), in paragraph (2), for sub-paragraph (bb) substitute –

'(bb) in any proceedings under Part 2 of the Sexual Offences Act 2003, or on appeal from any such proceedings;'.

Magistrates' Courts Act 1980 (c. 43)

26   (1) The Magistrates' Courts Act 1980 is amended as follows.

    (2) In section 103 (evidence of persons under 14 in committal proceedings), in subsection (2)(c), after 'the Protection of Children Act 1978' insert 'or Part 1 of the Sexual Offences Act 2003'.

    (3) In Schedule 7 (consequential amendments), omit paragraph 18.

Criminal Justice Act 1982 (c. 48)

27   In the Criminal Justice Act 1982, in Part 2 of Schedule 1 (offences excluded from early release provisions), after the entry relating to the Proceeds of Crime Act 2002 (c. 29) insert –

> ### 'Sexual Offences Act 2003
>
> Sections 1 and 2 (rape, assault by penetration).
> Section 4 (causing a person to engage in sexual activity without consent), where the activity caused involved penetration within subsection (4)(a) to (d) of that section.
> Sections 5 and 6 (rape of a child under 13, assault of a child under 13 by penetration).
> Section 8 (causing or inciting a child under 13 to engage in sexual activity), where an activity involving penetration within subsection (3)(a) to (d) of that section was caused.
> Section 30 (sexual activity with a person with a mental disorder impeding choice), where the touching involved penetration within subsection (3)(a) to (d) of that section.
> Section 31 (causing or inciting a person, with a mental disorder impeding choice, to engage in sexual activity), where an activity involving penetration within subsection (3)(a) to (d) of that section was caused.'

Police and Criminal Evidence Act 1984 (c. 60)

28   (1) The Police and Criminal Evidence Act 1984 is amended as follows.

    (2) In section 80(7) (sexual offences for purposes of compellability of spouse), after 'the Protection of Children Act 1978' insert 'or Part 1 of the Sexual Offences Act 2003'.

    (3) In Schedule 1A (specific arrestable offences), after paragraph 25 insert –

'Sexual Offences Act 2003

26. An offence under –

    (a) section 66 of the Sexual Offences Act 2003 (exposure);
    (b) section 67 of that Act (voyeurism);
    (c) section 69 of that Act (intercourse with an animal);
    (d) section 70 of that Act (sexual penetration of a corpse); or
    (e) section 71 of that Act (sexual activity in public lavatory).'

(4) In Part 2 of Schedule 5 (serious arrestable offences), after the entry relating to the Obscene Publications Act 1959 (c. 66) insert –

'Sexual Offences Act 2003

16. Section 1 (rape).
17. Section 2 (assault by penetration).
18. Section 4 (causing a person to engage in sexual activity without consent), where the activity caused involved penetration within subsection (4)(a) to (d) of that section.
19. Section 5 (rape of a child under 13).
20. Section 6 (assault of a child under 13 by penetration).
21. Section 8 (causing or inciting a child under 13 to engage in sexual activity), where an activity involving penetration within subsection (3)(a) to (d) of that section was caused.
22. Section 30 (sexual activity with a person with a mental disorder impeding choice), where the touching involved penetration within subsection (3)(a) to (d) of that section.
23. Section 31 (causing or inciting a person, with a mental disorder impeding choice, to engage in sexual activity), where an activity involving penetration within subsection (3)(a) to (d) of that section was caused.'

Criminal Justice Act 1988 (c. 33)

29 (1) The Criminal Justice Act 1988 is amended as follows.
   (2) In section 32 (evidence through television links), in subsection (2)(c), after 'the Protection of Children Act 1978' insert 'or Part 1 of the Sexual Offences Act 2003'.
   (3) In section 160(1) (possession of indecent photograph of child), at the beginning insert 'Subject to subsection (1A),'.

Criminal Justice Act 1991 (c. 53)

30 In section 34A of the Criminal Justice Act 1991 (power to release short-term prisoners on licence), in subsection (2)(da), for 'Part I of the Sex Offenders Act 1997' substitute 'Part 2 of the Sexual Offences Act 2003'.

Sexual Offences (Amendment) Act 1992 (c.34)

31 (1) Section 2 of the Sexual Offences (Amendment) Act 1992 (offences to which that Act applies) is amended as follows.
   (2) In subsection (1) (England and Wales) –

    (a) after paragraph (d) insert –

        '(da) any offence under any of the provisions of Part 1 of the Sexual Offences Act 2003 except section 64, 65, 69 or 71;';

(b)   in paragraph (e) for '(d)' substitute '(da)'.

(3)   In subsection (3) (Northern Ireland) –

    (a)   after paragraph (hh) insert –

        '(ha) any offence under any of sections 15 to 21, 47 to 53, 57 to 59, 66, 67, 70 and 72 of the Sexual Offences Act 2003.';

    (b)   in paragraph (i) for '(hh)' substitute '(ha)'.

Criminal Justice and Public Order Act 1994 (c. 33)

32   (1)   The Criminal Justice and Public Order Act 1994 is amended as follows.

    (2)   In section 25 (no bail if previous conviction for certain offences), for subsection (2)(d) and (e) substitute –

        '(d)   rape under the law of Scotland or Northern Ireland;

        (e)   an offence under section 1 of the Sexual Offences Act 1956 (rape);

        (f)   an offence under section 1 of the Sexual Offences Act 2003 (rape);

        (g)   an offence under section 2 of that Act (assault by penetration);

        (h)   an offence under section 4 of that Act (causing a person to engage in sexual activity without consent), where the activity caused involved penetration within subsection (4)(a) to (d) of that section;

        (i)   an offence under section 5 of that Act (rape of a child under 13);

        (j)   an offence under section 6 of that Act (assault of a child under 13 by penetration);

        (k)   an offence under section 8 of that Act (causing or inciting a child under 13 to engage in sexual activity), where an activity involving penetration within subsection (3)(a) to (d) of that section was caused;

        (l)   an offence under section 30 of that Act (sexual activity with a person with a mental disorder impeding choice), where the touching involved penetration within subsection (3)(a) to (d) of that section;

        (m)   an offence under section 31 of that Act (causing or inciting a person, with a mental disorder impeding choice, to engage in sexual activity), where an activity involving penetration within subsection (3)(a) to (d) of that section was caused;

        (n)   an attempt to commit an offence within any of paragraphs (d) to (m).'

    (3)   Omit sections 142 to 144.

    (4)   In Schedule 10 (consequential amendments) omit paragraphs 26 and 35(2) and (4).

Criminal Law (Consolidation) (Scotland) Act 1995 (c. 39)

33   In section 5(6) of the Criminal Law (Consolidation) (Scotland) Act 1995 (which relates to construing the expression 'a like offence'), after paragraph (c) insert 'or

    (cc)   any of sections 9 to 14 of the Sexual Offences Act 2003;'.

Criminal Injuries Compensation Act 1995 (c. 53)

34   In section 11 of the Criminal Injuries Compensation Act 1995 (approval by parliament of certain alterations to the Tariff or provisions of the Scheme) –

    (a)   in subsection (3)(d), after 'rape' insert 'or an offence under section 30 of the Sexual Offences Act 2003';

    (b)   after subsection (8) insert –

'(9) In subsection (3) "rape", in relation to anything done in England and Wales, means an offence under section 1 or 5 of the Sexual Offences Act 2003.'

Sexual Offences (Conspiracy and Incitement) Act 1996 (c.29)

35 In the Schedule to the Sexual Offences (Conspiracy and Incitement) Act 1996 (sexual offences for the purposes of that Act), in paragraph 1 –

(a) for sub-paragraph (1)(b) substitute –

'(b) an offence under any of sections 1 to 12, 14 and 15 to 26 of the Sexual Offences Act 2003.';

(b) in sub-paragraph (2), for 'In sub-paragraph (1)(a), sub-paragraphs (i), (iv), (v) and (vi) do' substitute 'Sub-paragraph (1)(b) does'.

Sexual Offences (Protected Material) Act 1997 (c. 39)

36 In the Schedule to the Sexual Offences (Protected Material) Act 1997 (sexual offences for the purposes of that Act) –

(a) after paragraph 5 insert –

'5A. Any offence under any provision of Part 1 of the Sexual Offences Act 2003 except section 64, 65, 69 or 71.';

(b) in paragraph 6, for '1 to 5' substitute '5 and 5A'.

Sex Offenders Act 1997 (c. 51)

37 The Sex Offenders Act 1997 ceases to have effect.

Crime and Disorder Act 1998 (c. 37)

38 (1) The Crime and Disorder Act 1998 is amended as follows.

(2) Omit sections 2, 2A, 2B and 3 (sex offender orders and interim orders).

(3) In section 4 (appeals against orders) –

(a) in subsection (1), omit 'a sex offender order or an order under section 2A above', and

(b) in subsection (3), omit 'or 2(6) above'.

(4) Omit section 20.

(5) In section 21 (procedural provisions with respect to orders) –

(a) omit subsection (2);

(b) in subsection (4) –

(i) omit 'or (2)'; and

(ii) for 'either of those subsections' substitute 'that subsection';

(c) in subsection (5), omit 'or 20';

(d) in subsection (6), omit 'and sex offender orders' and 'or 20(4)(a)';

(e) in subsection (7)(b)(i), omit 'or, as the case may be, chief constable';

(f) omit subsections (7A) and (7B); and

(g) in subsection (10), omit 'or 20'.

(6) Omit section 21A.

(7) In section 22 (offences in connection with breach of orders), omit subsections (6) and (7).

(8) In Schedule 8 (minor and consequential amendments), omit paragraph 144.

Criminal Justice (Children) (Northern Ireland) Order 1998 (S.I. 1998/1504 (N.I. 9))

39   In paragraph 1 of Schedule 1 to the Criminal Justice (Children) (Northern Ireland) Order 1998 –

(a)   omit sub-paragraphs (c), (e) and (j);

(b)   after sub-paragraph (l) insert –

'(m) Section 69 of the Sexual Offences Act 2003.'.

Criminal Justice (Northern Ireland) Order 1998 (S.I. 1998/2839 (N.I. 20))

40   In the Criminal Justice (Northern Ireland) Order 1998, omit Articles 6, 6A, 6B and 7.

Youth Justice and Criminal Evidence Act 1999 (c. 23)

41   (1)   The Youth Justice and Criminal Evidence Act 1999 is amended as follows.

(2)   In section 35 (cross examination of child witnesses), in subsection (3)(a), after sub-paragraph (v) insert 'or

(vi) Part 1 of the Sexual Offences Act 2003;'.

(3)   In section 62 (meaning of 'sexual offence' etc.), for subsection (1) substitute –

'(1) In this Part "sexual offence" means any offence under Part 1 of the Sexual Offences Act 2003.'

Criminal Evidence (Northern Ireland) Order 1999 (S.I. 1999/2789 (N.I. 8))

42   (1)   The Criminal Evidence (Northern Ireland) Order 1999 is amended as follows.

(2)   In Article 3(1) (meaning of 'sexual offence'), after sub-paragraph (gg) insert –

'(ga) any offence under any of sections 15 to 21, 47 to 53, 57 to 59, 66, 67, and 70 to 72 of the Sexual Offences Act 2003.'.

(3)   In Article 23 (protection of child complainants and other child witnesses) –

(a)   in paragraph (3), after sub-paragraph (c) insert –

'(cc) any offence under any of sections 15 to 21, 47 to 53, 57 to 59, 66 to 72 of the Sexual Offences Act 2003;';

(b)   in paragraph (4)(a), after '(3)(a)' insert 'or (cc)'.

Powers of Criminal Courts (Sentencing) Act 2000 (c. 6)

43   (1)   The Powers of Criminal Courts (Sentencing) Act 2000 is amended as follows.

(2)   In section 91 (power to detain offenders under 18 convicted of certain offences), for subsection (1)(b) and (c) substitute –

'(b) an offence under section 3 of the Sexual Offences Act 2003 (in this section, "the 2003 Act") (sexual assault); or

(c)   an offence under section 13 of the 2003 Act (child sex offences committed by children or young persons); or

(d)   an offence under section 25 of the 2003 Act (sexual activity with a child family member); or

(e)   an offence under section 26 of the 2003 Act (inciting a child family member to engage in sexual activity).'.

(3) In section 109 (life sentence for second serious offence), in subsection (5), after paragraph (f) insert –

'(fa) an offence under section 1 or 2 of the Sexual Offences Act 2003 (in this section, "the 2003 Act") (rape, assault by penetration);

(fb) an offence under section 4 of the 2003 Act (causing a person to engage in sexual activity without consent), where the activity caused involved penetration within subsection (4)(a) to (d) of that section;

(fc) an offence under section 5 or 6 of the 2003 Act (rape of a child under 13, assault of a child under 13 by penetration);

(fd) an offence under section 8 of the 2003 Act (causing or inciting a child under 13 to engage in sexual activity), where an activity involving penetration within subsection (3)(a) to (d) of that section was caused;

(fe) an offence under section 30 of the 2003 Act (sexual activity with a person with a mental disorder impeding choice), where the touching involved penetration within subsection (3)(a) to (d) of that section;

(ff) an offence under section 31 of the 2003 Act (causing or inciting a person, with a mental disorder impeding choice, to engage in sexual activity), where an activity involving penetration within subsection (3)(a) to (d) of that section was caused;

(fg) an attempt to commit an offence within any of paragraphs (fa) to (ff);'.

(4) In section 161 (definition of 'sexual offence' etc.), in subsection (2) –

(a) after paragraph (f) insert –

'(fa) an offence under any provision of Part 1 of the Sexual Offences Act 2003 except section 52, 53 or 71;';

(b) in paragraph (g), for '(a) to (f)' substitute '(f) and (fa)'.

(5) In Schedule 9 (consequential amendments), omit paragraphs 189, 190 and 193.

Criminal Justice and Courts Services Act 2000 (c. 43)

44 (1) The Criminal Justice and Courts Services Act 2000 is amended as follows.

(2) Omit sections 39 and 66.

(3) In section 68 (sexual and violent offenders for the purposes of risk assessment etc.), in subsection (2), for 'Part I of the Sex Offenders Act 1997' substitute 'Part 2 of the Sexual Offences Act 2003'.

(4) In section 69 (duties of local probation boards in connection with victims of certain offences), in subsection (8)(b), for 'Part I of the Sex Offenders Act 1997' substitute 'Part 2 of the Sexual Offences Act 2003'.

(5) In Schedule 4 (offences against children for the purposes of disqualification orders) –

(a) in paragraph 1, for sub-paragraph (m) substitute –

'(m) an offence under any of sections 5 to 26 and 47 to 50 of the Sexual Offences Act 2003 (offences against children).';

(b) in paragraph 2, for sub-paragraph (n) substitute –

'(n) an offence under any of sections 1 to 4, 30 to 41, 52, 53, 57 to 61, 66 and 67 of the Sexual Offences Act 2003.';

(c) in paragraph 3, after sub-paragraph (s) insert –

'(sa) he commits an offence under section 62 or 63 of the Sexual Offences Act 2003 (committing an offence or trespassing with intent to commit a sexual offence) in a case where the intended offence was an offence against a child.'.

(6) Omit Schedule 5.

Sexual Offences (Amendment) Act 2000 (c. 44)

45   (1)   The Sexual Offences (Amendment) Act 2000 is amended as follows.

    (2)   In section 1 (reduction in age at which certain sexual acts are lawful), omit subsections (1) and (2).

    (3)   In section 2 (defences available to persons under age), omit subsections (1) to (3).

    (4)   Omit sections 3 and 4 (abuse of position of trust) except so far as extending to Scotland.

    (5)   Omit section 5 (notification requirements for offenders under section 3).

    (6)   In section 6 (meaning of 'sexual offence' for the purposes of certain enactments), omit subsection (1).

Proceeds of Crime Act 2002 (c. 29)

46   (1)   The Proceeds of Crime Act 2002 is amended as follows.

    (2)   In paragraph 4 of Schedule 2 (lifestyle offences: England and Wales), for sub-paragraph (2) substitute –

> '(2) An offence under any of sections 57 to 59 of the Sexual Offences Act 2003 (trafficking for sexual exploitation).'.

    (3)   For paragraph 8 of that Schedule substitute –

'Prostitution and child sex

8   (1)   An offence under section 33 or 34 of the Sexual Offences Act 1956 (keeping or letting premises for use as a brothel).

    (2)   An offence under any of the following provisions of the Sexual Offences Act 2003 –

        (a)   section 14 (arranging or facilitating commission of a child sex offence);

        (b)   section 48 (causing or inciting child prostitution or pornography);

        (c)   section 49 (controlling a child prostitute or a child involved in pornography);

        (d)   section 50 (arranging or facilitating child prostitution or pornography);

        (e)   section 52 (causing or inciting prostitution for gain);

        (f)   section 53 (controlling prostitution for gain).'.

    (4)   In paragraph 4 of Schedule 5 (lifestyle offences: Northern Ireland), for sub-paragraph (2) substitute –

> '(2) An offence under any of sections 57 to 59 of the Sexual Offences Act 2003 (trafficking for sexual exploitation).'.

    (5)   In paragraph 8 of that Schedule –

    (a)   after sub-paragraph (1) insert –

> '(1A) An offence under any of the following provisions of the Sexual Offences Act 2003 –
>
>   (a)   section 48 (causing or inciting child prostitution or pornography);
>
>   (b)   section 49 (controlling a child prostitute or a child involved in pornography);

    (c)   section 50 (arranging or facilitating child prostitution or pornography);

    (d)   section 52 (causing or inciting prostitution for gain);

    (e)   section 53 (controlling prostitution for gain).';

(b)   omit sub-paragraphs (2) to (5).

Adoption and Children Act 2002 (c. 38)

47   In section 74 of the Adoption and Children Act 2002 (status conferred by adoption not to apply for the purposes of certain enactments), in subsection (1) for paragraphs (b) and (c) substitute 'or

    (b)   sections 64 and 65 of the Sexual Offences Act 2003 (sex with an adult relative).'.

Nationality, Asylum and Immigration Act 2002 (c. 41)

48   In the Nationality, Asylum and Immigration Act 2002, omit sections 145 and 146 (traffic in prostitution).

Criminal Justice (Scotland) Act 2003 (asp 7)

49   In section 21(9) of the Criminal Justice (Scotland) Act 2003 (power of adjournment where person convicted of sexual offence or offence disclosing significant sexual aspects to behaviour in committing it), for the words from ' – (a) "three weeks"' to 'each case' substitute '"four weeks" there were'.

Protection of Children and Vulnerable Adults (Northern Ireland) Order 2003 (S.I. 2003/417 (N.I. 4))

50   In paragraph 1 of Schedule 1 to the Protection of Children and Vulnerable Adults (Northern Ireland) Order 2003, after sub-paragraph (n) insert –

    '(o) any offence under any of sections 15 to 21 and 47 to 50 of the Sexual Offences Act 2003.'.

Access to Justice (Northern Ireland) Order 2003 (S.I. 2003/435 (N.I. 10))

51   In Schedule 2 to the Access to Justice (Northern Ireland) Order 2003, in paragraph 2(d) –

(a)   omit sub-paragraph (x),

(b)   omit 'or' at the end of sub-paragraph (xi),

(c)   at the end of sub-paragraph (xii) insert 'or

    (xiii) under section 89, 90, 97, 100, 104, 108, 109, 114, 118, 123, 125 or 126 of the Sexual Offences Act 2003,'.

Criminal Justice (Northern Ireland) Order 2003 (S.I. 2003/1247 (N.I. 13))

52   In the Criminal Justice (Northern Ireland) Order 2003, omit –

(a)   in Article 19(4), sub-paragraph (a), and

(b)   in Schedule 1, paragraphs 1, 2, 20 and 21.

SCHEDULE 7   REPEALS AND REVOCATIONS   Section 140

Reference	Extent of repeal or revocation
Vagrancy Act 1824 (c. 83)	In section 4 except so far as extending to Northern Ireland, the words from 'every person wilfully' to 'female'. In section 4 as it extends to Northern Ireland, the words from 'wilfully, openly, lewdly' to 'any female; or'.
Town Police Clauses Act 1847 (c. 89)	In section 28 the words 'every person who wilfully and indecently exposes his person:'.
Offences Against the Person Act 1861 (c. 100)	Sections 61 and 62.
Criminal Law Amendment Act 1885 (c. 69)	Section 2(2) to (4), Section 11.
Vagrancy Act 1898 (c. 39)	The whole Act.
Criminal Law Amendment Act 1912 (c. 20)	Section 7.
Visiting Forces Act 1952 (c. 67)	In the Schedule, in paragraph 1(a) the words 'rape, buggery'; paragraph 1(b)(viii).
Army Act 1955 (3 & 4 Eliz. 2 c. 18)	In section 70(4), the words 'or rape'.
Air Force Act 1955 (3 & 4 Eliz. 2 c. 19)	In section 70(4), the words 'or rape'.
Sexual Offences Act 1956 (c. 69)	Sections 1 to 7, Sections 9 to 17, Sections 19 to 32, Sections 41 to 47. In Schedule 2, paragraphs 1 to 32.
Naval Discipline Act 1957 (c. 53)	In section 48(2), the words 'or rape'.
Mental Health Act 1959 (c. 72)	Sections 127 and 128.
Indecency with Children Act 1960 (c. 33)	The whole Act.
Sexual Offences Act 1967 (c. 60)	Section 1, Section 4, Section 5, Sections 7 and 8, Section 10.
Theft Act 1968 (c. 60)	In section 9(2), the words 'or raping any person'.
Children and Young Persons Act (Northern Ireland) 1968 (c. 34 (N.I.))	In section 21, in subsection (1) the words 'or the prostitution of,' and in subsection (2) the words 'or the prostitution of,' and 'or who has become a prostitute,'.
Criminal Justice Act 1972 (c. 71)	Section 48.
National Health Service Reorganisation Act 1973 (c. 32)	In Schedule 4, paragraph 92.
Sexual Offences (Amendment) Act 1976 (c. 82)	Section 1(2), Section 7(3).
Criminal Law Act 1977 (c. 45)	Section 54.

Reference	*Extent of repeal or revocation*
National Health Service Act 1977 (c. 49)	In Schedule 15, paragraph 29.
Internationally Protected Persons Act 1978 (c. 17)	In section 1(1)(a), the word 'rape,'.
Suppression of Terrorism Act 1978 (c. 26)	In section 4(1)(a), the word '11,'. In Schedule 1, paragraph 11.
Magistrates' Courts Act 1980 (c. 43)	In section 103(2)(c), the words from 'the Indecency with Children Act 1960' to '1977 or'. In Schedule 1, paragraphs 23, 27 and 32. In Schedule 7, paragraph 18.
Criminal Attempts Act 1981 (c. 47)	In section 4(5), paragraph (a) and the word 'and' immediately after it.
Magistrates' Courts (Northern Ireland) Order 1981 (S.I. 1981/1675 (N.I. 26))	In Article 29(1), the words from 'or with an offence under section 1(1)(b) of the Vagrancy Act 1898' to 'homosexual act'. In Schedule 2, paragraphs 5(c), 10(c) and 22.
Criminal Justice Act 1982 (c. 48)	In Schedule 1, in Part 1, paragraph 2, and in Part 2, the cross-heading immediately before paragraph 12, and paragraphs 12 to 14.
Mental Health (Amendment) Act 1982 (c. 51)	In Schedule 3, paragraphs 29 and 34.
Homosexual Offences (Northern Ireland) Order 1982 (S.I. 1982/1536 (N.I. 19))	In Article 2(2), in the definition of 'homosexual act', the words from ', an act of gross indecency' to the end. Article 3, Article 7, Article 8, Article 10(2)(a) and (b). In Article 11(1), the words ', or gross indecency with,'. Article 12(1). Article 13. In the Schedule, paragraphs 3, 4 and 7.
Mental Health Act 1983 (c. 20)	In Schedule 4, paragraph 15.
Police and Criminal Evidence Act 1984 (c. 60)	In section 80(7), the words from 'the Sexual Offences Act 1956' to '1977 or'. In Schedule 1A, paragraph 4 and the cross-heading immediately before it. In Part 1 of Schedule 5, paragraphs 4 and 6 to 8. In Part 2 of Schedule 5, paragraph 2 and the cross-heading immediately before it. In Part 1 of Schedule 6, paragraph 9.
Sexual Offences Act 1985 (c. 44)	Section 3. Section 4(2) and (3). Section 5(2).
Mental Health (Northern Ireland) Order 1986 (S.I. 1986/595 (N.I. 4))	In Schedule 5, in Part II, the entry relating to the Homosexual Offences (Northern Ireland) Order 1982.
Criminal Justice Act 1988 (c. 33)	In section 32(2)(c), the words from 'the Sexual Offences Act 1956' to '1977 or'.
Children Act 1989 (c. 49)	In Schedule 12, paragraphs 11 to 14 and 16.
Criminal Justice and Public Order Act 1994 (c. 33)	Sections 142 to 144. In Schedule 10, paragraphs 26 and 35(2) and (4).
Criminal Procedure and Investigations Act 1996 (c. 25)	Section 56(2)(a).

Reference	*Extent of repeal or revocation*
Sexual Offences (Conspiracy and Incitement) Act 1996 (c. 29)	In the Schedule, paragraph 1(1)(a).
Sexual Offences (Protected Material) Act 1997 (c. 39)	In the Schedule, paragraphs 1 to 4.
Crime (Sentences) Act 1997 (c. 43)	Section 52.
Sex Offenders Act 1997 (c. 51)	The whole Act.
Crime and Disorder Act 1998 (c. 37)	Sections 2, 2A, 2B and 3. In section 4, in subsection (1) the words ', a sex offender order or an order under section 2A above' and in subsection (3) the words 'or 2(6) above'. Section 20. In Section 21, subsection (2); in subsection (4), the words 'or (2)'; in subsection (5), the words 'or 20'; in subsection (6), the words 'and sex offender orders' and 'or 20(4)(a)'; in subsection (7)(b)(i), the words 'or, as the case may be, chief constable'; subsections (7A) and (7B); and in subsection (10), the words 'or 20'. Section 21A. Section 22(6) and (7). In Schedule 8, paragraphs 36 and 144.
Criminal Justice (Children) (Northern Ireland) Order 1998 (S.I. 1998/1504 (N.I. 9))	In Schedule 1, paragraph 1(c), (e) and (j).
Criminal Justice (Northern Ireland) Order 1998 (S.I. 1998/2839 (N.I. 20))	Articles 6, 6A, 6B and 7.
Youth Justice and Criminal Evidence Act 1999 (c. 23)	In section 35(3)(a), sub-paragraphs (i) to (iv).
Powers of Criminal Courts (Sentencing) Act 2000 (c. 6)	Section 161(2)(a) to (e). In Schedule 9, paragraphs 189, 190 and 193.
Care Standards Act 2000 (c. 14)	In Schedule 4, paragraph 2.
Criminal Justice and Courts Services Act 2000 (c. 43)	Section 39. Section 66. In Schedule 4, paragraphs 1(c) to (i), 2(g) to (m) and 3(b) to (r). Schedule 5.
Sexual Offences (Amendment) Act 2000 (c. 44)	Section 1(1), (2) and (4). Section 2(1) to (3) and (5). Sections 3 and 4 except so far as extending to Scotland. Section 5. Section 6(1).
Armed Forces Act 2001 (c. 19)	In Schedule 6, paragraphs 2 and 59.
Proceeds of Crime Act 2002 (c. 29)	In Schedule 5, paragraph 8(2) to (5).
Police Reform Act 2002 (c. 30)	Sections 67 to 74.
Nationality, Immigration and Asylum Act 2002 (c. 41)	Sections 145 and 146.
Access to Justice (Northern Ireland) Order 2003 (S.I. 2003/435 (N.I. 10))	In Schedule 2, in paragraph 2(d), sub-paragraph (x) and the word 'or' at the end of sub-paragraph (xi).

Reference	*Extent of repeal or revocation*
Criminal Justice (Northern Ireland) Order 2003 (S.I. 2003/1247 (N.I. 13))	In Article 19(4), sub-paragraph (a). In Schedule 1, paragraphs 1, 2, 20 and 21.

INDEX

CLSA Duty Solicitors' Handbook

2nd edition

Andrew Keogh

The only book to provide complete coverage of procedure in both the police station and magistrates' court.

This updated and extended 2nd edition incorporates the very latest legislative changes, including:

- Magistrates' Association sentencing guidelines
- key guideline cases including *Kefford*, *Ghafoor*, *Oliver* and *McInerney*
- new PACE Codes of Practice reproduced in full
- updated to reflect changes to the general criminal contract
- section on funding of criminal cases
- coverage of anti-social behaviour orders, youth court procedure, bail and magistrates' court procedures
- convention rights
- all the important cases of the last 12 months.

'Provides no-nonsense solutions in an easy-to-find, easy-to-follow handbook that covers the frequent and infrequent problems that arise with police station work.'
Independent Lawyer (of first edition)

Available from Marston Book Services:
Tel. 01235 465 656

1 85328 975 2
600 pages
£44.95
Nov 2003

The Law Society

Criminal Defence

Second edition

*Roger Ede and
Anthony Edwards*

This book covers practice and
procedure in all criminal courts
(Youth, Crown, Magistrate and
Appeal). It prompts readers when
actions need to be considered,
when investigations need to be
made, and when information needs
to be gathered.

The new edition of this well respected text includes:

- advice on public funding following the introduction of the Legal
  Services Commission and the Criminal Defence Service
- reference to the revised Legal Services Commission Transaction
  Criteria
- recommendations following the introduction of Legal Services
  Commission Specialist Quality Mark
- complete text of the Code for Crown Prosecutors 2000, the mode
  of trial guidelines and sentencing guidelines.

Criminal Defence is endorsed by the Criminal Law Committee of the
Law Society and welcomed by the national inter-agency Trials
Issues Group.

Available from Marston Book Services:
Tel. 01235 465 656.

1 85328 830 6
400 pages
£44.95
2002

The Law Society

Criminal Justice Act 2003

A Guide to the New Law
Andrew Keogh

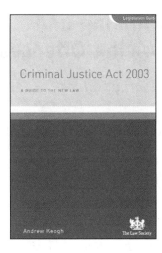

Controversial and far-reaching, the new Criminal Justice Act 2003 is one of the most important pieces of criminal legislation ever passed.

This comprehensive guide offers a clear explanation as to how the new law will affect current practice. It provides a quick overview of each of the new provisions, followed by a more detailed analysis with reference to appropriate cases and the existing legislative framework.

Major proposals contained in the Act include:

- new charging methods for offences
- reverse presumptions under the Bail Act for offending while on bail, failing to appear, and abolition of High Court bail
- overhaul of disclosure provisions
- retrial for serious offences
- overhaul of hearsay provisions
- new definition of bad character and overhaul of admissibility provisions.

The book includes a copy of the Act reproduced in full.

Available from Marston Book Services:
Tel. 01235 465 656

1 85328 877 2
480 pages
£34.95
Feb 2004

The Law Society

Drinking and Driving Offences

Jonathan Black

This guide provides practitioners with a logical route through the maze of legislation, practice and case law that has developed around the subject of drink-driving.

The book:

- analyses relevant case law on the statutory provisions relating to drinking and driving
- examines all major challenges in courts to breathalyser law
- reviews statutory provisions relating to Human Rights Act '98
- includes details of Magistrates' Courts sentencing guidelines
- provides helpful checklists at the end of every chapter.

Contents: An overview of the procedure; The screening breath test; The arrest; Protection for hospital patients; Driving or in charge whilst under the influence; The 'in charge' statutory defence; Drinking whilst over the prescribed limit; Evidence of analysis; Using specimen evidence, post-accident consumption and back-calculation; Failure to provide a specimen; Causing death whilst under the influence of drink or drugs; Sentencing.

Available from Marston Book Services:
Tel. 01235 465 656.

1 85328 851 9
208 pages
£29.95
2002

The Law Society

Forensic Practice in Criminal Cases

Lynne Townley and Roger Ede

This is a practical guide to understanding the uses, strengths and limitations of forensic practice.

Advised by experts and written by lawyers in a modern, accessible style, *Forensic Practice in Criminal Cases* takes readers through the nature and uses of forensic evidence and explores specific areas of expertise.

The book offers practical coverage of:

- the types of forensic investigation which should be carried out
- how investigations can go wrong
- what further investigations need to be carried out
- what documentary records of the investigation should be made
- how to instruct a forensic scientist to provide or challenge scientific evidence.

'At last a new and innovative book which brings together the theory and practice of criminal law and forensic science in an accessible way.' Robert Brown, President of the London Criminal Courts Solicitors Association

Available from Marston Book Services: Tel. 01235 465 656

1 85328 821 7
504 pages
£44.95
Dec 2003

The Law Society

Understanding Legal Aid

A Practical Guide to Public Funding

Vicky Ling and Simon Pugh

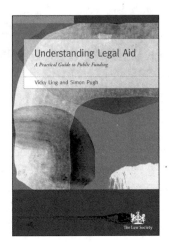

An indispensable quick reference guide to the various types of public funding available and the context in which they operate. The emphasis is on the practical implementation of the schemes and wherever possible tactical advice and checklists are provided.

- covers both civil and criminal legal aid schemes
- providing useful insights into other services performed by the Legal Services Commission, such as the Community Legal Service and Public Defender Service
- includes cross-references to official sources of information for other areas.

Written by a leading consultant and a specialist practitioner, *Understanding Legal Aid* is an easily comprehensible guide to doing publicly funded work, applicable equally to solicitors, the not-for-profit sector and the Bar.

Available from Marston Book Services:
Tel. 01235 465 656.

1 85328 895 0
256 pages
£29.95
2003

The Law Society